D0718078

# THE
# BRISTOL
# BOOK
## OF
# DAYS

## D.G. AMPHLETT

*To Beth, for her love and support.*

First published 2011

The History Press
The Mill, Brimscombe Port
Stroud, Gloucestershire, GL5 2QG
www.thehistorypress.co.uk

British Library Cataloguing in Publication Data.
A catalogue record for this book is available from the British
Library.

ISBN 978 0 7524 6038 3

Typesetting and origination by The History Press
Printed in India
Manufacturing managed by Jellyfish Print Solutions Ltd

# *January 1st*

**1701:** In pursuance of an ancient custom, the sheriffs of Bristol presented the Mayor with a new scabbard for the state sword usually borne before him. It was made of silver gilt, costing the sheriffs about £80. On retirement, the Mayor probably retained the ornament as a souvenir. In return, the sheriffs received a pair of gold-fingered gloves costing around £20. (John Latimer, *Annals of Bristol*, Kingsmead, 1970)

———•◆•———

**1864:** Rail passengers entering down-line of the Patchway Tunnel near Bristol may catch sight of a commemorative plaque reading: 'BRISTOL & SOUTH WALES UNION RAILWAY OPENED SEPTEMBER EIGHTEEN HUNDRED & SIXTY THREE. CHRISTOPHER JAMES THOMAS CHAIRMAN. RAILWAY PIERS DESIGNED BY ISAMBARD KINGDOM BRUNEL.' The Union Railway ran from Bristol to New Passage on the River Severn, connecting with a ferry to convey passengers across the river to Portskewett, and connecting with trains to South Wales. This date marked the opening of a short (51 chains) railway branch from Portskewett to the South Wales main line and passengers could purchase a single ticket from Bristol to Cardiff. Previously passengers had to purchase three separate tickets – one for the train from Bristol to New Passage, one for the ferry, and another railway ticket for a train into South Wales. (John Norris, *The Bristol & South Wales Union Railway*, Railway and Canal Historical Society, 1985)

# January 2nd

**1894:** Christopher James Thomas, a soap manufacturer, was born on August 16th 1807 at Llangadog, Carmarthenshire. He was educated until the age of 12 at Taliesin School, Merthyr Tydfyl, when he had to leave school to help out in his family's business. In 1830 he moved to Bristol to work in the family's soap business at the Red Lion Yard in Redcliffe Street. The firm merged with soap manufacturers Fripp & Co. in 1841 and the firm continued to innovate throughout the nineteenth century, for example using silicate of soda to fill soaps and patenting the extraction of glycerine from lyes in 1879. Thomas also played a role in the civic life of Bristol, becoming Liberal Councillor for St Phillip's ward (1845-1887), serving on the Bristol Docks Committee (1848-1878) and was a member of the Bristol Chamber of Commerce (1853-1877). He died on this date in 1894 and was buried at the Lewins Mead Unitarian Chapel. The epitaph on his grave reads: 'he bore testimony to the simple truths of Unitarian belief whereon this heart ever stayed.' (*Oxford Dictionary of National Biography*, OUP)

# January 3rd

**1920:** The following extract is a newspaper report of a robbery that took place on this day: 'As a poor labouring man was returning home from Bristol to Redland, through Pugley's field, he was accosted by two fellows, with a demand of money or life. The poor man, having purchased a new jacket with part of his wages, had but 7s remaining, and this he refused to give up. One of the fellows hereupon knocked him down, and rifled his pockets of their whole contents, further insisting upon the surrender of his new jacket, for which one of them gave him his own in exchange. Arriving home, and searching the pockets of the ill-conditioned wrapper of iniquity, the poor man was agreeably astonished to find in it a *ten-pound Bank of England note!* – doubtless, a recently-made prize, obtained from some less fortunate victim.' (*The Times*)

———— • ◆ • ————

**1941:** A major bombing raid on Bristol took place, with Temple Meads and the City Docks particularly badly affected. One hundred and forty-nine people died and 133 were seriously injured. The bitter cold meant that water streaming from the fire hoses caused icicles to form on the buildings and created sheets of ice on the roads below, hampering the attempts to quench the fires. (Reece Winstone, *Bristol in the 1940s*, 1961)

# January 4th

**1977:** The Albion Dockyard closed completely. The construction of the Bristol Floating Harbour in 1809 allowed for the building of the Albion Dockyard, which was then known as the New Dockyard, and it was built for the firm Hillhouse, Sons & Company. In 1827 Charles Hill, who had been an accountant at the company, became a partner in the firm. In 1845 the firm became Charles Hill & Son and the business remained there until the closure of the dockyard. In 1848 the New Dockyard was renamed the Albion Dockyard. The last Bristol ship to be built there was the *Miranda Guinness*, which was launched on July 9th 1976. The *Miranda Guinness* was the first bulk beer carrier to be registered with Lloyds and the ship was able to carry two million pints of beer. The ship was launched by Lady Iveagh, the wife of the joint chairman of Arthur Guinness, Son & Co. The closure of the Albion Dockyard became inevitable after Bristol City Council pushed through a Parliamentary Act to close the docks' commercial shipping in 1970. (*The Times* / www.bristol-rail.co.uk)

# January 5th

**1753:** An early Bristol newspaper, *Felix Farley's Journal*, records that the rural populace celebrated Christmas on this date. Why was this so? During 1752 a series of reforms to the calendar had taken place which aligned it with the Gregorian calendar that was used on the Continent. These changes resulted in the year beginning on January 1st rather than March 25th and the year 1752 was shortened by eleven days during September, so that September 14th followed September 2nd. These reforms seem to 'have been especially obnoxious to the uneducated classes who held certain fixed festivals, who could not understand why they should be deprived of nearly half a month, and who, many of them, believed that their lives would be shortened to a corresponding extent.' In many towns farmers were noticeably absent from their stalls on this day as they were celebrating Christmas according to the old calendar. In rural areas *Felix Farley's Journal* also records that 'to gratify the feelings of their parishioners, many rural clergymen preached nativity sermons on the following Sunday.' (*Felix Farley's Journal*, quoted in John Latimer, *Annals of Bristol*, Kingsmead, 1970)

# January 6th

**1854:** Those reading *The Times* on this date were treated to an unusual case of theft heard at the Bristol Quarter Session. Richard Harris, who had a reputation for being a 'cunning man', stole money from two women servants from a respectable house. They were Miss Boley and Miss Tracey, aged 21 and 23 respectively. Harris claimed to be able to make a charm that 'would compel towards them the affections of the male sex' and that they would be able to have whom they wanted as husbands. Harris demanded to be lent a sovereign to make a charm and the women gave all they had, amounting to 13s 6d. Harris drew a heart on some paper and pretended to wrap the coins in it, telling them that they should keep this charm in their pockets for nine days and in their bosoms for three days more. These credulous women pocketed the charm but later took a closer look at it. The half sovereign they had given Harris had been 'converted' into a sixpence, a half-crown into a penny and a shilling into a farthing. For these crimes Harris was sentenced to four months' imprisonment with hard labour. (*The Times*)

# January 7th

**1851:** At the Bristol Quarter Sessions James Simpson, described as 'a young man of respectable appearance and connexions', was sentenced to ten years transportation. Simpson was the head of a gang of thieves which had 'long infested that portion of the Great Western Railway between Bristol and Bath', on which Simpson had made repeated trips, always travelling in first class. However, on November 2nd 1850, a lady named Cook, with her servant, travelled from Bath to Bristol. While the servant was busily engaged with her mistress' luggage, Simpson pushed against her and, shortly afterwards, she noticed that the money from her pocket was gone. Alerting some of the railway officials, Simpson was stopped and a large sum of money found in his pocket, plus twelve gold sovereigns in a purse. Through the exertions of Superintendent Burton of the Railway Police, the purse was identified by a Miss Powell as belonging to her. It had been stolen from her only a day or two previously whilst waiting on a platform to see a friend off. On sentencing, Simpson threw up his hand pretending to faint, but on removal from the dock he was observed to poke his tongue out at his fellow prisoners. (*The Times*)

# January 8th

**1930:** The 2.40 a.m. express passenger train from Shrewsbury to Penzance ran into a stationary goods train at Lawrence Hill at 5.45 a.m. Fortunately for the thirty to forty people on board the train, no one was injured. A more serious disaster was averted owing to the prompt actions of the driver and fireman of the locomotive. When the driver of the express train, James Burroughs, saw the tail-lights of the goods train in front, he applied the brakes with the assistance of his fireman, A. Paul. Although collision seemed inevitable both men stayed on the footplate of their locomotive. The speed of the impact was estimated to have been 45mph. Frank Boobyer, guard of the goods train, jumped down from his van as he saw the express train approaching. His van was flung down the embankment into a brick-built shed and smashed. In total four goods trucks were derailed and destroyed, with the front of the express train described as being buried in wood and coal. Only the rear driving wheels of the express train were left on the track. The guard of the express train, a man named Saunders, had his van smashed but escaped unhurt. A special train was put on to allow the passengers to complete their journey. (*The Times*)

# January 9th

**2001:** Prime Minister Tony Blair was hit by a tomato thrown by a protester when he visited Bristol to open the City of Bristol College. As the Prime Minister arrived at the college several protesters surged forwards towards his car but were held back by police, some of whom were on horseback. Several tomatoes were thrown before one hit the Prime Minister. Mr Blair ignored the incident as he went in to officially open the college. Demonstrators held placards with the slogans such as 'People are more important than oil' and 'Cut the war tax'. The protest came amid pressure from EU allies to reconsider the sanctions on Iraq, which critics claimed had led to many civilian deaths. The second Iraq War did not start until March 2003. Alistair Campbell, Communication Secretary to the Prime Minister, also faced a hostile reception at the City of Bristol College in April 2004, when he attended a question and answer session with media and politics students. Four youths pelted his car with eggs. Later, he spotted two of the perpetrators and is reported to have said, 'You are the people who threw eggs at me earlier ... are you going to find some rashers of bacon?' (*Daily Mail / Daily Telegraph / London Evening Standard*)

# January 10th

**1750:** Captain Carbry arrived back in Bristol after his ship, *Phœnix*, was seized by pirates on December 22nd. *Phœnix* was stopped by an Algerine Corsair of thirty guns just off the coast of Lisbon, and under the pretence that one of the European passes was a forgery, the ship was seized and the ship's crew ordered to make for Algiers under the control of six Turks. Carbry, assisted by three of his crew, recovered his ship after flinging two of the pirates overboard. (John Latimer, *Annals of Bristol*, Kingsmead, 1970)

───────◆─•─────

**2010:** An unusual cargo arrived at the Royal Portbury Docks. Two 1940s Stanier 8F steam locomotives that had been sent out to Turkey as part of the war effort were returned to Britain by steam enthusiasts who hope to restore them. The locomotives had been rusting in Turkey before the railway enthusiasts went over to Turkey to free the wheels so the trains could be transported as part of a freight convoy to the port of Izmir – a 500-mile journey. Restoration of locomotives 45166 and 45170 are to be undertaken by two restoration groups at Barry in South Wales and Morepeth in Northumberland. (BBC News website)

# January 11th

**1877:** Six children named Daniel Baker, George Edwards, William Edwards, Henry Moore, William Durdan and George Wilk, each around 10 years old, were discovered at Bristol stowing-away in a goods train. They had been playing in a goods yard at Plymouth when a guard shouted at them and the boys hid in a truck. That truck was placed on a goods train bound for Penzance. When the train reached Truro the boys got out and tried to walk back towards Plymouth. It rained heavily so they went back to Truro station and, unobserved, got into another truck which they thought would take them back to Plymouth. However, the truck was actually part of a train that went straight through to Bristol. By the time they arrived at Bristol, three days and nights had elapsed since they went missing and several of the boys were so weak as to be unable to stand. The next day they were put in front of Bristol Police Court on charges that they did not pay their fare on the Great Western Railway. The magistrates remanded the children for a day to allow for further enquires but were of the opinion that it was hardly a case of defrauding the railway company. (*The Times*)

# January 12th

**1815:** James West was indicted for stealing bank notes and bills from the Bristol Mail Coach amounting to £1,357 17s 6d. C. King, clerk at the Montgomery Bank, made up the parcel and was directed to Mr Fothergill in London. The parcel was first given to Lee, guard of the Swansea coach, to deliver to the Bristol mail. It was then given to Morris, porter of the Bush Inn at Bristol, who delivered it to Lewis, clerk of the coach-office, who placed it on the back seat of the mailcoach. When the coach reached London, John Painter, clerk of the Swan with Two Necks, in Lad Lane, London, could not find the parcel. West was arrested on December 8th when he tried to use the stolen bank notes at the banking-house and the notes were immediately identified. Another witness, James Ball, porter at the Stock Exchange, claimed that West used him to change the bank notes, which were immediately identified. In giving his defence, West stated that he had got the notes at a gamming-house in the West End. He said that he had lately returned from sea and that the stolen notes could have passed through many hands before they came to him. The jury was unconvinced and found him guilty. (*The Times*)

# January 13th

**1881:** After an intense frost, snow began to fall heavily and temperatures remained low for a fortnight. Railway services were particularly affected, as this description shows: 'During the snowstorm, a fast train, which left Bristol for London at half-past five in the evening, did not reach its destination until seven o'clock the following evening, having been snowed up near Didcot. The chairman of the Great Western Railway Company, at the half-yearly meeting held soon afterwards, stated that 111 miles of their lines had been drifted up, and 64 trains were buried in drifts, exclusive of 141 temporary blocks sustained by others. The clearing of snow added many thousands of pounds to the working expenses of the company. Postal communication in some parts of the country was suspended for three days.' (John Latimer, *Annals of Bristol*, Kingsmead, 1970)

———— ◆ ————

**1888:** 'We had a repetition of the fog in Bristol ... and when the darkness set in traffic on the suburbs was only safely carried on with extreme care. The fog was dense upon the river and greatly interfered with shipping movements. On the hills the fog was thicker than in the more central parts of the town.' (*Bristol Times*)

# January 14th

**1908:** The University College of Bristol had been taking students since it first opened on October 10th 1874. It had been founded through the efforts of John Percival, headmaster of Clifton College, who had observed that the provinces of Britain usually lacked a university and produced a pamphlet entitled *The Connection of the Great Universities and the Great Towns*. This was well received by Benjamin Jowett, master of Balliol College at Oxford, who became a financial backer of the new university. Unusually for the time, when the University College of Bristol opened, it accepted men and women on an equal basis, except in the area of medicine. By the 1900s it had become desirable to seek a charter. However, it was difficult to raise the endowment of the college above £30,000 until H.O. Wills, on January 14th 1908, promised to donate £100,000 provided the charter could be granted in two years. Within twenty-four hours more money had been raised for the university than had been raised in the previous three decades. On May 24th 1909 the charter, approved by King Edward VII, came into effect and the University College of Bristol became Bristol University. (Bristol University website)

# January 15th

**1928:** A fire at St Mary's Church, Shirehampton left most of the church gutted. At 1.13 a.m. the Central Fire Brigade received a call, and on arriving at the scene they targeted their jets at the belfry louvers as it was feared that if the bell, weighing half a ton and supported on wooden transom, came down it would also bring down the steeple. The fire, which started in the west gallery, found ready fuel as the gallery, the roof supports and the pews were all made of wood. The vicar, with the support of the fire brigade, went in through the vestry in order to remove the safe containing the church's sacred vessels and oils. (*Bristol Times and Mirror*)

———◆———

**1930:** The consecration of the new St Mary's Church, Shirehampton by the Bishop of Malmesbury took place on the exact day it was destroyed by fire two years previously. During the ceremony the bishop knocked three times upon the door, saying, 'Open the gates of righteousness; that I may go in and give thanks' (Psalm 118: 19). The church was crowded and several people had to stand at the back. The church was designed by P. Hartland Thomas. (*Bristol Times and Mirror*)

# January 16th

**1777:** An attempt was made to destroy Bristol Harbour. A ship called the *Savannah La Mar*, which was bound for Jamaica, was daubed during the night with pitch and set on fire, but the fire was quickly quenched and did not spread. This was not the end of the story, however, as on the same night a warehouse owned by Corn Street druggist James Morgan also had a lucky escape after entry had been forced into the building. Here a box of tow moistened with turpentine was used as the accelerant. Fortunately the fire failed to take hold. Three days later, the warehouses in Bell Lane were targeted. These fires were started by torches surrounded by flammable material and several other torches were also found in the city. Patrols were started and rewards for information offered in an attempt to catch the perpetrators. The mystery was not solved for some weeks until suspicion turned to a 25-year-old man named James Aitken, who went by the alias Jack the Painter. When the authorities caught up with him, he confessed to the arson attacks in Bristol and also to the other attacks in Portsmouth. For his crimes he was hanged at Portsmouth on gallows 67ft high. (John Latimer, *Annals of Bristol*, Kingsmead, 1970)

# January 17th

**1817:** At Leigh Down workmen discovered a large quantity of Roman coins which had apparently been buried 6 inches below the ground. Up to 1,000 coins were found, although half of them disappeared into the labourers' pockets. The coins ranged in date from the reign of Nero to Constantius II, suggesting that the hoard was buried around AD 350. (John Latimer, *Annals of Bristol*, Kingsmead, 1970)

———◆———

**1881:** The Council decided to experiment with electric light as a replacement for gas lighting and on this day erected seven streetlights on the thoroughfares converging at the Council House. The experiment was not a success, owing to the apparatus used to generate electricity proving faulty. One of the chief objections was the cost of the electric motors used for the production of electricity. A scheme was suggested whereby the tide could be used to generate electricity for the lights, but this came to nothing. Other experiments in Bristol using electricity proved more successful. Electric light was used in Bristol Cathedral a couple of years previously, on November 28th 1878, and, according to contemporary reports, was the first ecclesiastical building to use them. The effect was said to have been 'exceedingly fine'. (John Latimer, *Annals of Bristol*, Kingsmead, 1970)

# January 18th

**1904:** Cary Grant, christened Archibald Alec Leach, was born at 15 Hughenden Road in Bristol. Between 1932 and 1966 Cary Grant made seventy-two feature films, becoming one of the best paid and most famous of Hollywood film stars. He did not have the happiest of childhoods in Bristol, for when he was 9 his mother was committed to a sanatorium. Nobody seems to have told Leach and he thought that she had died. His childhood was spent around music halls in Bristol and at 14 he left school to join a company of acrobatics, stilt walkers and slapstick comics. They toured Britain before sailing to America in 1920 to complete a long run of performances at the New York Hippodrome. Leach continued to perform and went to Hollywood in 1931, securing a five-year contract with Paramount. In 1932 he first performed under the name Cary Grant (legally changing his name in December 1941). When his father died in 1935, he found his mother and visited her many times before she died in 1973. Cary Grant is best known for such films as *The Awful Truth* (1939), which established him as a leading comedy actor, and *North by Northwest* (1959). He died in Iowa on November 29th 1986. (*The Guardian / Oxford Dictionary of National Biography*, OUP)

# January 19th

**Since 1204:** This date marks the feast of St Wulfstan, who was canonised by Pope Innocent III in 1203. Wulfstan was a Benedictine monk who became the bishop of Worcester in 1062. He was the first English bishop known to make systematic visitations of his diocese and was responsible for the building of many churches. One of his most notable achievements was the abolition of the slave trade that operated between Bristol and Viking Ireland through his persistent preaching efforts. (*Oxford Dictionary of Saints* / Henry Sebastian Bowden, *Miniature Lives of the Saints*, Donald Attwater (ed.), Burns, Oates & Washbourne, 1959)

⸭

**1913:** In 1862 James Williams Arrowsmith (1839-1913) joined his father's printing business at 11 Quay Street. They worked together publishing railway timetables and occasional books but printing was the mainstay of the business. In 1881 Arrowsmith decided to develop the business by publishing books. The first two books were not successful. However, when Arrowsmith published *Call Back* in 1883 it was reviewed favourably by Henry Labouchre. It was continuously in print until 1933 and secured the business. Arrowsmith continued to publish a number of successful titles, including Jerome K. Jerome's *Three Men in a Boat* and Weedon Grossmith's *Diary of a Nobody*. Arrowsmith died at his Clifton residence on this date in 1913. (*Oxford Dictionary of National Biography*, OUP)

# January 20th

**1607:** What has become known as the Great Flood occurred on this day. Low-lying land on each bank of the River Severn downwards was inundated with water, covering at least 200 square miles and killing around 2,000 people. Water travelled up the Severn at speeds of up to 30mph and up to 25ft in height. The cause of the flood was thought to have been high tides combined with a storm surge, although some experts have suggested that a tsunami may have in fact been to blame. One later description of events stated that 'a greater number of people were saved only by climbing upon trees, haystacks, and roofs of houses. In Bristol the tide being partially dammed back by the bridge, flowed over Redcliff Street, Thomas and Temple Streets to a depth of several feet. St Stephen's Church and the quays were deeply flooded and the loss of goods in cellars and warehouses was enormous.' A pamphlet to commemorate the disaster produced at the time was entitled 'God's warning to the people of England by the great overflowing of the waters or floods'. (BBC News website / John Latimer, *Annals of Bristol*, Kingsmead, 1970)

# January 21st

**1853:** The numerous colliery accidents of the period is evidenced by the opening line of the *Daily News*, which read: 'Another of those fatal accidents at collieries, which unhappily have become of much too frequent occurrence of late.' The accident in question took place at Shortwood Colliery, Mangotsfield. Four men were being lowered down a shaft in a wooden cart by means of a drawing engine at 10 a.m. at the beginning of the shift, when a malfunction of the engine caused the cart to lose control and descend rapidly to the bottom of the shaft – a depth of over 230 yards. The cause of the malfunction was a broken wheel owing to defective casting. Three of the men survived the accident. They were Samuel Bryant, 38; Isaac James, 32; and a 16-year-old boy named Gingell. Isaac James was carried home by friends to recover. The others were taken to Bristol Royal Infirmary suffering from fractures. The fourth man, Samuel Bennett, died five to six hours later from internal injuries that he sustained in the fall, leaving a wife and three children. (*The Morning Post / Daily News*)

# January 22nd

**1633:** 'Between Thursday the 22 January after noon, and Friday being the 23 of the same, fell such a store of snow all England over, as like hath not been seen in many years before, which was so much greater, not only for that every day after unto the end of the month fell some continually; but more especially in some places it was more deep and dangerous, by reason of great wind forcing the same, which made it very dangerous for traveller; by means whereof many Christians and cattle perished. It hindered the coming of barks to our fair, and trowes could not come down from the Seaverne [Severn] for ice in a month after. After Candlemas Day [2 February] commandment was give to rid away the snow from our streets, which was so hard frozen that it put our city to great charges, and people were forced to break and dig it up with pickaxes, bar of iron and hatches, being so thick and hard like unto great stones digged out of rocks, and may well be called the last great snow for many years after, for all our halliers and carters were hired and compelled many days to carry it and throw it into the river.' (William Adams, *Adams's Chronicle of Bristol*, J.W. Arrowsmith, 1910)

# January 23rd

**1855:** An attempted burglary was thwarted by the actions of a quick-thinking police constable in the early hours of the morning. The attempt took place at the premises of Mr Tovey, a wine and spirit merchant at Stokes Croft. At 1.15 a.m., a police constable noticed an upstairs light and, knowing that portion of the premises was unattended, aroused his suspicion. He dispatched another police constable to the station for backup and then a search was made. Four panes of glass had been removed from a window by a portico. The four burglars still inside the building heard footsteps and one of them, William Baker, tried to make his escape by jumping off the portico – a distance of approximately 14ft (4.3m). Despite attempting to run away he was captured by the police in St James' churchyard. A large iron safe containing a number of trade books had been forced and the burglars, in their hurry to escape, left a quantity of housebreaking instruments, including skeleton keys, lock picks, and some crowbars. It was thought that the gang were originally from Birmingham and had recently been responsible for a number of crimes in the neighbourhood. (*The Times*)

# January 24th

**1837:** 'The last local duel to which any reference can be made in the local press was fought on Durdham Downs. The antagonists were described as "a gentleman of Hotwells and a foreigner residing in the neighbourhood." After some shots were fired they managed to effect an arrangement.' (John Latimer, *Annals of Bristol*, Kingsmead, 1970)

———◆———

**1907:** At Lawford's Gate Petty Sessions George Kendall, a haulier of Hanham, was charged with stealing five bricks from Mount Hill Brick Works on January 15th. Kendall had taken a load of 600 bricks from the yard and explained that he had only taken the five bricks as a sample. However, Kendall was seen putting the five bricks on his cart and taking them into his premises by Sergent Bradley of Hanham, who was on duty at Stone Hill. He later challenged Kendall to account for the bricks and asked to see the ticket showing the number of bricks that was on the cart. After Kendall was cautioned for the theft of the bricks he admitted stealing them. He was ordered to pay 20 shillings in damages or spend fourteen days in jail. (*Bristol Times and Mirror*)

# January 25th

1830: 'The month of January 1830 was remarkable for a protracted snowstorm, which blocked up the roads in all parts of the country, communication between the towns being almost suspended for several days. A local newspaper, in recording the incidents of the season, stated that on 25th January a party of nineteen labourers dragged into the city a wagon containing upwards of two tons of flour, which they succeeded in hauling from Melksham, a distance of twenty-five miles. They had been promised by a baker, and received 28s 4d for performing this arduous task.' (John Latimer, *Annals of Bristol*, Kingsmead, 1970)

---

1916: Francis Pigou, dean of Bristol Cathedral, dies. Pigou had been ordained in 1855 by Bishop Samuel Wilberforce. His first curacy was at Stoke Talmage, where the 92-year-old rector, who was fond of Port, gave him all his sermons and those of his father. Pigou later held various posts, including the chaplaincy of Marboeuf Chapel, Paris. In 1891 he became Dean of Bristol and ensured that each altar in the cathedral was furnished with a cross, candlesticks and flowers, and provided cassocks and surplices for the choir. He was also noted for his sermons when leading parochial missions and retreats. (*Oxford Dictionary of National Biography*, OUP)

# January 26th

**1832:** Richard Vines was reprieved from the sentence of execution for his role in the Bristol Riots. Following the rejection of the Parliamentary Reform Bill, which sought to end rotten boroughs and organise a fairer distribution of seats in the House of Lords on October 8th 1831, widespread popular protests took place in many parts of the country and rioting occurred in Bristol. On January 17th, the sentence of death was handed out to five Bristolians for their part in the riots. They were William Clarke, Richard Vines, Christopher Davis, Thomas Gregory and Joseph Kayes. All men collapsed in fits of tears, some protesting their innocence. Shocked by the severity of the sentence, a campaign was started and 10,000 people signed a petition to the King 'praying for a commutation of the punishment'. The execution was appointed for January 27th but only one of the men, Richard Vines, was reprieved owing to his insanity and the allegation that one of the witnesses was guilty of perjury. The behaviour of the crowd was strangely subdued when compared to other executions of the period, and they quickly and quietly dispersed after the sentence had been carried out. (Geoffrey Amey, *City Under Fire: The Bristol Riots and their Aftermath*, Lutterworth Press, 1979)

# January 27th

**1728:** *Felix Farley's Journal* reported the following on the activities of bodysnatchers: 'The shoo-maker that hang'd himself last week ... was bury'd in the Cross Road called Dungen's Cross, but we hear that some young Surgeons have since caused it to be taken up again to anatomise.' The only legal supply of bodies for medical students to study at this time came from convicted murderers, and apprehension of murderers was not common enough to meet demand. Consequently, bodies were sourced from those recently interred. (John Latimer, *Annals of Bristol*, Kingsmead, 1970 / Hubert Cole, *Things for the Surgeon*, Heinemann, 1964)

———— •◆• ————

**1827:** 'A grave was ordered to be made in St Paul's burying-ground, Bristol, of ten feet deep, and to be finished by ten o'clock in the morning; fortunately, the undertaker was punctual to the time, for on the arrival of the corpse for internment, the grave was found nearly filled up, and groans were heard issuing from underneath; assistance was immediately procured, and after doffing some depth a hat and wig came up, and soon after the grave-digger himself made his appearance. He was taken out in a very exhausted state and carried home; had he remained a short time longer, he must have expired.' (*The Times* quoting the *Bristol Gazette*)

# January 28th

**1729:** News from around the world took time to arrive. A letter from Bristol in the *Gloucester Journal* on this date announced the murder of Captain Holliday and his crew of last May on the African coast by the people they were trying to enslave. (John Latimer, *Annals of Bristol*, Kingsmead, 1970)

———— • ◆ • ————

**1767:** Hickson, a notorious highwayman, was captured near Lawford's Gate. In an earlier trial in 1754, he was convicted of robbery at Worcester and sentenced to transportation to America. Within a month of landing he stole money from a merchant's office in Boston, allowing him to secure a berth on a boat back to England to resume his criminal career. He moved to a manor house in Frenchay after one of his brothers was executed for returning from transportation. Here he lived the life of a country gentleman, keeping horses and a pack of hounds until he was arrested at Lawford's Gate. Lack of evidence meant he was acquitted of robbery and he moved to Carmarthenshire, were he committed two burglaries. For these crimes he was sentenced to death. However, representations from an earl were reported in a newspaper and consequently delayed his execution; until it was proved that the representation was a forgery. He was executed in November 1767. (John Latimer, *Annals of Bristol*, Kingsmead, 1970)

# January 29th

**1753:** The famous Bristol historian John Latimer describes the entertainment enjoyed by the City Council on this day: 'The magnates of the Corporation, although standing much of their dignity, occasionally condescended to patronise the entertainments offered to the dull city by roving showmen. On the 29 January, "the famous fire-eater, Mr Powell," was requested to display his skill at the Council House, before the mayor, aldermen, councillors, and "other persons of distinction," which probably meant the ex-mayoresses and other worshipful females. Mr Powell's advertisements informed the world that "He eats red-hot coals of the fire as natural as bread; he fills his mouth wide with red-hot charcoal, and broils a slice of beef upon his tongue, and any person may blow fire with a pair of bellows; he melts a quantity of resin, bees-wax, sealing wax, brimstone and lead in a chafing dish and eats the said combustibles with a spoon." The performance was rewarded by the pitiful payment of 21s out of corporate funds; but the poor conjurer may have been satisfied, for, unless he obtained the mayor's leave, he was liable to six months imprisonment as a rogue and vagabond if he exhibited his tricks to the public.' (John Latimer, *Annals of Bristol*, Kingsmead, 1970)

# January 30th

**1823:** The trial of the 'Bedminster Case' resurrection men took place at Wells. Here five Bristol men intending to be surgeons were indicted on several charges, including conspiracy to raise dead bodies, disturbing a grave, and assault on members of the patrol, including the Chief Constable. At the trial, the council for the prosecution stated that there was a plentiful supply of bodies that could be used for anatomical research rather than the recently interred. In reality the opposite was the case. In their defence it was stated that Hippocrates, Galen and other distinguished surgeons had often forcibly acquired bodies to study. The court, deciding that the case was of a 'serious and novel nature', chose to adjourn sentencing until other judges could be consulted. (*The Times*)

# January 31st

**1532:** St Bartholomew's Hospital had been founded by Roger de la Warre (d.1320) and the hospital was maintained by an annual endowment. By the 1530s the endowment barely maintained the master and brethren of the hospital and the de la Warre family had insufficient funds to raise necessary capital for the hospital. Hence on this date a legal document was signed between de la Warre and Robert Thorne, with the cooperation of the master of the hospital that the estate be transferred to Thorne, who undertook to convert the building into a school and the estate transferred to the Corporation. Assent was gained from Henry VIII regarding Throne's 'laudable purpose', but Thorne died a few months afterwards. The St Bartholomew's estate eventually passed to his brother, Nicolas Thorne, who took no steps to convey the property to the Corporation. When he died the estate passed to his son, who was not yet of age and so nothing could be done. On the death of the youth in 1557, the estate passed to his brother, also called Nicolas, who survived into adulthood, when, at the insistence of the Corporation, the estate was acquired when Nicolas became of age. The school founded by Nicolas Thorne is known as Bristol Grammar School. (John Latimer, *Annals of Bristol*, Kingsmead, 1970)

# February 1st

1872: Clara Ellen Butt was born on this date in Sussex. Her family moved to Bristol and she was educated at South Bristol High School. It was here that her teacher noticed her singing talent and asked bass Daniel Rootham to hear her. He trained her voice and enrolled her in the Bristol Festival Chorus, which he conducted. She won a three-year scholarship to the Royal College of Music, which was extended for a fourth year, enabling her to spend three months studying in Paris under V.A. Duvernoy, with Queen Victoria paying for her expenses. During the First World War she organised a series of charity concerts to contribute to the war effort, including six successive performances of *The Dream of Gerontius*, which raised £2,700 for the Red Cross. She was awarded a DBE in 1920, and died in 1936. (*Oxford Dictionary of National Biography*, OUP)

——— ◆ ———

1910: Joe Gainard, 56, died from the effects of smoke inhalation in a fire at Easton Colliery. Gainard was working underneath an engine making repairs when he dropped a lighted candle, igniting a quantity of greasy fluff. The jury at the subsequent inquest expressed the opinion that the engine room should have been kept cleaner and that a lamp should have been used instead of a candle. (*The Times*)

# February 2nd

**1745:** Hannah More was born in Fishponds, Bristol. She is best known for her writing and as a philanthropist. Hannah was an intelligent child, learning Latin, mathematics and French. In 1762 her first publication, *The Search after Happiness*, was a pastoral play for schoolgirls to perform and 10,000 copies had been sold by the mid-1780s. Her play *Percy* brought her widespread acclaim in 1777 and established her reputation. More also wrote on educational matters, particularly for women, and her writings upheld the prevalent attitudes regarding the difference between men and women in terms of natural abilities and social roles. She campaigned in support of William Wilberforce for the abolition of slavery. From the 1780s her Evangelical faith grew stronger, which influenced her writing, and she became concerned about the manners of society, publishing anonymously *Thoughts on the Importance of the Manners of the Great to General Society* in 1788. As a philanthropist she founded several schools in the Mendips, starting with a school at Cheddar. Eventually twelve such schools were established. The impact of the French Revolution encouraged More to write a series of anonymous tracts to counter the ideas of Thomas Paine's *The Rights of Man*. It is for these tracts that she is perhaps best known. (*Oxford Dictionary of National Biography*, OUP)

# February 3rd

**1957:** A Vampire jet fighter aircraft was flown under the Clifton Suspension Bridge, nearly hitting it, before crash landing 2 miles away on the Somerset side of the Avon Gorge, near Pill. The crash killed the experienced pilot, Flying Officer J.G. Crossley, aged 28. The accident occurred on the day that 501 (County of Gloucester) Squadron of the Royal Auxiliary Air Force were making their final parade before disbanding to the Duke of Gloucester, who was honorary Air Commodore of the squadron, based at Filton. The impact caused the aircraft to go up in flames and also resulted in a small landslip, which fortunately missed the railway below. At the time Squadron Leader M.C. Collings stated that although the aircraft was being tested as a reserve for the fly-past at the sqaudron's final parade, no set route was prescribed and no permission was given for Crossley to fly under the Suspension Bridge. At the subsequent inquest it was revealed that two officers of 501 Squadron had tried to stop Crossley from taking off as he had not followed proper take-off procedures and was said to be in a hurry. A verdict of accidental death was recorded. (*The Times*)

# February 4th

**1709:** Bristol sea captain Woodes Rogers departed Bristol aboard the *Duke* on August 2nd 1708, on a privateering voyage around the world. The ship rounded Cape Horn but, caught in a violent storm, was pushed much further to the south. Due to the cold weather they headed to the Juan Fernandez Islands, which they reached on January 31st 1709. A few days later, on February 4th 1709, some members of the crew went ashore and found a man clothed in goatskins. That man was Alexander Selkirk, who had been marooned on the island for four years. On Rogers' return to his native Bristol he published *A Cruising Voyage Around the World*, telling his story to the world. It made Rogers famous and influenced Daniel Defoe in his writing of *Robinson Crusoe*. Later, Rogers became the Colonial Governor of the Bahamas and restored the defences at Nassau. Nevertheless, he constantly complained to the Board of Trade about the lack of protection to defend the colony against the Spanish. Eventually he went to London to plead his case but ended up in prison for debt. Owing to the ineffectiveness of Roger's successor to the Bahamas governorship, he was asked to return. He died in Nassau on July 15th 1732. (*Oxford National Dictionary of Biography*, OUP / John Latimer, *Annals of Bristol*, Kingsmead, 1970)

# *February 5th*

**1171:** Robert FitzHarding was a burgess and merchant of Bristol and lived in a large stone house on the High Street, near Frome Bridge. He was the grandson of the Saxon thegn Eadnoth the Staller, who died in 1068 near Bristol after resisting an invasion by one of Harold Godwineson's sons. As a financier, FitzHarding's clients included St Peter's Abbey in Gloucester and Henry FitzEmpress, who fought against King Stephen during the Civil War. FitzHarding was rewarded for his support with social connections and tenurial gains. Nevertheless, FitzHarding's influence extended only regionally. In 1140 FitzHarding established the Abbey of St Augustine's on his Billeswick property, which later became Bristol Cathedral from 1542. FitzHarding retired from public life and died, at the abbey, as a canon, on this date in 1171, and was subsequently buried there. FitzHarding also caused the chapter house to be built, which is one of the few surviving Norman aspects of Bristol Cathedral. According to tradition, FitzHarding's wife, Eva, founded and became prioress of the Priory of St Mary Magdalene on St Michael's Hill, close to St Augustine's Nunnery. When she died she too was buried at St Augustine's Abbey. (*Oxford Dictionary of National Biography*, OUP; Bristol Cathedral website; Nikolaus Pevsner, *The Buildings of England: North Somerset and Bristol*, Penguin, 1958)

# February 6th

**1878:** A tragic accident occurred at St Phillip's railway station. A schoolboy heard groans and discovered Private William Harris on the rails beneath the carriages of a train standing at the platform. He immediately alerted the driver, fireman and the guard of the train. Nevertheless, William Harris died from his injuries shortly afterwards. The deceased had been a solider serving in the Indian regiment and has arrived at Bristol at 7.21 p.m. He was, however, the worse for liquor, so much so that another solider had to get out his ticket to present it to the inspector. Although the station was well lit, it seems that Harris fell in front of a moving train as carriages were being shunted into the station. St Philip's station had opened in Bristol in 1870 as a terminus station for local services from Gloucester, Fishponds, Yate and Bath, and relieved congestion at Bristol Temple Meads. The location of St Philip's station gave ease of access to the Old Market shops until many of the buildings were lost during the Second World War. The station closed to passengers in 1953, when services were transferred to Bristol Temple Meads. (*Bristol Mercury and Daily Post* / Mike Oakley, *Bristol Suburban: Temple Meads, Local Stations, Halts and Platforms 1840-1990*, Redcliffe, 1990)

# February 7th

**1839:** An accident occurred during the construction of tunnels at Brislington on the Great Western Railway, and was reported in *The Times*: 'Some workmen employed in the formation of the centring of the arch in tunnel No.1 were alarmed by a portion of brickwork giving way, and before they able to escape the masonry fell upon them, and three of them were killed on the spot. A number of labourers engaged in another part of the tunnel ran to their assistance and almost immediately they reached the spot a still larger mass of brickwork fell in, by which two others sustained very severe fractures of the skull, and seven or eight others were injured. At an inquest held on the bodies of the deceased a verdict of "Accidental Death" was returned. The Bristol Infirmary is an institution which over affords immediate aid to those who suffer from these calamities, and should therefore be met with liberal support from the directorate of public companies, the hazardous nature of whose works renders it impossible to prevent the dreadful accidents which so frequently occur.' (*The Times*)

# February 8th

**1904:** Alfred Ainger, a Church of England clergyman and writer, died from pneumonia at the home of his niece at Darley Abbey, near Derby. Ainger was born in London on February 9th 1837 and was educated at Joseph King's School, where a schoolmaster took him to hear Fredrick Denison Maurice preach. This turned Ainger away from the Unitarianism of his father and towards the Church of England. Charles Dickens also discovered the youth's acting talent and he performed in various amateur dramatic performances at Dickens's house. He later studied at King's College, London, where he became the first president of the college's Shakespeare Society. He later went on to study at Trinity Hall, Cambridge, and was ordained deacon in 1860 and priest in 1863. Ainger wrote considerably on the life and work of Charles Lamb and lectured on literary subjects, frequently lecturing at the Royal Institution from 1889. His influence as a preacher grew steadily and as a result he became a canon of Bristol Cathedral in 1887. In 1895 he was made honorary chaplain, then, in 1896, chaplain-in-ordinary to the Queen. He held a canonry at Bristol Cathedral until the end of 1903, following an attack of influenza. (*Oxford Dictionary of National Biography*, OUP)

# *February 9th*

**1880:** George Jackson appeared at Bristol Police Court charged with stealing a quantity of clothing and a pair of boots from the Victoria Hotel, Temple Meads. On a Saturday afternoon he walked into an upper apartment of the hotel and was spotted by a hotel worker whilst walking back down the stairs. As Jackson rushed out of the hotel, he was followed by the hotel worker, who shouted, 'Stop Thief!' He was captured by a policeman outside the hotel. Jackson made an unreserved confession, stating that he did not want to put the police to any trouble. He was sentenced to a week on remand. Mary Williams also appeared at the court. She was charged with stealing two shirts and some clothes to the value of 16*s* from pub landlord George Wintle, whose premises were on Ashley Road. The clothes had been left in a bundle for a friend but after she left, the clothes were found to be missing. The bundle was later found with her whilst she was at another pub. She later admitted to the crime and said she was sorry for not putting the bundle back on the counter. For 'repenting too late' she was sentenced to twenty-one days' imprisonment with hard labour. (*Bristol Mercury and Daily Post*)

# February 10th

**1824:** Although born in Bristol, Samuel Plimsoll spent much of his adult life in London, working as a coal merchant. It was here that he realised the danger of men in so-called 'coffin ships'. These were ships that were overloaded and undermanned by unscrupulous owners and often insured for an amount that was many times their actual value. In 1868 Plimsoll became Liberal MP for Derby and was now in a position to do something about them. His first step was to publish a book entitled *Our Seamen*, which began: 'I have no idea of writing a book. I don't know how to do it ... Now there are many hundreds of lives lost annually by shipwreck, and as to far the greater part of them, they are lost from causes that are easily preventable.' The book also contained a map of the British Isles, indicating all the shipwrecks that took place in 1871 – nearly 2,000 in total. It was a catalyst for reform and in 1876 the Merchant Shipping Act was passed, ensuring that a load line, or Plimsoll line as it has become known, which is a disc 1ft across and with a line 1½ft across, would thenceforth be painted on all British ships. Its position marks the maximum safe draft. (Marguerite Fedden, *Bristol Bypaths*, Rankin, 1954)

# February 11th

**1906:** An inquest into the death of John Lewis, 29, was held at the Grapress Inn, Frampton Cotterell. Lewis had been excavating clay at the Stoke Gifford Brickworks when he met his death from falling earth. Although a verdict of accidental death was recorded, the jury considered that the foreman was careless in his duties, undertaking insufficient supervision of the work to ensure correct procedures were followed in shoring up the hole, and no written rules were displayed at the site. (*Bristol Times and Mirror*)

---

**1927:** *The Times* records that on this day Percy Gibbs, 28, a dentist of Bristol, accompanied by three friends, Stanley Wilcox, 28, Charles Norton, 26, and Percy Davis, 30, was driving a motorcar along Gloucester Road and travelling into the city. At a bend in the road Gibbs overtook a bus but collided with an oncoming tram. His car was wrecked and all four men were taken to Bristol Royal Infirmary in a serious condition. The incident was written up in *The Times* on February 14th and forms part of a column in the newspaper with the heading 'Motoring Accidents'. Such stories seem to have been a staple for the newspaper at the time, with a column dedicated to recording them in the 1920s. (*The Times*)

# February 12th

**1839:** The construction of the Bristol and Exeter Railway led to regular reports in the newspapers of archaeological finds. *The Times* on this day reported the discovery of numerous coins from the reign of Constantine, some bronze spoons of 'elegant shape', a jar, and two coffins containing the skeletons of the deceased. It is alleged that the bones were of gigantic size, including one 7ft long, although this seems to be exaggerated. The bones crumbled to dust shortly after being exposed to the air. (*The Times*)

————— •◆• —————

**1934:** In 1932 the Gem cinema on Broadweir closed as a cinema and became a boxing club. During an unlicensed fight, held on this date, Jimmy Cooper, aged only 14, collapsed and died after being knocked down by his 22-year-old competitor. The boxing club closed and concerns were expressed by the coroner. As a cinema, the Gem was one of the last in Bristol to introduce sound films, owing to the lack of space to house the sound equipment. When the new projection equipment was installed the beam shone through the circle so that when someone stood up their shadow would show on screen, much to other patrons' annoyance. (Dave Stephenson & Jill Willmott, *Bristol Cinemas*, The History Press, 2005)

# February 13th

**1975:** Racing driver Ben Collins was born in Bristol. He is best known for his on-screen performances in the BBC programme *Top Gear* as The Stig. Collins has competed in many different categories of racing, including Formula 3 and Indy Lights. In addition Collins runs his own company, Collins Autosport, for television and film-makers, including the James Bond film *Quantum of Solace*, where Collins completed car driving stunts for actor Daniel Craig, who plays the lead role. In 2004 Collins took up the role of The Stig, an unidentified racing driver clad in a white racing-driver's suit and helmet, who tests cars for speed on the *Top Gear* test track. However, he was sacked from the show after publishing his autobiography *The Man in the White Suit*, which revealed he was The Stig. The BBC tried to prevent its publication by taking the publisher, Harper Collins, to court, but failed to get an injunction and the book was duly published. Collins, in one newspaper report, claimed that he started writing the autobiography when he feared losing his job from the BBC. He is now a co-presenter on Channel 5's show *Fifth Gear*. (*The Mail* / *Wikipedia* / *The Telegraph*)

# February 14th

**1879:** The inquest was opened into the death of 5-year-old Charlotte Tomlin, who died in tragic circumstances. It seems that poison had got into a pudding cooked by her mother. Four other family members also suffered from the effects of eating the pudding and were taken to the Bristol Infirmary. The inquest was adjourned until some of the family were well enough to attend. Evidence for Charlotte's death came from her older brother Henry, aged 10. He was 'much affected while giving his testimony, and cried so much that his statement was rather confused.' He was standing on the table in order to reach from a cupboard when he found a parcel containing a white powder 'just like flour.' He told his mother of the discovery, who asked his sister to fetch the parcel. His sister took the parcel to her mother, who, believing it to be flour, mixed it with the rest of the flour in the pan. Later all who had eaten the pudding suffered severe vomiting. Only the father was not affected as he was in bed having worked the previous night. Subsequent tests showed the cause of the poisoning to be arsenic. (*Bristol Mercury and Daily Post*)

# *February 15th*

**1880:** Charles Branwhite, landscape painter, dies at his Clifton residence. He was born in Bristol on July 7th 1817, son of Nathan Cooper Branwhite, a miniature portrait painter. He studied art with his father and initially pursued sculpture, with a measure of success, winning silver medals of bas-reliefs at the London Society of Arts in 1837 and 1838. Possibly influenced by William James Müller, he took up landscape painting and exhibited annually at the British Institution between 1823 and 1857, and intermittently at the Royal Academy between 1845 and 1856. Typically he exhibited snow and frost scenes. On February 12th 1849 he was elected an associate member of the Society of Painters in Watercolours and exhibited there for thirty years. A keen angler, he was fond of rivers and painted many watercolour scenes in Devon and Wales. The failure of the West of England Bank aggravated the symptoms of his heart disease, as he was a major shareholder. After his death he was buried at Arnos Vale. (*Oxford Dictionary of National Biography*, OUP)

# February 16th

**1878:** The boys of Clifton College were drilled in how to use a rifle and took the train to Avonmouth to a range to practice. The boys returned by the 5.40 p.m. train from Avonmouth, where one of the students, Edward Hughes Hemming, aged 18, was having a conversation while demonstrating how one of the younger pupils held his rifle with his own when the rifle went off – a cartridge having been left in the gun. The bullet hit Alexander Fletcher Jones, a mathematics teacher at Clifton College, who had been sitting in the adjoining carriage. The train at this point had reached Sea Mills station. Since no doctor was known to be in vicinity the train proceeded hastily to Redland station in order to seek medical help. The college boys who formed a cadet force were required to have their guns examined by an officer in charge or the sergeant-instructor when the order to cease firing was given so that any unused cartridges might be removed from the gun. It is possible that Alexander Fletcher Jones may have unknowingly caused his own death because as a sergeant-instructor he did not follow procedure and check Hemming's rifle at the end of the practice. A verdict of accidental death was recorded at the subsequent inquest. (*Bristol Mercury and Daily Post*)

# February 17th

**1899:** During the afternoon 'the utmost excitement prevailed ... when a bull, breaking away from its keepers, ran loose, and several persons passing at the time were in serious danger. Henry Perkins and Henry Celes were taking the bull from Mr Baggs Farm, Redland Green, to its owner Mr Bence of Stapleton Road, to be slaughtered ... as they were passing through Zetland Road, it became unmanageable. Despite efforts ... to restrain it, the bull dashed from one side of the road to the other, and rushed with lowered head at everything that attracted its attention. The pedestrians quickly took refuge behind the gates of the houses, but there were several narrow escapes. The traffic along this road was stopped for some time, as it was impossible to pass through without the animal making a rush. Happily no one was injured, although some were not a little frightened at the antics of the bull. However, the rope attached to the ring in its nose was caught, and it was tied to a tree; but tearing the ring from its nose the bull again made its rushes at people, but in the meantime the owner had been informed of the occurrence, and a man named George Jones arrived on the scene with a gun and shot it.' (*Bristol Mercury and Daily Post*)

# February 18th

**1947:** The Bristol to Severn Beach line once extended through to Pilning, which is situated on the main line to South Wales. After Avonmouth a freight-only line from Filton joins the branch at Hallen Marsh Junction. On this day the 9.20 p.m. Avonmouth to Salisbury freight train was accidentally diverted along the single line to Pilning at Hallen Marsh Junction and collided head-on with the Cardiff to Avonmouth freight train at around 5.30 a.m. All six people aboard the train sustained injury, although five were released from hospital the same day. The Cardiff train had just passed Severn Beach station when the drivr saw the headlights of an approaching locomotive. Unfortunately he did not have time to apply the brakes or blow his whistle before the trains collided. The driver of the Salisbury-bound train did not notice he was on the wrong line until it was too late. Both engines and tenders were damaged and some of the wagons were smashed in the incident. Some difficulty was had in clearing up the wreckage with three inches of snow on the ground and a risk of explosion from some full petrol tanks. (Ministry of Transport's Accident Report)

# February 19th

**1910:** Sir George White registered The British and Colonial Aviation Aeroplane Company and, together with his brother Samuel and son G. Stanley White, subscribed £25,000 to start the company. Hence all risks that the new venture may have were underwritten by the family. With the vast sums involved, perhaps it was no wonder that Sir George's colleagues at the Bristol Stock Exchange thought that he had taken leave of his senses. Two sheds were leased from the Bristol Tramways Company's northern terminus at Filton. Success came early on when they built the Bristol Biplane, otherwise known as the Boxkite, with the first examples produced in June 1910. The Boxkite was a very near copy of the Henri Farman biplane, which shared its dimensions, although the Boxkite had more refined metal fittings. Because of the similarity of design, solicitors acting for Farman Friers were prepared to sue the directors of the Bristol company for infringing patent law. The directors responded by sending a defence and claimed numerous substantial improvements over the Henri Farman. The result was that no further action was taken against the company. The Boxkite continued to be produced until 1914, by which time seventy-six had been built. (C.H. Barnes, *Bristol Aircraft Since 1910*, Putnam, 1970)

# February 20th

**1739:** George Whitfield, who introduced Methodism to Bristol in 1737, had a meeting with Revd Reynolds, the Chancellor of Bristol, at which Whitfield was told to stop his preaching activities in Bristol as he had no licence for such activities. Whitfield responded that he thought that the custom was now obsolete and asked why a certain Irish clergyman, who preached only a few days previously, was not asked the same question. Reynolds then referred to Whitfield's ordination service and other particulars of Church law. Whitfield replied, 'I apprehended those Canons did not belong to professed ministers of the Church of England' and refered to a canon that prevented clergymen frequenting a tavern or playing cards asking, 'why is not that put into execution?' Reynolds replied that if someone complained of them then he would. Reynolds claimed that Whitfield preached false doctrine. Whitfield did not answer the charge but stated that he would continue to proceed as before. Reynolds threatened Whitfield that if he continued without a licence he would be suspended and then excommunicated. Whitfield was as good as his word and preached no less than three times that day, including at Newgate Prison. (George Whitfield, *Whitfield's Journals*)

# February 21st

**1587:** On August 4th 1586, the privy council considered how 'the 100 turkes brought by Sir Francis Drake out of the West Indyes, may upon their arrival' be 'conveyed home and presented to [William Harborne] the Ambassador unto the Grand Seigneur.' The task fell to Laurence Aldersey, who set sail from Bristol on this date commanding the *Hercules of London*. Aldersey's journal records that on their arrival in Patras: 'they brought us to the house of Cady, who was made then to understand of the 20 turks that we had aboard, which were to go to Constantinople, being redeemed out of captivity by Sir Francis Drake, in the West Indies ... that he might see them, and understood how strangely they were delivered, and he marvelled much, and admired the Queen's Majestie of England.' Such admiration for England does not seem to have lasted for 'there grew a great controversie between the mariners of the Hercules, and the Greeks of the town of Sio, about the bringing home of the Turks, which the Greeks tooke in ill part, and so a broile beganne.' Aldersey's account of his voyages was published by Richard Hakluyt in the 1589 edition of *Principall Navigations*. (*Oxford Dictionary of National Biography*, OUP)

# *February 22nd*

**1906:** An inquest was held at the Coroner's Court into the death of Thomas Reed, 31, formerly of Millpond Avenue, Baptist Mills, who died at the Eastville Workhouse on February 19th. Reed worked for Sir John Avid & Co. in the Avonmouth Dock until an accident occurred on August 19th 1904. A crane was at work above him and was conveying a load to a truck. Whilst the crane was carrying out this process some mud fell from the crane and struck Reed on the shoulder, knocking him over and causing his spine to fracture. It was not the first time that mud had fallen out of the grab of the crane, but it was the first time that the mud had hit anyone. Reed was hospitalised at Bristol General Hospital for three months before being allowed home to recuperate. However, his condition deteriorated so that the last month of his life was spent in the Eastville Workhouse Infirmary. At the inquest the jury returned a verdict of accidental death. (*Bristol Times and Mirror*)

# February 23rd

**1980:** More than thirty football supporters appeared before Bristol magistrates following a match between Bristol Rovers and Chelsea, held on this date, on charges of criminal damage, threatening behaviour and assault on police officers. Thirty-five people were also taken to hospital as a result of the trouble, which started at the game and spilled out onto the streets surrounding Bristol Rovers' ground at Eastville. It later emerged that an unnamed WPC saved a colleague caught up in the fight. PC John Brandon noticed a large group of Chelsea supporters throwing stones at a group of Rovers supporters. PC Brandon grabbed Michel O'Reilly, a Chelsea supporter, by the shoulder and as they struggled the PC was punched in the face. A struggle took place and PC Brandon found himself on the ground, being kicked by a number of Chelsea fans. The WPC threw herself on the ground to cover PC Brandon's face and prevent further injury until additional help arrived. Following the match two supporters were jailed and £4,850 was levied in fines to a total of fourteen other people. Bristol Rovers had won the game 3-0. (*The Times*)

# February 24th

1936: 'Two express trains from the North came into collision just outside Temple Meads Station, Bristol, early this afternoon. The 10.40 Great Western train from Wolverhampton to Penzance and a London Midland and Scottish train from Bradford were running into the station when, about 200 yards outside it, the Bradford train apparently failed to take the points and the second of its two engines struck the last coach but one of the Great Western train, throwing it on its side and tearing off the front bogie. On account of their nearness to the station both trains were running slowly and were able to pull up quickly. Station officials and railwaymen engaged on work nearby assisted passengers to leave the overturned coach through the upper most windows. Several of the passengers suffered from shock and Mr George Herniman, 33, of Sidney Street, Ashton Gate, Bristol, suffered a torn ear. He was treated at Bristol General Hospital. Two other coaches of the Great Western train were derailed in the collision, but remained upright. The second engine and one coach of the Bradford train were derailed, but no one in that train complained of injury. It was nearly 6 o'clock before the line was cleared and normal traffic resumed.' (*The Times*)

# February 25th

**1885:** The official trial of a floating fire engine took place on the Floating Harbour. The fire engine was built by Messrs Strand, Mason & Co. of Blakfriars, London and had been transported via the Kennett and Avon Canal for severe and repeated testing by Mr F.W. Gladstone, engineer to the docks, where it had 'given the greatest satisfaction.' The 53ft (16.1m) boat was fitted with steam-driven pumps capable of pushing through 1,100 gallons of water per minute with a jet that could force the water 200ft (61m) into the air or four jets that could work simultaneously and force the water 150ft (45.7m) into the air. The boat could travel up to speeds of nine knots. The trial started at midday in front of civic dignitaries including the Mayor. At a given signal some fires were lit and in nine minutes the boiler pressure of the boat was sufficient for the craft to proceed from St Phillip's Bridge towards a point near the steam cranes by the harbour railway wharf, where the various hoses were used by the municipal fire brigade, headed by Supt Wingfield, to put out the fire. They showed that they had 'perfect acquaintance with the various apparatus' and the trial was deemed a success. (*Bristol Mercury and Daily Post*)

# February 26th

**1723:** The *Gloucester Journal* of March 4th 1723 contained the following account of a Shrove Tuesday tradition that took place in Bristol each year: 'The blacksmiths of this city assembled in a body in St Thomas's Street, in order to engage their annual combatants, the coopers, carpenters and sailors there; which last bore so hard upon the weather quarter of smith's anvils (notwithstanding the furious discharge of their wooden thunderbolts) that they drove every Vulcan into his fiery mansion. The noise of this defeat alarmed the whole posse of weavers, who joined the smiths, and made a general attack on the wrong wing of their enemies, for they then totally routed them, sending them home in the utmost disorder to show their wives &c., a parcel of broken loggerheads. However, we understand the smiths and weavers are resolved to form another campaign next year, and try their success at arms on the same day therein.' *Felix Farley's Journal* of February 26th 1757 shows that the custom was still taking place when, during the evening of Shrove Tuesday, a fight ensued on the quay where several were wounded including a carpenter, who had his skull fractured. (John Latimer, *Annals of Bristol*, Kingsmead, 1970)

# February 27th

**1927:** Emma Saunders died. She was a member of the Railway Mission, which she joined in 1881. Her involvement began when Louisa Stevenson had to give up because of ill-health and Emma took over her patch, which covered the Clifton Extension Railway, the Severn Tunnel and Loop Line at Pyle Hill. Over time her mission extended to cover all of Bristol's railways and she had passes to enable her to travel on locomotives and brake vans. On her visits to railwaymen and their families she distributed small gifts and religious literature. Another team of women would help package the gifts. In an attempt to keep railwaymen – especially the young – away from the temptations of the pub, Emma also helped to set up the Bristol and West of England Institute. It provided a canteen, billiard rooms, bagatelle and a skittle alley. There were also rooms for engineering classes and religious services. She was well respected by the railwaymen of Bristol, and on the occasion of her 80th birthday she was presented with an armchair and settee, for which 5,000 GWR and Midland railwaymen had subscribed. A memorial plaque describing her as 'the railwaymen's friend' currently stands outside the entrance to Bristol Temple Meads station. (Redland Church website)

# February 28th

**1910:** John Latimer was born on May 7th 1824 in Newcastle-upon-Tyne. His first job was at a local newspaper as a cashier, but his writing talent was soon recognised and he wrote articles for the paper. He became interested in local history and his first book, *Local Records*, was published in 1857. In 1858 he moved to Bristol, becoming editor of the *Bristol Mercury*. He collected information for a continuation of John Evans's *Chronological History of Bristol* (1824), but the project was delayed until Latimer's retirement as soon the newspaper was expanded to a daily publication. The first volume of his *Annals of Bristol* was published in 1887, detailing the nineteenth century, and other volumes were subsequently published detailing the seventeenth and eighteenth centuries. Latimer's *Annals of Bristol* were not strong sellers and to ensure that the third volume of the seventeenth century was published, his friends organised a collection and a cheque for £163 14s was handed to Latimer on this date, in a presentation ceremony held at the Council House. His *Annals of Bristol* fulfil the aim of a 'comprehensive sketch of the political, municipal, commercial and social life' of the city. (Patrick MacGrath's introduction to John Latimer, *Annals of Bristol*, Kingsmead, 1970 / *Bristol Mercury*)

# February 29th

**2008:** BBC News reported that Mark Boyle, 28, had failed in his attempt to walk from Bristol to Porbandier in India, the birthplace of Ghandi. He set out with only some T-shirts, a bandage and sandals, and had hoped to rely on the kindness of strangers to provide him with food and lodging for the 9,000-mile trek. He had set out some four weeks previously and made a promising start, having been given two free meals whilst in Glastonbury, and was joined by two companions in Dover. The three men then made it across the English Channel to Calais. However, it was there that their luck ran out and Boyle recorded in his on-line journal of the trip that 'We now were pretty much out of food, hadn't slept in days and were really cold; we had to reassess the whole situation.' Boyle also describes how people in Calais perceived them as 'a bunch of freeloading backpackers' or asylum seekers because they were not able to speak French. Mark Boyle is a member of the Freeconomy Movement, which wants the world to do without money. (BBC News website / Freeconomy Community website)

# March 1st

**1809:** A duel took place in a field near the Monagu Hotel in Clare Street between Henry Smith, an attorney, and Richard Priest, a tailor, following a quarrel at a theatre. Richard Priest was fatally wounded in the thigh and died a few hours later. Smith fled to Portugal but later surrendered. At the assizes in April 1810, charges were dropped owning to a technical breach in the court documents. (John Latimer, *Annals of Bristol*, Kingsmead, 1970)

———— • ◆ • ————

**1859:** Mary Ann Villers was charged with having fraudulently obtained £3 10s from the Governess's Benevolent Fund. She first made an application for assistance in February 1856, claiming to be the daughter of a medical man who had deserted his family. Other family members had died and she said that she had been forced to sell jewellery, plate and books to avoid destitution. Further letters followed asking the society for assistance. The letters were generally characterised by their religious tone and one particular letter aroused suspicion. She claimed that after returning from France, from a governess position where the children had died, she had become ill and close to the point of death. Further enquires discovered that she had solicited assistance from the Bristol Mendicity Society as early as 1850. (*The Times*)

# March 2nd

**1879:** Frank Sedgbeer failed to keep his engagement with Emily Tripp, 20, who therefore left St Andrew's Church after the evening service and went in the company of another man. When she returned to her lodging she found Sedgbeer waiting to speak to her. She initially refused to see him on the grounds that it was late, but later consented to meet him for ten minutes. Sedgbeer asked her who the man she was talking to after church but Tripp refused to tell him, whereupon he pulled out a revolver and pointed it at her. She exclaimed, 'If you do not put that away I will call a policeman.' He put the gun away but pulled it out again when she again refused to tell him who she had been speaking to after church. This time Sedgbeer fired it at her. The first bullet was stopped by the steel stays of her corset but a second entered through her right shoulder-blade. Sedgbeer then turned the gun on himself. At the inquest a verdict of suicide was reached on Frank Sedgbeer, and thus he was buried without the customary funeral rites. (*Bristol Mercury and Daily Post*)

# March 3rd

**1141:** Archbishop Theobald of Canterbury came to Bristol, staying until April 7th. Here he attended the council of Winchester. During this time a Charter was issued by Theobald, confirming Turstin of Bristol as priest of St Ewen's Church, which stood in Corn Street and was one of Bristol's earliest churches until its demolition in the 1820s. The Charter was written on a small piece of parchment and is currently the oldest document in the care of Bristol Record Office. The Charter was probably written because St Ewen's Church was founded by Robert, Earl of Gloucester, and Tewkesbury Abbey was attempting to remove Robert's candidate and install their own priest. The Charter was known as the 'Curse of St Ewen' as Archbishop Theobald threatened that if anyone should threaten Turstin or his church then they would be 'firmly bound up in the chains of anathema', meaning to suffer damnation. (Bristol City Council website)

———— • ◆ • ————

**1928:** Ronnie Dix, aged 15, became the youngest League goal scorer when he scored Bristol Rovers' second goal against Norwich City twenty minutes from the end of the game. He also remains the only player in the club's history to have played for Rovers before his sixteenth birthday. (Stephen Bryne & Mike Jay, *Bristol Rovers Football Club: The Definitive History 1883-2003*, Tempus, 2003)

# March 4th

**1889:** The Local Marine Board, at the offices in Prince Street, made a presentation to Captain John William Harvey of the SS *Napier* of North Shields for his role in a courageous rescue of the crew of the SS *Domingo* during a heavy gale in the Atlantic. During the night of November 26th 1888, the *Domingo* had got into difficulties when her engines and rudder stopped working. The *Domingo* was also taking on water. All bar one of her lifeboats had been washed away during the course of the gale. A distress flare was sent up when the *Napier* was spotted but high waves prevented the *Napier* coming alongside to affect a rescue. The first plan was that if the crew of the *Domingo* could keep their ship afloat then the *Napier* would attempt to tow the ship to a port. However, the *Domingo* continued to take on water and the order was given to abandon ship. The captain of the *Napier* sent lifeboats to the *Domingo* at great risk, owing to the high seas, but they succeeded in rescuing all the men aboard the stricken ship. (*Bristol Mercury and Daily Post*)

# March 5th

**1496:** John Cabot, who would later become the first European to set foot on the Continent of North America, was granted letter patent stating: 'Be it known and made manifest that we have given and granted ... to our beloved John Cabot, citizen of Venice ... free and full authority ... to sail to all parts, regions and coasts of the eastern, western and northern seas, under our banners and ensigns, with five ships or vessels.' Cabot previously tried to elicit sponsorship from the Kings of Spain and Portugal for such a voyage but without success. (Peter Firstbrook, *The Voyage of the Matthew*, BBC Books, 1997)

———— ◆ ————

**1853:** The *Bristol Journal* reported the following: 'Not withstanding the many failures of the steam-carriage on common roads, it has again made its appearance between Bath and Bristol; and this time owing to several most ingenious improvements in the machinery employed, has thoroughly realized the expectations of its projectors. The rate of travelling is about twelve miles an hour, and the cost is most trifling – say *6d* for the journey.' The historian John Latimer could find no further references for this venture and consequently concludes that, like so many steam-carriage businesses, this too failed. (John Latimer, *Annals of Bristol*, Kingsmead, 1970)

# March 6th

**1856:** A report from *The Times* concerning how ships could get stranded at Nelson's Point, a shallow section of the River Avon between Avonmouth and Bristol, read: 'About a month since the *Sabrina* steamer, plying between Bristol and Cork, was stranded on Nelson's Point, on her outward voyage from the former port. The vessel lay there till Thursday [March 6th], when, with the return of the spring tides, she was floated off, and taken back to Bristol to have the extent of her damage ascertained'. The next morning 'the *Phoenix* steamer, for Dublin, was run aground at the same point, and, if she in not got off today, will in all probability lie there for at least a fortnight, if not a month. Both vessels are the property, or, at least, are running under the direction of the Bristol Steam Navigation Company. The injuries sustained by the *Sabrina* are said to be very slight, Nelson's Point being, in fact, an accumulation of soft mud. The occurrence of two accidents, similar in all respects, to the vessels belonging to the same company, would seem to indicate want of proper care on the part of their commanders, and the existence of such a point is hardly creditable to the river authorities.' (*The Times*)

# March 7th

**1876:** A Frenchman wanted for fraud was staying at the Grand Hotel in Bristol. When the police called to question him, they waited whilst he made assurances that he would be out of his room in a few minutes. After an hour had elapsed, the policemen gave an ultimatum to the man inside, threatening to break down the door, but consented to giving the man two more minutes, 'remembering how particular Frenchmen are about their toilet.' The policemen asked again after two minutes but received no reply, and, with assistance, broke down the door. The man had escaped by using the hour to knot together the bedsheets, allowing him to descend to the road some 50ft below. The criminal was later caught. (*Bristol Mercury*)

———— • ◆ • ————

**1889:** In 1883, a Bristol football team was formed known as the Black Arabs. A year later the club name changed to become Eastville Rovers. On this date in 1899 a meeting of the Gloucestershire Football Association was held in the White Hart Hotel in Old Market Street. A letter was read out asking if there was any objection in allowing Eastville Rovers to become Bristol Rovers. It was unanimously agreed to reply that the Council had no objection. (Bristol Rovers website / *Bristol Mercury and Daily Post*)

# March 8th

1965: 'There used to be an Army maxim which ran "Order, counter-order, blankety disorder." Bristol's motorists might be forgiven for putting this interpretation on changes being made her in some of the city's traffic signs. They are the result of new regulations governing signposting of waiting restrictions as part of the Worboys Committee's recommendations.' The Worboys Committee recommended adopting many European road signs, which they believed were clearer to understand and see, and which included new road markings. As part of these changes, the now familiar double yellow, single yellow and broken yellow lines were introduced. However, Bristol already had its own system of yellow lines painted on the roads, for example, broken yellow lines previously told Bristol motorists that they were in a meter zone and could not park. From this date these markings instead meant limited waiting. Furthermore a single yellow line in Bristol once meant that a loading or unloading order was in force. From this date the single yellow line now meant 'No waiting Monday – Saturday 8 a.m.-6 p.m.' To help the Bristol motorist avoid confusion, 100,000 windscreen stickers detailing the new arrangements were issued. (*The Times*)

# March 9th

**1629:** Merchant John Whitson was born in either 1553 or 1555 in Clearwell, in the Forest of Dean. He was apprenticed to Nicolas Cutt, a rich Bristol vintner. Whitson is alleged to have seduced Cutt's young widow, Bridget, in the wine cellar and the two married on April 12th 1585. Whitson's mercantile activities were mainly with France, Spain and the Mediterranean, trading lead, cloth and leather in exchange for wine, alum and currants. He was involved in local and national politics, becoming Mayor and MP of Bristol. After the death of his first wife he married again on April 21st 1609, to Magdalen Hynde, a penniless but attractive widow of William Hynde, a London salter. After she died he married Rachel Aubrey, another widow, whose dowry was said to have been £2,000. He was stabbed by a litigant in November 1626, leaving him with a permanent scar on his cheek. Shortly afterwards he wrote *An Aged Christian's Farewell to the World*. He died falling from his horse in Bristol on February 27th and was buried with full military honours on this date in 1629. With no direct heirs he bequeathed much to charity, including the founding of the Red Maid's School, which still exists today and is the oldest girls' independent school. (*Oxford Dictionary of National Biography*, OUP)

# March 10th

**1741:** The foundation stone of the Corn Exchange was laid by the Mayor 'amidst much rejoicing, to which a bountiful distribution of ale to the populace may have contributed.' The building was designed by John Wood the Elder. Outside the Corn Exchange are four so-called brass 'nails', that is they are baluster shaped with a small tabletop, on which business could be transacted. Two of these nails can be dated to Elizabethan times, whilst the other two nails date from 1625 and 1631. (John Latimer, *Annals of Bristol*, Kingsmead, 1970 / Nikolaus Pevsner, *The Buildings of England: North Somerset and Bristol*, Penguin, 1958)

---

**1788:** The sculptor Edward Hodges Bailey was born in Bristol. He is best known for the 16ft (4.9m)-high sculpture of Nelson, which stands on Nelson's Column in Trafalgar Square, London. George IV also employed him to make sculptures for Buckingham Palace and Admiralty Arch. In his native Bristol examples of his work are comparatively few, but one such example is the frieze over the Freemasons' Hall in Park Street. Bailey also sculpted several monuments, such as Bishop Grey's, which is located in Bristol Cathedral. (www.about-bristol.co.uk / Nikolaus Pevsner, *The Buildings of England: North Somerset and Bristol*, Penguin, 1958)

# March 11th

**1893:** The Clifton Rocks Railway opened. The cliff railway ran from Hotwell Road to Zion Hill, a distance of 500ft (152m). Unusually for a cliff railway, it ran inside a tunnel, as it was felt that a cutting would have a detrimental visual impact on the Avon Gorge. The tunnel was 27½ft (8.3m) wide and 18ft (5.5m) high. The gradient was reported as 1 in 2.223 which, according to a contemporary newspaper report, 'is of course an exception to those accustomed to use anything in the way of railways, but as a lift railway the engineers consider it a good comfortable slope, while steep enough to admit a good shaft of light descending down from the heights above to the waiting room in the Hotwell Road ... For those unaccustomed to travel on cliff railways in this remarkably steep ascent, we may add that the greatest care has been taken to provide for the safety of the cars.' The safety features included a form of automatic braking and double ropes of steel wire. The railway was not a financial success and continued deficits meant that the railway closed on October 1st 1934. A charitable trust is currently working on the restoration of this former attraction. (*Bristol Mercury and Daily Post* / www.cliftonrocksrailway.org.uk)

# March 12th

**1994:** The first women priests were ordained into the Church of England at Bristol Cathedral. Thirty-two women were ordained at the service which lasted two-and-a-quarter hours. Demonstrations were held on College Green outside the Cathedral; however these were largely in favour of the ordination of women. Rt Revd Barry Rogerson, the Bishop of Bristol, was assisted by the Rt Revd Peter Firth, the Bishop of Malmesbury. Each of the candidates had chosen four priests to lay hands on them. The laying on of hands was proceeded by a huge burst of applause and at the peace which followed the hugging and kissing went on for fifteen minutes. The first woman priest in the Church of England is regarded as Angela Berners-Wilson, as she was the first candidate to receive the laying-on of hands. The other women were Waveney Bishop, Christine Clarke, Judith Creighton, Faith Cully, Brendan Dowie, Canon Carol Edwards, Margaret Embry, Annis Fessey, Janet Fortune-Wood, Susan Giles, Jane Haywood, Jean Kings, Karen MacKinnon, Audrey Maddock, Canon Charmain Mann, Helen Marshall, Glenys Mills, Jilliane Norman, Clare Pipe-Wolferstan, June Plummer, Susan Restall, Susan Rose, Susan Shipp, Margery Simpson, Sylvaia Stephens, Judith Thompson, Anita Thorne, Shelia Tyler, Pauline Wall, Sister Rosemary Dawn Watling and Valerie Woods. (*Church Times*)

# March 13th

**1892:** The body of William Boult Monks was recovered from the mine at Easton Colliery. Monks, one of the members of the company that owned the mine, was in his sixties when the accident occurred. He had gone missing two days previously, on the Saturday, when, owing to the cessation of work for a week, he had stayed on at the mine to ensure that everything was in good order and was last seen at 5 p.m. His family, who lived at The Grange, Hanham, became concerned when he did not return home and the next morning made inquiries at the mine. The worse was feared when his coat was found at the top of a shaft to the mine. The shaftsman, George Rax, lowered himself down to recover the body. Monks had fallen 300 fathoms and his body was badly mutilated. The pocketwatch Monks had been wearing was said to be 'doubled-up in the most extraordinary manner' owing to the violence with which Monks landed. As testament to the dangerous nature of mining at the period, it was reported that George Rax had, during the course of his working life, assisted in the recovery of over 300 bodies of his co-workers. (*Bristol Mercury and Daily Post*)

# March 14th

**1941:** Henry Walford Davies was born in Oswestry, Shropshire on September 6th 1869. He was admitted as a boy chorister to St George's Chapel, Windsor in 1882 and, after his voice broke, he became assistant organist there. In 1919 he became chairman of the National Council of Music for Wales – a post he held until his death. He was particularly known as a recitalist of Victorian organ works, particularly those by Herbert Parry. During the First World War, Walford Davies had been assisting with the 'Fight for Right' movement, organising musical events which included the commissioning of Parry's setting of 'Jerusalem'. He was knighted for his services to music in 1922. In 1926 he was appointed music advisor for the BBC and commissioned a variety of programmes, including *Music and the Ordinary Listener* (1926-29) and *Everyman's Music* (1940-41). As a composer he is best known for his miniature works, including the introit *God be in Head* and the *R.A.F. March Past*. On the outbreak of the Second World War he moved to Bristol with the BBC's Religion Department, where he died on March 11th 1941. His funeral took place on this date at Bristol Cathedral and his ashes were laid in the cathedral garden. (*Oxford Dictionary of National Biography*, OUP)

# March 15th

**1872:** An exhibition held at the Colston Hall, which starred the 'two-headed nightingale', finished. The 'two-headed nightingale' were in fact Millie and Chrissie McKoy, African-American conjoined twins. Their parents, Jacob and Monemia, were slaves owned by Jabez McKay, a blacksmith. He recognised the twins' commercial value and sold them when they were just 10 months old for $1,000. By the time they were six they had been sold three times. When slavery was abolished they chose to stay with their owner, Joseph Pearson Smith. They were able to speak five different languages, play the piano and the guitar, and possessed good singing voices. Queen Victorian even invited them to Buckingham Palace, where they were presented with diamond hairclips in 1871. They later became involved with assisting African-American schools and churches in the southern USA. They died from pneumonia in 1912. (Nicola Sly, *A Grim Almanac of Bristol*, The History Press, 2011 / *American National Biography Online*)

———•◆•———

**1932:** A fire engine from Avonmouth Fire Station was responding to a call in the Lawrence Weston area of the city when it veered off the road. The firemen, 'undismayed at this mishap, ran the last part of the way to the fire.' (Dennis Hill, *Firefighting in Bristol 1877-1974*, The History Press, 2007)

# March 16th

**1941:** One of the worst air raids Bristol suffered during the Second World War started shortly before 8.30 p.m. It lasted for more than five hours before the 'Raider's Passed' was sounded. However, the raid began anew only ten minutes later and continued until 4.12 a.m. Bombing was heavy and persistent and an estimated 700-800 high explosives and several thousand incendiary bombs fell upon the city. It left 257 injured and 391 people dead. St Barnabus' Church crypt suffered a direct hit and fifteen bodies were later discovered. Bombing affected a wide area of the city but especially the districts of Whitehall, Eastville and Fishponds. The districts of Easton, Montpelier, Kingsdown and St Paul's were also affected. During this raid St Michael's Church was set on fire. (Reece Winstone, *Bristol in the 1940s*, 1961)

---

**1999:** Pero's Bridge, which links Narrow Quay and Queen's Square with Millennium Square, was dedicated. It was designed by artist Ellis O'Connell in partnership with engineer's Ove Arup. The bridge is named after a slave owned by Bristol merchant and plantation owner John Pinney, who had estates on Nevis in the Leeward Islands. Pero became his manservant and first came to Bristol in 1783, dying in 1798 after becoming ill. (Bristol City Council website / *Oxford Dictionary of National Biography*, OUP)

# March 17th

**1775:** The unfortunate death of Revd Thomas Newnham occurred. Newnham, a minor canon of Bristol Cathedral, went with his sister and two friends on an excursion to a cavern near Brentry on the edge of Bristol, known as Pen Park Hole. Newnham wished to know the depth of the cavern and clung to an ash branch overlooking the entrance to the cave in order to drop a plumb line. However, the branch from which he was hanging suddenly snapped and he fell 200ft (60m) into a deep pool of water at the bottom of the cave. Repeated attempts were made to recover his body but it was not until over a month later, on April 25th, that a successful attempt was made. He was thought to have been around twenty-five years of age. Pen Park Hole was one of the first caves to be surveyed, as early as 1683. Its formation owes to geothermal water and is the only cave known in Britain to be formed in such a way. Access to the cave is controlled by the City Council. (John Latimer, *Annals of Bristol*, Kingsmead, 1970 / *University of Bristol Speleological Society Newsletter Spring 2007*)

# March 18th

**1880:** Robert Henry Tilstone Barnes was walking home across the Clifton Suspension Bridge at around 10 o'clock at night when he noticed a man's coat and hat in the middle of the roadway. He looked towards the trelliswork and saw that a tall man was about to jump off the 245ft (76m)-high bridge. Barnes put his hands through the balustrade and grabbed the man's arms, and, despite the man's efforts to work himself loose, Barnes kept hold of him until help arrived. By that time the man attempting suicide had gradually slipped through the rescuer's hands so that Barnes only held the man by one of his wrists. Barnes's efforts to save the would-be suicide victim from a near-certain death was much appreciated by his fellow citizens, for 558 of them subscribed to a fund to present him with a gold watch and chain. The names of the subscribers were written in a book and presented to Barnes in the presence of the Mayor of Bristol on May 10th. The Mayor wished that Barnes would for many years to come wear the watch and chain that he was being presented with. (*Bristol Mercury and Daily Post*)

# March 19th

**1791:** Reports emerge of an elopement involving schoolgirl Clementina Clarke, who was under 15 years of age and in the care of Miss Mills, a schoolmistress in Park Street. Clementina was an heiress to her uncle's fortune, which had been made in Jamaica and brought an income of £6,000 a year. This fortune had come to the attention of an apothecary named Richard V. Perry, who furtively sought the attentions of Clementina whilst she was promenading with her companions. During one such promenade, Perry slipped in to her hand a note that she should go off with him and be married at Gretna Green. Bribing a servant allowed Clementina to escape the safety of Miss Mills. Following the elopement the schoolmistress pursued the couple as far as Belgium, but without any success. On Perry's return to England he was arrested on suspicion of abduction, but was acquitted at his trial in April 1794 when Clementina swore that she had left of her own accord. The couple eventually separated and Clementina died in poverty in Bath in 1812. Perry, however, moved to Jamaica and lived under the name of Ogilvie in magnificent style, and was even a candidate for the House of Assembly in 1816. (John Latimer, *Annals of Bristol*, Kingsmead, 1970)

# March 20th

**1855:** The iron bridge carrying the Bath Road across the River Avon was struck by a Cardiff steam barge, completely destroying the structure. The vessel that caused the accident had delivered a cargo of coke to the railway works and was returning downstream. A strong current, coupled with unskilful boat handling, allowed the vessel to strike the iron ribs of the bridge with such force that it led to the structure collapsing, which, according to an eyewitness, collapsed 'like a child's house of cards'. Two people lost their lives in the accident, one of whom was a wagoner whose cart was found the day after the accident at downstream Rownham. The building of the iron bridge was not without incident, for on February 20th 1806 the bridge suddenly collapsed when it was nearing completion. Two workmen lost their lives but the design of the bridge was not changed when work commenced on a replacement, leading many to predict the bridge's collapse. After collapsing for the second time a replacement was duly ordered and a ferry established during construction. By June 5th 1855, the work had advanced sufficiently to allow people to walk across. (John Latimer, *Annals of Bristol*, Kingsmead, 1970)

# March 21st

**1985:** Sir Michael Scudamore Redgrave, actor, was born at St Michael's Hill, Bristol on March 20th 1908. Soon afterwards he was taken by his parents to Australia, where his father was acting. His parents divorced three years later and he returned with his mother to Britain. Michael was educated at Clifton College before going on to study medieval and modern languages and English at Magdalene College, Cambridge. Whilst here he undertook much acting and edited university magazines. After graduating he had a brief spell as a modern languages teacher at Cranleigh School, Surrey, until he left to act at the Liverpool Playhouse. He met his wife, Rachel Kemoson, in a production of *The Flowers of the Forest* and they had three children, Vanessa, Corin and Lynn, who also went on to become well-known actors. He acted in a wide variety of plays, including Shakespeare, and reluctantly went on to star in films when Hitchcock cast him in *The Lady Vanishes* in 1939. He was awarded a CBE in 1952 and was knighted in 1959. Redgrave's books include *The Actor's Ways and Means* (1953) and *Mask or Face* (1958). His autobiography was published in 1983. He died in a nursing home at Denham, Buckinghamshire on this date in 1985. (*Oxford Dictionary of National Biography*, OUP)

# March 22nd

**1744:** On October 27th 1743, a farmer named Winter of Charlton had gone to Bristol market with some cattle. Two men, Andrew Burnet and Henry Payne, waited for his return along the Stoke's Croft to Durdham road, believing that he would return with the proceeds of the sale, which they intended to steal. However, Farmer Winter remained in Bristol overnight. Travelling back along that road was a man named Richard Ruddle, coachman to Sir Robert Cann, who had also been in Bristol. Near Stoke Court the robbers struck Ruddle with such brutality that he died from his injuries. The robbers escaped with a watch. About a week later a man entered a watchmaker's shop and asked for a watch to be repaired. The watchmaker, being suspicious, asked the man where he had obtained the watch; whereupon the man replied that he had obtained it from a man in a pub. The man was taken to the pub by a constable, who recognised the assailants and was able to make their arrest. The men were condemned at the next assize to be hanged and gibbeted on Durdham Down. On March 22nd 1774 they were conveyed to the place where the crime occurred and the sentence carried out. (John Latimer, *Annals of Bristol*, Kingsmead, 1970)

# March 23rd

**1811:** 'A trifling riot took place in our market this morning, which we are induced to notice in this manner, in order to prevent the ill effects of any exaggerated statements which may be circulated amongst our country friends on the subject. A material advance in the price of fresh butter having taken place, this article having been sold yesterday for *2s 6d* per pound, a party of the lower orders of workmen and colliers met the market-people at Ashton turnpike this morning, took forcible possession of the butter and sold it at a shilling a pound, returning the money to the owners of the butter but in most instances the parties in this outrage, who were themselves the purchasers, disposed of it again at *2s* a pound!' Similar disturbances took place at the High Street market, where the populace seized butter in order that it was sold at what the perpetrators considered a fair price and also gave it to the market people to whom they had plundered. This continued until all the butter had been sold and a party of constables arrived and 'the market was soon cleared, and half a dozen most active in the disturbance have been sent to brood over the exploits of the day in Bridewell.' (*The Times*)

# March 24th

**1761:** An early reference to Joseph Fry is contained in the following announcement in the *Bristol Journal* of this date, stating that 'Joseph Fry, Apothecary, is removed from Small Street to a house opposite Chequer Lane in Narrow Wine Street, where he makes his chocolate as usual.' In November 1761, Fry had taken over the patent once held by Walter Churchman, who had been manufacturing chocolate in the city since 1728. Fry's firm initially concentrated on producing cocoa rather than chocolate, which was sold on the basis of its health properties. Chocolate was not developed as a luxury product until the 1860s. Fry's expanded rapidly in the later half of the nineteenth century and opened seven new factories in Bristol between 1860 and 1907. Production moved to a new site at Keynsham as Fry's merged with Cadbury's in 1919. In 1935 the firm became a subsidiary of Cadbury-Schwepps. The company was taken over by Kraft, which, although initially promising to keep the Somerdale plant open, stopped production at the site in January 2011, causing a great deal of anger locally. (John Latimer, *Annals of Bristol*, Kingsmead, 1970 / Helen Reid, *Bristol & Co.*, Redcliffe Press, 1987 / BBC News website)

# March 25th

**1517:** 'The Mayor [Richard Hobbey] died on 25 March and John Jay succeeding him. Also this year whereas there was a custom in Bristow for the relief of prisoners in Newgate that every one that bought in any thing to be sold in the market should pay the jailer for pitching down of every pot a halfpenny; because of the jailers did convert it to their own profit and wronged the poor prisoners thereby, one Mr Richard Abbington to reform the abuse, and ... with the consent of the Mayor, this Mr Jay, put down this disordered custom; and the said Abbington of his own costs purchased a maintenance for the prisoners.' (William Adams, *Adams's Chronicle of Bristol*, J.W. Arrowsmith, 1910)

———◆———

**1571:** 'The market place in St Thomas's Street built this year with land purchased from the Queen by Mr Michael Sowdley an apothecary. On this day it was proclaimed at the High Cross that this market was to be kept forever upon Thursdays starting next week.' (William Adams, *Adams's Chronicle of Bristol*, J.W. Arrowsmith, 1910)

———◆———

**1808:** A double duel took place at Stapleton involving four French prisoners, two of whom were mortally wounded. A verdict of manslaughter was reached against the two survivors at the next Gloucester Assizes but they were acquitted the following month. (John Latimer, *Annals of Bristol*, Kingsmead, 1970)

# March 26th

**1603:** 'Our King was proclaimed at the High Crosse of Bristoll by John Aldworth sheriff, and as Philip Jenkins writeth and another he was proclaimed on the 29th March 1603 by Sir George Snig our recorder, by whom myself [John Adams, author of *Adams's Chronicle of Bristol*] was then an eyewitness, First Trigs the trumpeter sounded 4 times solemnly and mournfully, turning himself 4 several ways upon the cross, for the death of her Majestie; then 4 times and 4 ways joyfully for the entrance of King James; and then our recorder read and pronounced the proclamation aloud; and on 25th July 1603 our King was crowned at Westminster by Doctor Whitegift Archbishop of Canterbury.' (William Adams, *Adams's Chronicle of Bristol*, J.W. Arrowsmith, 1910)

———— ◆ ————

**1938:** The Ambassador cinema in Kingswood opened. The Art Deco building had a stained-glass window celebrating cricketing hero W.G. Grace, who once lived in nearby Downend. During the Second World War a mine exploded at the rear of the premises. No one was hurt but a salesgirl was blown out of the cinema and into the foyer. The cinema was renamed the Odeon after being taken over by Oscar Deutsch after the war, and closed on March 11th 1961. (Dave Stephenson & Jill Willmott, *Bristol Cinemas*, The History Press, 2005)

# March 27th

**1906:** Fireman Arthur Wale died whilst tackling a blaze at Derham's seven-storey boot and shoe factory. He was killed when the front wall of the factory collapsed and was the first member of Bristol Fire Brigade to die attending a blaze. He left behind a widow and eight children. On the occasion of his funeral his coffin was carried to St Mary Redcliffe Church on a fire tender. Bristol Fire Brigade had been formed on July 1st 1877 directly as a result of a series of devastating fires in the city. Prior to this, half a dozen insurance companies had provided a limited number of firemen equipped with manual fire engines. The police constabulary also had limited equipment to fight fires. However, this was felt inadequate and five of the insurance companies handed over their fire-fighting equipment to Bristol City Council, who also purchased a steam-powered horse-drawn fire engine. The new brigade of twelve men operated from Bridewell Street police station. Bristol Fire Brigade existed until 1974, when it became part of the Avon Fire Brigade, created when the new county was formed. (Dennis Hill, *Firefighting in Bristol 1877-1974*, The History Press, 2007)

# March 28th

**1764:** The foundation stone of the new Bristol Bridge was laid after a somewhat protracted process to procure a replacement. A committee had been formed as early as 1758 in order to work out the best way to acquire funds. The aptly named James Bridges produced a design for the replacement. However, this design proved controversial and sparked debates as to whether the river should be bridged in a single span or using the existing piers. It took two years and seventy-six meetings, accompanied by angry pamphlets and letters in the newspapers from rival architects and their supporters, before it was decided to bridge the river using the existing piers according to the design of James Bridges. Bridges though had enough of the wrangling and the replacement bridge was eventually built by Thomas Paty. The new bridge opened in September 1768, with the Mayor being the first to cross it in a carriage. It was felt desirable to replace the original medieval bridge, which was thought unsafe owing to the numerous shops and houses that had been built on it, impeding the flow of traffic over it and causing numerous accidents. A wider road was built across the bridge in Victorian times on top of the Georgian structure. (John Latimer, *Annals of Bristol*, Kingsmead, 1970 / Andrew Foyle, *Pevsner Architectural Guides: Bristol*, Yale University Press, 2004 / www.buildinghistory.org)

# March 29th

**1628:** Tobias Matthew, Archbishop of York, dies. He was born around the year 1544 at Bristol Bridge, which was then the heart of Bristol's mercantile community. Whilst at Oxford he came under the influence of James Calfill, a Scottish Protestant, who apparently persuaded Matthew to be ordained – something that upset his parents. Matthew was something of a 'rising star' at Oxford, known for the depth of his learning and his eloquence. His promotions in the Church at this stage seem to have been to support his Oxford career. As a theologian he was committed to the Calvinist viewpoint. In 1581 Edmund Campion published *Decem Rationes*, which was a defence of the Roman Catholic Church in which he accused Matthew of not being sufficiently read in scriptures. He wrote a defensive sermon preached in October of that year, which was circulated widely in manuscript form. In 1583 he became Dean of Durham and was Bishop of the diocese from 1595. Here he used a network of spies to root out Papists and increased the numbers of licensed preachers. He became Archbishop of York in 1696 and continued to have great influence in religious affairs until his death. (*Oxford Dictionary of National Biography*, OUP)

# March 30th

**1962:** A report from *The Times* 'Special Correspondent' read: 'Extensive studies in local broadcasting have been made by the BBC; and here today it was the turn of the commercial interests to show for the first time how they would handle the situation if local broadcasting, in one form or another, eventually becomes a fact in Britain. The demonstration by South Western Broadcasting Ltd was on a closed circuit. It was attended by MPs, representatives of more than fifty registered local radio companies from other parts of Britain, the press and principles of most of the leading advertising agencies – and the BBC.' A full day's radio schedule of twenty hours was shortened to two hours for the demonstration and local news was provided by the *Bristol Evening Post*. Just over eight years later, BBC Radio Bristol first began broadcasting, on September 4th 1970. The station's first programme was *Morning West* and was presented by Joanthan Fullford, with the familiar voices of Kate Adie and Roger Bennet, who went on to host the show. (*The Times* / BBC News website)

# March 31st

**1718:** John Bracegirdle, a tide surveyor, appeared before the Mayor giving information regarding a seditious sermon that he heard preached by the Revd Edward Blisse a few days previously at St George's Church, near Pill. The controversial sermon was a tirade against both George I, the reigning monarch, and the previous king, William III, claiming they were usurpers to the throne. Blisse argued that the country was doomed to failure unless the rightful king, James III, was restored to the throne and whom Blisse referred to as his master. The pretender, James III, was the son of James II, who had fled England owing to the threat of invasion from William of Orange in 1685, during the Glorious Revolution. Blisse had taken the oath of allegiance to George I, which Anglican clergy were required to make, but in wishing to make amends for this, Blisse vented his opinions around the country. The following November he was convicted at the assize for Wiltshire, Buckinghamshire and Somerset and sentenced to be imprisoned for four years, to be exposed twice in the pillory, and was fined £600. Since he had taken the oath the authorities were not able to deprive him of his livings, which he held for several years. (John Latimer, *Annals of Bristol*, Kingsmead, 1970)

# April 1st

**1974:** Bristol lost its county status, held since 1373, and became a district of the new county of Avon, formed from Bristol City, southern Gloucestershire and parts of Somerset. The last council meeting ended at midnight and it became the first meeting of the district council. The new district Mayor, Bert Peglar, was given his Chain of Office at midnight by Jack Fisk, the former Bristol County Mayor. (*Western Daily Press*)

---

**1979:** The first bungee jump in the UK was undertaken by members of the Oxford University Dangerous Sports Society, off Clifton Suspension Bridge; creating a new extreme sport. The students were dressed in top hat and tails and performed a four-man simultaneous jump. They were arrested shortly afterwards. (http://library.thinkquest.org/C0123122/historybungee.htm)

---

**1996:** After twenty-two years as a county, road signs marking the county of Avon were uprooted today as four new super councils were formed as part of major local government reorganisation. Bristol City regained its county status, lost in 1974. The Lord Mayor, Mrs Joan McLaren, celebrated the occasion by riding through Bristol in a carriage drawn by two shire horses. (*Western Daily Press*)

# April 2nd

**1809:** With Bristol in urgent need of improvements to its harbour to accommodate shipping, William Jessop suggested the construction of a floating harbour. His scheme was duly adopted and the first boats entered the Bathurst Basin on this date. The official opening came on May 1st 1809. (John Latimer, *Annals of Bristol*, Kingsmead, 1970)

———— •◆• ————

**1980:** A riot started in the St Paul's district of the city when police raided the Black and White Café, a known drugs den. It is not known the exact cause of the riot, which went on for several hours. Over 200 policemen went into the St Paul's district to try and restore law and order. Ten police cars were burnt in the disturbances and Lloyds Bank and a post office were also set on fire. Nineteen police officers and six civilians required hospital treatment. Protected by riot shields, the police slowly fought off a crowd of youths who threw bricks and bottles. *The Times* highlighted the racial tensions that existed between the predominantly black community of St Paul's and the police. Although around 130 people were arrested during the riots, no one was prosecuted for any crime. (*The Times*)

# April 3rd

**1817:** A young woman was discovered in Almondsbury wearing a black turban and speaking an unknown language. She had long black hair, brown eyes and very white teeth. She gained the sympathy of Elizabeth Worrell, the wife of Bristol's Town Clerk, who rented Knole Park manor house. Her husband, however, felt that she should be tried for vagrancy and she was imprisoned at Bristol prison. While there, she was identified by a Portuguese sailor, Manuel Enes, who claimed to understand her language and stated that she was from an island called Javasu. He said that she had been kidnapped by pirates, but had managed to jump overboard into the Bristol Channel. He gave her name as Princess Caraboo. That summer, Caraboo spent her time at Knole and performed an exotic war dance, archery, provided written examples of her language and swam naked in the lake. Caraboo's origins were in fact far more humble, for it transpired that Caraboo was actually Mary Wilcox, daughter of a Devon cobbler. Apparently, after suffering from a bout of rheumatic fever as a child, she had, according to her father, 'never been right in the head.' Her later years were spent in Bedminster, supplying leaches to the local infirmary. She died on Christmas Eve 1864 and was buried in Hebron Road burial ground. (*Oxford Dictionary of National Biography*, OUP)

# April 4th

**1876:** A Chapter meeting was held at Bristol Cathedral, at which petitions and protests were voiced against statues that had recently been placed in niches in the north porch of the cathedral. The statues, sculpted by James Redfern, depicted saints with their traditional attributes: the Virgin Mary, the Virgin Mary with Christ Child, St Gregory crowed with Papal tiara, St Ambrose carrying a triple scourge, St Jerome in a cardinal's hat and St Augustine carrying a burning heart. The figures led to protests by some Protestants, who claimed that they were evidence for a creeping Catholicism in the Church of England. Without consultation, the Dean engaged a gang of workmen to remove the statues from their niches. The Dean's action brought a series of protests from the architect of Bristol Cathedral's nave, G.E. Street, who wrote to both the Dean and the *Guardian* newspaper alleging that the Dean's actions had damaged the statues and that the offending Catholic attributes could have easily been removed. The statue of the Virgin Mary was badly damaged during the removal but the others were repaired and were removed by Street to the East Heslerton church in the East Riding of Yorkshire. The niches were later filled with depictions of the four Evangelists. (Joseph Bettey, *Bristol Cathedral: The Rebuilding of the Nave*, Historical Association, 1993)

# April 5th

**1755:** The *Bristol Journal* contained the following advertisement 'inviting handicraft tradesmen, husbandmen, and boys to go over to the city of Philadelphia in a ship of 200 tons burthen, lying at the Quay, the captain held out the usual bait of "a new suit to each passenger."' Emigration to America in the eighteenth century was somewhat limited. Many who left England were often so poor that they were unable to pay for their passage and could thus be forced to work as servants for a certain number of years. (John Latimer, *Annals of Bristol*, Kingsmead, 1970)

---

**2011:** BBC News reported that a would-be thief was trapped inside a clothes-recycling bin near Bradley Stoke for four hours after he tried to steal used clothes. CCTV images showed the man being helped into the small opening of the bin by an accomplice. When security staff approached, the accomplice ran off and the fire brigade were called to cut open the top of the bin in order to get the thief out. A 28-year-old man was arrested by police on suspicion of theft and was issued with a caution. (BBC News website)

# April 6th

**1719:** A letter of this date from Sir William Daines stated that he represented Bristol in Parliament for over twenty years at a cost to himself of over £10,000. As small compensation, he asked that his sister's son, Thomas Cary, be appointed landing-waiter in the Custom House. It was decided that the request would be granted upon a vacancy. The letter is indicative of the system of political patronage at this time. (John Latimer, *Annals of Bristol*, Kingsmead, 1970)

———— ◆ ————

**1817:** The Bristol mail coach journeying towards London was robbed of a parcel containing £80 in silver. 'The person to whose care the package was entrusted, left Bristol by the mail on Sunday evening, having placed the parcel in the seat-box of the coach. On arriving at Bath, he looked in the place, and at that time the parcel was perfectly safe. He gave himself no farther concern about it, until the coach stopped at Hounslow, when he again examined the seat-box, and, to his great consternation, discovered that the package was gone ... A man who came inside from Marlborough to Newbury is suspected to be the person by whom the robbery was committed.' (*The Times*)

# April 7th

**1824:** Hugh O'Neill, best known as an architectural draughtsman, was born in Bloomsbury, London on April 20th 1784. Although little is known of his early life, between 1800 and 1804 exhibited at the Royal Academy, and in 1803 he won a silver palette from the Society of Artists. His pictures were often published, for example many of his drawings were included in *Skelton's Antiquities of Bristol* and his drawings of the ruined Christ Church, Oxford after the 1809 fire were engraved and subsequently published. He tended to keep the original drawings, selling only copies. In 1821 he moved to Bristol and made over 500 drawings of the city. He died in poverty in Princes Street on this date in 1824. (*Oxford Dictionary of National Biography*, OUP)

———— ◆ ————

**1978:** Lord Beswick, chairman of British Aerospace, and the Lord Mayor of Bristol, Ted Wright, opened Bristol Industrial Museum in the M Shed, Princes Wharf. (David J. Eveleigh, *A Century of Bristol*, The History Press, 2007)

# April 8th

**1819:** The execution of William Burton for the murder of William Symns took place following his trial at the Gloucester Assizes. On November 3rd 1818, the men had travelled together in a boat from Woolaston to Bristol, where William Symns had business. A witness saw the two men in the boat on the return voyage from Bristol, however, on reaching Woolaston, only Burton got out of the boat. Suspicions were soon aroused as Burton went to Bristol a pauper and came back with some unexpected riches. On November 27th a decomposed body was hauled from the Severn. Nevertheless, it was possible to identify the body as William Symns, who was killed with two blows to the head. Signs of blood were also found in the gun whales of the boat. In the end Burton acknowledged the justice of his sentence. (*The Times*)

———— ◆ ————

**1822:** The *Bristol Journal* records that 'the annual scenes of rude festivity and, may we add of low debauchery, known by the name of the "Bedminster revels", took place on Monday, as usual at this period of the year; and a fight of no interest was exhibited on Durdham Down between two combatants of little note and less skill.' (Quoted in John Latimer, *Annals of Bristol*, Kingsmead, 1970)

# *April 9th*

**1969:** Concorde's first flight in the UK took place, travelling from Filton Airport to RAF Faiford, and piloted by Brian Tubshaw. The flight lasted a mere twenty-two minutes. Concorde did not fly supersonic on this occasion and was limited to 10,000ft (3,000m) and 250kt. Although it was the first flight of Concorde in Britain, the very first flight by Concorde had been made from Tolouse Airport on February 2nd 1969, piloted by Andre Turcat, who said on landing the new supersonic jet that 'finally the big bird flies, and I can say it flies pretty well.' The noise of the crowd witnessing that first flight was drowned out by the sound of the four Olympus 593 engines, which were built jointly by the Bristol division of Rolls-Royce and the French SNECMA organisation. The first supersonic flight was not made until October 1st that same year. There followed an exhaustive testing of the aircraft, which took Concorde to many destinations around the world. It took 5,000 hours of test flights before the first commercial service started on January 21st 1976, when British Airways flew from London to Bahrain and Air France from Paris to Rio de Janeiro. (BBC News website / Peter R. March, *The Concorde Story*, Sutton, 2005)

# April 10th

**1835:** The trial of Mary Ann Burdock for murder began and lasted two days. The victim was an elderly woman named Clara Ann Smith, who had died on October 23rd 1833. Clara Smith had been lodging with the accused in College Street. Relatives of the deceased had heard nothing from her for about a year and became concerned for her welfare. They made enquires at Burdock's house but did not find the answers given by her satisfactory, nor did they find any of the considerable property that Clara was known to have possessed. The body was disinterred fourteen months after burial and it was discovered that the stomach contained traces of arsenic. Other evidence against the accused included the fact that Burdock had administered all of Clara's food to her and had purchased a quantity of arsenic. Furthermore, £800 had been received by Clara shortly before her death, and after her death Mary Burdock had become suddenly rich. The jury found Burdock guilty and she was sentenced to death. After the trial Burdock showed indifference to her fate. She asked her brother not to spend more than £2 on her coffin and gave instructions to be provided with a 'warm, comfortable shroud'. She was hanged on April 15th in the presence of 50,000 spectators. (John Latimer, *Annals of Bristol*, Kingsmead, 1970)

# April 11th

**1941:** The final tram in Bristol ran from Old Market to Kingswood. It was the last tram scheduled for that day and was crewed by Driver Webster and Conductor Arthur Brittan. The bombing of Bristol that night began at 10 p.m. as the tram was heading for the relative safety of the suburbs. At 10.30 p.m. the tram came to a sudden halt; the bombing had taken out St Phillips Bridge and disconnected the power supply. Left without any power, the driver and conductor thought that a push from behind would get the tram to the top of the next downward slope, which ran to Kingswood Depot at the end of the line. With some assistance from members of the public the tram was once again moving on its own, with gravity providing the necessary force as it travelled down Hill Street. Driver Webster did not apply the brakes of the tram until it had swung in through the gates of the depot and brought the tram to a halt just outside the main shed. It was not possible to restore the power supply for the tramways and so the Regional Traffic Commissioner authorised the closure of the tramways network. (John B. Appleby, *Bristol Trams Remembered*, 1969)

# April 12th

**1894:** At 7.30 in the evening a group of eighteen football enthusiasts met in the home of Fred Keenhan on Milford Road, Southville. Their topic of conversation was the future of the game in south Bristol following the disbanding of Bristol South FC after they had won the South Bristol and District League. As a result of this meeting a new club was formed, known as Bristol South End. Twelve days later a general meeting was held to announce this decision. The new team would play in red shirts and dark navy shorts. Gaining entry to the Bristol and District League proved difficult and so the organisers arranged that Bristol South End would play against any club who would give them a game. The first match eventually took place on September 1st of that year against Swindon Town, who were then West of England Champions. The event attracted 3,500 spectators but Swindon Town won 4-2. In that season all the local clubs played against the new team. The only exception was Bedminster FC, who were aggrieved that this new club had poached some of their players. On May 10th 1896 the club changed its name, becoming what it is known as today – Bristol City. (Peter Godsiff, *Bristol City: The Complete History of the Club*, Wensum Books, 1979)

# *April 13th*

**1808:** An 'extraordinary inundation' of the River Frome took place on this date and by the following morning some parts of the city was under up to 4ft of water. A stream of water was said to be 'rushing with the utmost impetuosity through Newfoundland Street, Milk Street, Rosemary Land, Old King Street, Merchant Street, Broadmead and St James's Back.' The flood took three days to subside. (*The Times*)

❖

**1873:** Easter Sunday in 1873 fell on this date and J.S. Fry, whose factory was then located in Union Street, produced the first chocolate Easter Eggs in the UK. An inspection report from 1866 details the treatment of workers at the factory. Employees were expected to be Christian, punctual and clean, and were fined for lateness, singing and eating the firm's products. The men worked from 6 a.m. to 6 p.m. and the women from 8 a.m. to 6 p.m., male and female workers being segregated. These hours were shorter than some of the other factories in Bristol. The workplace was clean, light and airy, and Fry's took an interest in the education and health of their employees. (Helen Reid, *Bristol & Co.*, Redcliffe Press, 1987 / *Easter Brand Factsheet* produced by Cadbury's and on their website)

# April 14th

**1965:** The new Plimsoll Bridge, built at a cost of £2,650,000, was opened by Mr Fraser, Minister of Transport. The new bridge, located at the Cumberland Basin, carries the A4 over the River Avon and can be swung open to allow tall vessels to pass through. However, a few hours after the official opening the bridge developed a fault in an electrical duct and the whole system had to be shut down. The fault prevented the 865-ton cantilever bridge from opening properly and traffic had to be diverted to a nearby swingbridge as engineers commenced emergency repairs. Police patrol cars and police motorcyclists used radio communication sets to keep in touch with the radio control room to sort out the rush-hour traffic. Mr Fraser was also taken to see the building of the Severn Bridge and the proposed Portbury Dock extension from the air by helicopter. However, due of thick fog, the minister was forced to land in a Somerset motel car park. He was taken to Bristol Airport by car to continue his journey back to London, albeit an hour and ten minutes late. (*The Times*)

# April 15th

**1892:** Amelia Edwards, best known for her work as an Egyptologist, died in Western-super-Mare and was subsequently buried in St Mary's churchyard, Henbury. Amelia first visited Egypt in 1873 and became fascinated with the place. On meeting some friends in Italy, they formed an expedition group and sailed up the Nile to Wadi Halfa. Whilst at Abu Simbel the party discovered and excavated a small, unknown temple with a painted chamber. The experiences gained on this visit were written up in Edwards' book *A Thousand Miles up the Nile* and illustrated with her own watercolours. From 1878 she contributed to weekly journals on the subject of Egypt to stimulate interest in the region. Whilst in Egypt Amelia became troubled by the neglect and vandalism of ancient monuments by the visitors. An opportunity arose to form a scientific expedition looking at Egypt's ancient monuments and the *Egypt Excavation Society* was formed on March 27th 1882, Amelia taking an active role raising funds, lecturing and reporting the society's findings to the press. In 1886 Smith College in Massachusetts awarded her an honorary LLD – the first woman to be awarded this distinction. She contracted a lung infection in October 1891 whilst supervising the arrival of antiquities from Egypt at London Docks and died a few months later. (*Oxford Dictionary of National Biography*, OUP)

# April 16th

**1468:** William Canynges (1402-1474), a successful Bristol merchant and shipbuilder, was ordained priest by Bishop John Carpenter of Worcester. Before this point Canynges had concerned himself with temporal affairs – with businesses interests and a political role in the governance of Bristol. He became the city's bailiff in 1432 and was elected Mayor for the first time in 1441. He held the post an additional four times. In 1429 he married Joan Burton, the daughter of another prominent Bristol family. They had two sons whom Canynges attempted to set up as country gentlemen. However, although his sons were married, they died before their father and were both childless. In 1467 Canyges's wife also died and this event marks a turning point for Canynges, who studied for holy orders and when ordained priest became a canon in Westbury-on-Trym Church and preband of Goodringhill. He enriched the fabric of St Mary Redcliffe Church by establishing two chantry chapels. He was made Dean at Westbury-on-Trym in June 1469. He died on either the 17th or 19th of November 1474 and is buried at St Mary Redcliffe Church in the south transept alongside his wife. An effigy of Canynges in canonical vestments, said to have come from Westbury-on-Trym Church during the time of the Dissolution, is also nearby. (*Oxford Dictionary of National Biography*, OUP)

# April 17th

**1956:** The new Bristol Council House was formally opened by HM the Queen. The building, which was begun in 1938, was designed by E. Vincent Harris. Of particular note are the two 12ft (4m)-high bronze unicorn statues on the roof at either end of the building, designed by sculptor David McFall. The unicorns arrived at the building in October 1950 and caused much confusion at the Council. The workmen, noting two flat plinths on top of the roof, assumed that that was where they were to go and made preparations to get the two statues up and onto the roof. However, an order to stop came from Alderman Frank Sheppard, chairman of the city's building committee, and the unicorns were placed under tarpaulin with Sheppard stating that 'we know nothing about the unicorns until today, and we decided to postpone their erection until the committee had considered the matter and the architect Mr Vincent Harris had been given a chance to explain.' The architect was on holiday in Italy and so it was a few weeks before the go-ahead to allow the erection was given. The architect had substituted them for a length of ornamental ridging which would have cost £600 more. (*The Mail / The Express / Bristol Evening Post*)

# April 18th

**1867:** The railway line between Bristol and Portishead opens. It was built by the Bristol and Portishead Railway Company. A line had first been proposed by Isambard Kingdom Brunel in 1839. The line is closed to passengers but the freight only branch currently serves Portbury Docks. (John Latimer, *Annals of Bristol*, Kingsmead, 1970)

---

**1932:** A new Bristol newspaper was published entitled the *Bristol Evening Post*. The first editorial thanked the public for their support before going on to state that 'we do not propose to replicate the facts that are perfectly well known to all, but in regard to our policy we may be permitted to emphasise that we seek to be perfectly impartial, both denominationally and politically. Being human, we do not pretend that we shall never err, but we are going to do our level best to hold the balance evenly ... being owned, directed and produced by the men of the West – the vast proportion born and bred in Bristol – should be able to share so entirely with the feelings, aspirations and desires of our fellow citizens.' Messages of support for the new venture were also printed from the Lord Mayor, the Bishops of Bristol and Clifton, and MPs from the two Bristol constituencies. (*Bristol Evening Post*)

# April 19th

**1785:** With the first manned balloon flight having taken place only a couple of years previously in a balloon made by Montgolfier Brothers in France, there was considerable interest in this country on the matter. *The Times* frequently reported on these early flights: one such report states that 'the inhabitants of Chippenham were agreeably surprised by the appearance of a balloon over that town, which ascended Bristol about three the same day, with Mr Dicker Jun. in a gallery below to conduct it. The wind was so boisterous, that Mr Dicker met with a rather disagreeable journey, being frequently darted upon the ground; and instantly carried to a surprising height in the air, by which the balloon was much damaged, and he was in some degree a sufferer from the trees, having great difficulty to maintain a proper equilibrium.' On landing near Chippenham he was carried on horseback to the town, with many joyful acclamations. It was the first manned balloon flight in Bristol. Previously, in January 1784, a small, unmanned balloon had been launched from Bath, landing on a spot near Kingswood. This spot is today known as Air Balloon Hill. (*The Times* / John Latimer, *Annals of Bristol*, Kingsmead, 1970)

# April 20th

**1832:** George Müller was born in Germany in 1805 and studied to become a preacher, but spent most of his father's allowance on drinking and gambling. His wild ways continued until he attended a religious meeting, when he beleived that God intervened in his life and he announced he was going to become a missionary. He came to England in 1829, settling in Teignmouth as a minister and travelling preacher. On this date in 1832 Müller set out for Bristol. Here he established his first orphanage in Wilson Street, St Paul's, in 1836. He relied on God alone and the generosity of others to ensure that he had sufficient funds to run his orphanages and refused to advertise or solicit donations. One morning, while the children were waiting for breakfast, Müller prayed, 'Father, we thank thee for what Thou are going to give us to eat.' At that moment a baker arrived with fresh bread, claiming that he had been unable to sleep worrying about the hungry orphans. In 1849 Müller re-established his orphanages at Ashley Down – the £100,000 cost raised without any fundraising. He died on March 10th 1898 and is buried in Arnos Vale Cemetery. (*Bristol Evening Post* / A.T. Pierson, *George Müller of Bristol*, Inglis, 1900)

# *April 21st*

**1886:** The funeral of Colonel John Charles Campbell Daunt took place at Redland Green Chapel (now Redland parish church) with full military honours. Colonel Daunt gained the Victoria Cross for acts of heroism during the Indian Mutiny of 1857. On October 2nd 1857 he saw action against the Ramghur Battalion mutineers at Chrota Nagpore, when he was a lieutenant. Two enemy guns were causing problems for British forces during the fight and so, with Sergeant Denis Dynon, Daunt rushed forward, firing a pistol at the two enemy gunners and managed to stop further shooting. A month later, on November 2nd 1857, Daunt, together with Rattray's Sikhs, an infantry regiment of the British Indian Army, pursued a large body of mutineers of the 32nd Bengal Native Infantry into an enclosure, where he was severely wounded. Despite his wounds the preservation of his company was largely put down to his gallantry. In 1886 he was residing at Overy House in Belgrave Road, Bristol, where he was on leave from the army. His health had deteriorated and an extension to his leave was granted. He died suddenly from 'an affection of the heart' on April 13th and was buried in the grounds of Redland church. (*Bristol Mercury and Daily Post* / Redland Church website)

# April 22nd

**1876:** The first public meeting of the Bristol and Gloucestershire Archaeological Association took place in the lecture room of the Bristol Museum and Library. The society's aims were to promote the study of history and of the antiquities of Bristol and the historic county of Gloucestershire. The society is still in existence today and each year publishes the *Transactions of the Bristol and Gloucestershire Archaeological Association*, featuring research on aspects of archaeology and history related to the area. Other activities include monitoring sites of historic and archaeological interest, giving grants to researchers studying the area's past and organising lectures. (Bristol and Gloucestershire Archaeological Association website)

———— ◆ ————

**1975:** The death of footballer Joe Payne. Joe Payne played for Luton Town and on April 13th 1936 he achieved an as yet unsurpassed record of scoring ten goals in a league match. The match in question took place against Bristol Rovers. The final result was 12-0 and remains the worst defeat by Bristol Rovers. (Stephen Bryne & Mike Jay, *Bristol Rovers: The Definitive History 1883-2003*, The History Press, 2003 / *The Times* / Wikipedia)

# April 23rd

**1822:** During the eighteenth and nineteenth centuries a network of turnpike roads was developed throughout Britain. Development was piecemeal as initiatives to create turnpike roads were locally overseen by parliamentary regulation. Gates were placed across roads, for which a toll was levied to maintain a stretch of road which would typically be 20 miles in length. The following description tells the opening of a turnpike road, notable for the grandeur of the ceremony: 'Coronation Road, Bedminster, a new turnpike road from Harford's Bridge to the new Ashton road, was opened on April 23rd 1822 with some ceremony. The dowager Lady Smyth of Clift House, in a coach and four, preceded by Captain Symth's troop of Yeomanry, took part in the inaugural ceremony. The road, which has been under construction for about a year, had received its name when the workmen employed upon it regaled on the coronation day of the new king.' That king was George IV, who was crowned a year previously on July 19th. Turnpikes are only thought to have accounted for around one sixth of all roads and all turnpikes were removed following Acts of Parliament in 1873 and 1878. (John Latimer, *Annals of Bristol*, Kingsmead, 1970)

# April 24th

**1752:** The execution of highwayman Nicholas Mooney took place. Highwaymen were looked upon by some as local heroes and their executions attracted souvenir hunters. A young woman is said to have travelled 15 miles for the rope that was used in Mooney's hanging; and which she got. It was believed by some that the rope from hanged men would charm away the ague and perform many other cures. During the execution the executioner attempted to pull off Mooney's shoes as the cart drew away, but only managed to break his head in the attempt. (F.C. Jones, *The Glory that was Bristol*, St Stephen's Bristol Press, 1946)

---

**1909:** The FA Cup final was played between Bristol City and Manchester United at Crystal Palace. Manchester United won the game after a goal was scored by Sandy Turnball in the second half. (Manchester United website / Bristol City website)

---

**1956:** A.N. Tupolev, designer of the Russian TU-104 jet aircraft, and S.N. Krushchev, son of the Russian President, visited the Bristol Aeroplane Company at Filton. They were shown the production lines of the Britannia aircraft. Tupolev said, through an interpreter, 'We have seen the excellent engines made by this firm,' adding in English, 'Very good motors they are too.' (*The Times*)

# April 25th

**1719:** *Robinson Crusoe*, written by Daniel Defoe, is first published. Inspiration for this story may have come from Bristol sea captain Woodes Rogers (*c.*1679-1732). Rogers set sail from Bristol in 1708. On rounding Cape Horn the ship was blown much further to the south and, owing to the cold, the ship headed towards Juan Fernandez. When some of the crew were sent ashore they found a man clothed in goatskins gesticulating wildly to get their attention. This man was William Selkirk, who had been marooned there for four years. Rogers was a friend of Daniel Defoe and it seems likely a source of information for his book. Defoe was also well known for his travel writing. In his publication *A Tour Through the Whole Island of Great Britain divided into Circuits or Journeys*, Defoe comments on St Vincent's Rock at Hotwells: 'The water of this well possess'd its medicinal quality no doubt from its original which may be as ancient as the Deluge ... it is now famous for being a specific [cure] in that otherwise incurable disease the diabetes; and yet was never known to be so, 'till within these few years; namely, thirty years, or thereabout.' (*Bristol Evening Post; Oxford Dictionary of National Biography*, OUP / Daniel Defoe, *A Tour Through the Whole Island of Great Britain divided into Circuits or Journeys* / University of Indiana website)

# April 26th

**1986:** Bristol Rovers played their last match against Chesterfield at their spiritual home of Eastville Stadium. The game had started well for Rovers, who scored in the twenty-first minute. However a controversial penalty in the 55th minute allowed Chesterfield to equalise. The game ended in a 1-1 draw. The grounds had been purchased during the 1896/97 season from Sir Henry Greenville Smyth of Aston Court for £150 and was bounded by the River Frome, the gasworks and a railway viaduct. The first match at the grounds took place on April 3rd 1897 against Aston Villa. Villa won the game 5–0. The decision to leave the stadium was made on financial grounds in order to save the club £30,000 per annum, plus expenses in the hiring of Eastville Stadium. The grounds also had the dubious honour of being located near the M32, and an elevated section of the motorway cut across the corner of the grounds between the Muller Road terraces and the South stand. On match days a steady stream of cars would develop 'breakdowns' on the hard shoulder. After the last match Rovers relocated to Twerton Park, Bath, before returning to the Memorial Stadium in Bristol a decade later. (*Western Daily Press* / Stephen Bryne's *History of Eastville Stadium* on the Bristol Rovers' website)

# April 27th

**1240:** With increasing exports of wool, cloth, ropes and lead during the reign of Henry III, improvements were needed to Bristol's port. A decision was taken to divert the River Frome through a new channel to form a new confluence with the Avon and provide a greater harbour area, giving more space for ships to turn. Henry III in this writ of April 27th 1240 commands people to join this new enterprise: 'Henry, by grace of God, King of England ... to all worthy men dwelling in Redcliffe in the suburb of Bristol, greeting. Whereas our beloved burgesses of Bristol for the common good for the whole town of Bristol as of your suburb have begun a certain trench in the Marsh of St Augustine that ships coming to our port of Bristol may be able to enter or leave more freely without impediment; which trench indeed they will be unable to perfect without great costs ... Moreover, it may be very useful and fruitful for you to work in the trench aforesaid to be perfected successfully according as it concerns you together with our aforesaid burgesses to who as sharers in the liberties aforesaid you shall give like efficacious aid as they themselves do.' (Quoted in J.H. Bettey, *Bristol Observed*, Redcliffe, 1986)

# April 28th

2010: A blue plaque was unveiled at the Glenside Campus at the University of the West of England to commemorate the artist Stanley Spencer (1891-1959), who worked as a medical orderly there during the First World War when it was known as the Beaufort War Hospital. The plaque was unveiled by the Lord Mayor of Bristol, Christopher Davies, attended by the Vice-Chancellor, Professor Steve West, Pro Vice-Chancellor and Stanley Spencer expert, Professor Paul Gaugh and John Williams from Bristol Museums and Archives Service and co-coordinator of the blue plaque scheme. Stanley Spencer established a reputation as a war artist and from July 1915, when he was at the Beaufort War Hospital, he became interested in the human body under duress. The following year he was posted to Macedonia, serving in the field ambulance divisions and then, in August 1917, he volunteered for the infantry, joining the 7th battalion of the Royal Berkshire Regiment, but was invalided out of the army following a bout of malaria. Spencer's sketches of his time in Macedonia went missing so he recreated these in a series of preparatory wash-drawings. He was subsequently commissioned to paint several paintings for the Sandham Memorial Chapel, Hampshire in the 1920s. (*Oxford Dictionary of National Biography*, OUP / Bristol City Council website)

# April 29th

**1841:** An extensive fire at the terminus of the Great Western Railway, which started at eight o'clock the previous evening, was finally brought under control at half past four in the morning on this date in 1841. The fire started in a timber yard of the company, containing at least 100,000 loads of timber. The fire appears to have started in a large tank of creosote, which was then a relatively new way of preserving wood. The fire could be seen for several miles and *The Times* claimed that 40,000-50,000 people came to view the spectacle from as far afield as Bath. Initial efforts to stop the spread of the flames came to nothing and the fire was only brought under control when timber that had not yet caught fire in the yard was removed. The operation to remove the timber involved several hundred men and four to five teams of horses. These actions almost certainly prevented the fire destroying the Brunel terminus and surrounding factories. The damage to property was estimated to have been between £18,000 and £20,000. Fortunately nobody was killed in the incident and the only casualty was a man whose thigh was broken by a piece of falling timber. (*The Times*)

# April 30th

**1852:** Telegraphs found their first commercial application with the building of the railways and, with the main line from London to the West nearing completion, a room was set up in the Commercial Rooms of Shirehampton ready to receive telegraph signals to and from London. The new system was used for the first time on this date in 1852 for journalists to send information regarding parliamentary proceedings. The telegraphic office was subsequently moved to Bristol Quay and then to the Exchange. The cost of sending a message at the time was 2s 6d. The telegraph's arrival also stopped committee members of the Commercial Rooms having to employ a 'pill warner' whose job it had been to send notice to the Commercial Rooms regarding the arrival of ships at Kingroad. (John Latimer, *Annals of Bristol*, Kingsmead, 1970 / *Bristol Mercury*)

———— • ◆ • ————

**1858:** During the night the *Brigand* collided with the barque *William Campbell* in the Irish Sea. The *Brigand* had been sailing from Bristol and was on her way to Glasgow. The collision caused both vessels to sink within minutes. The *Brigand* was carrying eleven passengers and a crew of twenty. The only survivors were the captain, six of the crew and two passengers. (John Latimer, *Annals of Bristol*, Kingsmead, 1970)

# May 1st

**1851:** The Great Exhibition opened in London. Among the exhibits was a novel form of transport invented by Bristol schoolteacher George Pocock, namely the Charvolant – a kite-powered carriage. He found that a carriage, carrying up to four people, could be powered by a couple of kites of 10ft (3m) and 12ft (3.7m) high. The acclaimed top speed was around 25mph. Visitors to the exhibition could also be taken for demonstration rides. The vehicle was first exhibited in June 1828 at Ascot Races before George IV. Obtaining a patent, Pocock and his family travelled for many years by his kite-powered carriages, especially as the vehicle was exempt from turnpike tolls. (John Latimer, *Annals of Bristol*, Kingsmead, 1970)

———◆———

**Until 1958:** To celebrate May Day, the rector and choir of St Stephen's Church would climb to the top of the 130ft (40m) tower of the church for a short service. Generally the service took place at 6 a.m. unless it was a Sunday, when the time was 10 a.m. (Reece Winstone, *Bristol in the 1940s*, 1961 / *Bristol Evening Post*)

———◆———

**1972:** Bristol Parkway railway station opens to encourage commuters to take InterCity trains to London, Birmingham and Cardiff. (*The Times*)

# May 2nd

1894: An inquest was held at the General Hospital into the death of Sarah Simmons, 42, a domestic servant employed at the Hen and Chickens public house in Bedminster. She was discovered in her bedroom lying unconscious on the floor and a doctor was sent for. He advised her removal to the hospital. Simmons smelt strongly of liquor and on arrival the doctor thought that she had been drinking to excess. A piece of rubber tubing was later found in the pocket of her dress, which also smelt of liquor. At the pub some of the spirits were kept in six-gallon jars and it seems that Simmons used the rubber tubing to get at the liquor. Post-mortem results were inconclusive as all of Simmons's organs were found to be healthy except the lungs, which were described as 'congested', but the verdict was death from a coma, probably resulting from alcoholic poisoning. (*Bristol Mercury and Daily Post*)

# May 3rd

**1817:** The *Bristol Journal* records that a steam-packet, *Britannia*, had made the journey from Swansea to Bristol against the ebbing tide in twelve hours, a most impressive time by the standards of the day. The first steam ship in Bristol had been the *Charlotte*, which travelled between Bristol and Bath and carried up to twenty passengers and goods. The fare for cabin passengers was half a crown, while steerage passengers paid 1s 6d. Using steam to power boats was looked upon with suspicion despite the difficulties experienced when navigating by sail, as this description by S.C. Hall shows: 'In the year 1815 it was my lot to visit Ireland. I was then a schoolboy in Bristol; and my family resided in Cork; and the voyage from one port to the other occupied just six weeks...The packet boat under the best circumstances was miserable enough. There was no separate accommodation for the ladies...Salt junk and hard biscuit were the only food to be obtained if the voyage lasted above three or four days.' It was not until May 1822 that a steam ship service from Bristol to Ireland began operating. (John Latimer, *Annals of Bristol*, Kingsmead, 1970)

# May 4th

**1899:** Emma Marshall died after a bout of influenza. She was well known locally as an author of historic novels, which often took on a local character. These included titles such as *Bristol Diamonds*, which described the life of eighteenth-century Hotwells, and a romantic novel, *Bristol Bells*. She was also famous for *The Tower on the Cliff*, which tells the story of Cook's Folly – a tall, hexagonal tower which stood on Knoll Hill at Stoke Bishop. Her stories were relatively simple and unsophisticated. They were also morally upright in character. Her first novel, *Happy Days at Fernbank*, for which she only received 10 guineas, was published in 1861. Thereafter she continued to write between three and four novels per year until her death, when an uncorrected manuscript was found lying on a table. During her final illness, the toll keeper of Clifton Suspension Bridge sent her a bunch of wild flowers. As she received them she is reported to have said that she would not cross that bridge again. She died three months later and was buried at Long Ashton churchyard. (*Bristol Mercury and Daily Post* / Marguerite Fedden, *Bristol Vignettes*, Burleigh Press, 1957)

# May 5th

**1921:** On September 7th 1855, William Green (who, after marrying, became Friese-Green), was born at 68 College Street, Bristol. He became famous as a photographer and for developing motion pictures. He was first introduced to photography when apprenticed, aged 14, at the studio of Maurice Guttenburg. Four years later he had his own studio and married Victoria Mariana Helena Friese. On meeting John Arthur Roebuck Rudge (1837-1903), who had adapted the magic lantern to create the illusion of movement, Friese-Green became interested in moving pictures. In 1888 he developed a camera for taking a series of photographs. He then worked with Mortimer Evans, producing a patent for a camera that could take ten pictures a second. Because of his expensive interest in inventing cameras he went bankrupt twice – in 1891 and 1917. In 1905, Friese-Green perfected a system where successive images were taken through alternating filters and the printed frames being dyed the colours of the filters. When projected at sufficient speed it gave the impression of colour. On May 5th 1921 Friese-Green made a speech to film distributors in London. He died a few minutes afterwards with only 1s 10d in his purse – all the money he had. (*Oxford Dictionary of National Biography*, OUP)

# May 6th

**1806:** On this date Ann Yearsley, poet and writer, died. She was the daughter of John and Ann Cromartie and was baptised at St Andrew's Church, Clifton on July 15th 1753. Her mother was a milkwoman who trained her daughter in the same occupation. Ann married John Yearsley, a yeoman, in 1774, and together they had five sons and two daughters. Ten years later John was working as a labourer and the family fell into destitution until Hannah More learned of Ann's reputation as a poet and organised a subscription to publish *Poems, on Several Occasions*, which was released to critical acclaim in June 1785. Soon afterward More and Yearsley quarrelled over the book's profits, which More had put into a trust to stop Yearsley's husband spending it. Yearsley had her way and gained access to the money. The fourth reprint of the volume included the author's own account of the dispute with Hannah More. Another volume of poetry, *Poems on Various Subjects*, was published in 1787. In 1795 she published a four-volume historical novel *The Royal Captives: A Fragment of Secret History, Copied from an Old Manuscript*, followed by another volume of poetry, *Rural Lyre* in 1796. After her death she was buried at St Andrew's Church, Clifton, on May 12th 1806. (*Oxford Dictionary of National Biography*, OUP)

# May 7th

**1777:** This is the probable birth date of Henry Pearce, a pugilistic fighter known as 'The Game Chicken'. The name may have derived from Pearce's habit of signing his name simply as 'Hen'. Born in Bristol, he stayed in the city until he was 21, serving an apprenticeship with a Bristol tradesman. Pearce started fighting in and around Bristol and caught the attention of Jem Belcher, who was then the English Champion boxer. At Belcher's request he moved to London in 1803. In 1805 he fought against John Gully, who at the time was in Fleet Prison for debt. He was determined to fight his way out and he proposed a fight with Pearce for 100 guineas. The men fought for an hour and Gully was overwhelmed by the superior skill of Pearce. His last fight was against Belcher who, by this time, had retired from boxing and was blind in one eye. Belcher's friends tried to talk him out of the contest but the fight went ahead and, because of Belcher's weaknesses, Pearce was afforded an easy victory. It was Pearce's last fight as he died soon afterwards on April 30th 1809, undefeated. (*The Times* / Henry Downes Miles, *Pugilistica: The History of British Boxing*, 1906 / James B. Roberts & Alexander G. Skutt, *The Boxing Register*, McBooks Press, 2006 / Wikipedia)

# May 8th

**1885:** Sadly, history records numerous suicides by people jumping off Clifton Suspension Bridge. Sarah Ann Henley, 24, a barmaid from Easton, could have easily become part of this sorry statistic. However, despite jumping off the 245ft (76m)-high structure, she survived. The reason put forward for her survival include the fact that she remained in an upright position as she fell, allowing her crinoline skirt, worn by women of the period, to act as a parachute, slowing her descent. She landed uninjured in the thick mud at low tide. The *Bristol Magpie* reported at the time: 'The rash act was the result of a lovers' quarrel. A young man, a porter on the Great Western Railway, determined to break off the engagement, wrote a letter to the young woman announcing his intention. This preyed upon the girl's mind, and she, in a state of despair, rushed to end her life by the fearful leap from the suspension bridge.' Sarah Ann Henley later went on to marry and lived until she was 85. (John Latimer, *Annals of Bristol*, Kingsmead, 1970 / *Bristol Magpie* / G.W. Barnes & Thomas Stevens, *A History of the Clifton Suspension Bridge*, The Clifton Suspension Bridge Trust, 1970)

# May 9th

**1619:** Rowland Searchfield was consecrated Bishop of Bristol. He was probably born in London in 1564 or 1565 and, aged 17, he went to St John's College, Oxford, where he graduated with a BA on October 11th 1586. John Manningham described Searchfield as 'a dissembled Christian, like an intemperate patient which can gladly heare his physicion discourse of his dyet and remedy, but will not endure to obserue them.' In Searchfield's thesis for his BD degree he argued that no one could be saved by the faith of another, as other forms of religion were incompatible with the unity of faith. He became chaplain-in-ordinary to James I, preaching Lenten sermons to the monarch in 1617 and 1622. Searchfield gained nomination to the bishopric of Bristol on March 12th 1619 and was subsequently consecrated. On his first visitation held on Holy Cross Day (September 14th) 1619 he consecrated Chantmarle Manor Chapel, near Cattistock in Dorset, where he confirmed 500 people. Some people were left unconfirmed as he felt so weary that he had to retire to bed. As Bishop of Bristol he supported his clergy's unsuccessful attempt to increase their stipends by appealing to Bristolians to contribute more to their maintenance. He died on October 11th 1622 and was buried in the sanctuary of Bristol Cathedral. (*Oxford Dictionary of National Biography*, OUP)

# May 10th

**1917:** Henry Barclay Swete was born at Redlands, Bristol on March 14th 1835 and was educated at Bishop's College. He later studied at King's College, London, and at Cambridge. He took holy orders and assisted his father as curate of Blagdon. Consumptive illness allowed him to visit Egypt to recover. He believed that consumption was an hereditary disease and for this reason he never married. During the 1870s he began to publish essays on the history and doctrine of the Holy Spirit. In 1890 he became Regius Professor of Divinity of Cambridge during a period of biblical-criticism and doctrinal controversy, where he made many significant contributions to the study of theology. He started the divinity *testimonium* scheme where ordinands were encouraged to undertake some form of theological study; his publications reflect a wide range of theological interests from commentaries on St Mark's Gospel to editing three volumes of essays on contemporary theological issues. It was his initiative that caused the *Journal of Theological Studies* to be founded by a committee of scholars from Oxford, Cambridge and Durham universities in 1899. He retired to Hithin, Hertfordshire in 1915 and died suddenly at his home on this date in 1917. (*Oxford Dictionary of National Biography*, OUP)

# May 11th

**1838:** At three o'clock in the early hours of the morning a policeman on duty in Coronation Road noticed that some burglars had broken into Clift House. The policeman leaped over the fence, saw two men running across the lawn and gave chase. He managed to capture one of them, however the thief rounded upon him with a knife and plunged it upwards into the policeman's right side, penetrating his lung. The policeman still endeavoured to arrest the man and in the struggle both men fell down from the lawn to the river – a depth of 8ft. The robber then plunged the knife into the policeman's left side and back, inflicting very serious wounds, and then, having wrested the truncheon off of the policeman, proceeded to beat him with it. Still the policeman tried once more to arrest the man and this time grasped the robber by the throat, but the robber drew his knife across the policeman's hand, almost severing his fingers and compelling him to let go. The policeman was eventually found by another officer and was conveyed to the station with little hope for recovery. (*The Times*)

# May 12th

**1739:** The foundation stone of the 'New Room' was laid. It is the oldest Methodist building in the world and was founded by John Wesley. Wesley had first preached outdoors in Bristol the previous month on text from Luke's Gospel: 'The Spirit of the Lord is upon me, for he has anointed me to preach the good news to the poor.' Wesley was initially reluctant to preach in the open air, recording in his diary that 'I could scarcely reconcile myself at first to this strange way of preaching in the fields, of which he [George Whitfield] set me an example on Sunday; I had been all my life (till very lately) so tenacious of every point relating to decency and order that I should have thought the saving of souls almost a sin if it had not been done in a church.' The New Room was enlarged in 1748 when, subsequently, the chapel had to be registered as a 'dissenting chapel' despite the fact that Wesley was an ordained member of the Church of England and regarded himself as a Church of England member throughout his life. (*John Wesley's Journal* / Mark Topping, *The New Room: John Wesley's Chapel*, Jarrold, 2004)

# May 13th

**1943:** An interesting report appeared in the *Evening World* on this date detailing some of the difficulties faced by the BBC Symphony Orchestra, then conducted by Sir Adrain Boult, when the orchestra moved to Bristol at the beginning of the Second World War: 'There was an epic occasion when contributing to an epilogue under fire, Paul Beard played *Air on a G String* while kneeling on the floor of a tiny studio and Stuart Kibbard broadcast a reading from Scripture while sheltering underneath a table. But whatever the Luftwaffe did over the heads of the famous orchestra it never made Adrain bolt. He stuck to his guns, or rather his baton, though it all and so did his colleagues. The story of the prudence of the driver of the instruments van one night when bombs were falling and fires burning deserves to be recorded. Instead of taking the van to the garage, he drove it out into the country, and there guarded the instruments through the night. When he drove back to the garage during in the morning he found that a bomb had wrecked it.' (Article quoted in Reece Winstone, *Bristol Blitzed*, 1973)

# May 14th

**1892:** A major fire on the banks of the River Avon took place. The fire started at the warehouses of Bear Creek Oil and Shipping Company, located at Temple Back. The frontage of the company extended 200ft (61m) along the banks of the Avon and were completely destroyed in the blaze. The warehouses contained a great deal of flammable material, including 5,000 barrels of petroleum, 40 tons of seal oil, and 100 barrels of colza oil. The fire spread to surrounding buildings as well as to several boats on the Avon, including the *Albaque*, a dredger belonging to the Bristol Docks Board, and three barges. (*Pall Mall Gazette*)

———— ◆ ————

**1900:** At Bristol Police Court three youths, Robert Winter (17), William Thomas (16), and Henry Wilmot (12), appeared charged with gambling in the streets on a Sunday. They were caught by PC Gregg, who saw them playing at cards for money in the streets of St Paul's. The police had received numerous complaints about the problem. Winter and Thomas were fined 5 shillings each while Henry Wilmot was sentenced to go to the Workhouse for three days, presumably on account of his age. (*Bristol Mercury and Daily Post*)

# May 15th

**1944:** The last German bombing raid on Bristol took place on this night. Ten high explosives were dropped, each weighing over 13,000lbs. Two of the bombs fell in Kingsweston Lane and a serviceman was killed at a searchlight sight. He was the only fatality in the raid. Three bombs were dropped in Bedminster near St Peter's Rise and Gifford's Hill, damaging several houses. The remaining bombs fell over Abbot's Leigh. The raiders then left the area at seven minutes past three in the morning. (Reece Winstone, *Bristol in the 1940s*, 1961)

———— •◆• ————

**2006:** A protest was held against the controversial show *Jerry Springer: The Opera*, which was shown at the Bristol Hippodrome between the 15th and 20th of May. Objectors from some religious groups, including the Brislington Christian Centre, believed the show to be blasphemous. A press release from the theatre stated that, 'Our theatre is committed to presenting a rich and diverse programme of arts and entertainment ... It is not our role to act as censors, but for the adult ticket-buying public to make up their own informed decision.' The show continued to attract protests around the country wherever it was shown. (BBC News website)

# *May 16th*

**1762:** In December 1761, alleged supernatural phenomena started at the Lamb Inn, Old Market Street, run by Richard Giles. The disturbances first affected the landlord's daughters, Molly and Dobby, aged 13 and 8 respectively. They were tormented each night by an invisible force, which bit them on the neck and arms and pricked them with pins. Giles' wagons were also affected as one of them became stuck fast in the road at Hanham and eighteen horses were required to shift it. The case attracted the interest of Henry Durbin, a prosperous druggist of Redcliff Street. Durbin visited the inn several times and on one occasion he saw a wine glass rise a foot in the air with no apparent cause. Durbin communicated with the spirit which he believed to be the cause of the trouble. From this communication he learned that a witch from Mangotsfield was paid ten guineas by a rival carrier to instigate the manifestation. On May 12th Giles suddenly became ill and returned home on a gig. On reaching the spot where his wagons were usually affected the harness broke and he saw an old woman standing by the wheel. He did not have the courage to speak. He died shortly afterwards on this date in 1762. (John Latimer, *Annals of Bristol*, Kingsmead, 1970)

# May 17th

**1720:** The River Froom flooded part of Bristol. Earl's Mead was inundated and the water rose as 'high as the wall at the ducking stool.' Broadmead and Merchant Street were under water for several hours. (John Latimer, *Annals of Bristol*, Kingsmead, 1970)

* * *

**1927:** The first flight of the Bristol Bulldog, a two-seater bomber aircraft, took place, piloted by Cyril F. Unwins, chief test pilot for the Bristol Aeroplane Company between 1918 and 1947. This plane would become a developmental model for the Mark II production model, which first flew on January 21st 1928 with full-scale production commencing in May of that year. Production eventually ran to 443, with the RAF buying most of the planes. The plane was also exported to eight other nations, including Finland, Denmark, Sian (Thailand), Estonia and Australia. Pilots particularly liked the handling, with excellent manoeuvrability and well harmonised controls. Pilots were also able to dive the aircraft to its terminal velocity of 270mph without structural damage to the plane. The Bulldog's construction also allowed for cheap maintenance in the cash-strapped 1930s. The aircraft never saw active combat under a British banner although Finland used their against the Soviets in the Second World War. (C.H. Barnes, *Bristol Aircraft Since 1910*, Putnam, 1970 / www.militaryfactory.com / www.rafmuseum.org)

# May 18th

**1984:** The penultimate day of Billy Graham's 'Mission England' campaign in Bristol. 'Mission England' was a series of open-air revival meetings that used football stadiums as venues, beginning in Bristol. Ashton Gate, the home of Bristol City FC, was chosen for the revival in Bristol, which started on May 12th. Initial crowds over the weekend of the visit were 31,000 and 25,000 respectively, which was hailed by the organisers as an 'exceptional response'. Over 500 coaches were laid on to ferry the crowds to and from the venue. A closed railway station, Ashton Gate, reopened to facilitate the arrival of so many people to the football stadium. After an hour-long address given by Billy Graham, the evangelist asked people to come forward to say that they opened their heart to Christ. Over the initial weekend 4,000 people did so and were put in contact with trained counsellors to handle the experience. The sermons given by Billy Graham could be described as a spiritual homily peppered with personal anecdotes and no political message. (*The Times* / Mike Oakley, *Bristol Suburban: Temple Meads, Local Stations, Halts and Platforms 1840-1990*, Redcliffe, 1990)

# May 19th

**1494:** Every year at St Mary Redcliffe Church the 'Rush Sunday Service' is held. The service takes its name from the rushes and herbs that are strewn on the floor of the church. The tradition was started by William Spencer, a former Bristol Mayor who died in 1493. His will made provision for three sermons to be preached each year to commemorate William Canynge. Canynge was one of Bristol's richest merchants and was Mayor of Bristol five times (see April 16th). He gave up much of his wealth to become a priest and much of this money went to restore and improve St Mary Redcliffe Church. The will stated that the sermons should be preached at Whitsuntide. The first Rush Sunday service was held on this date in 1494, the day after Whit Sunday (Pentecost), with two further services held the next day and the day after. After the Reformation only one sermon was preached and the service moved to take place on the day of Whit Sunday. The preacher is normally the Vicar of St Mary Redcliffe Church. The service is a great civic occasion and is attended by the Mayor, aldermen and councillors, who are attired in scarlet robes. (Maurice Fells, *Bristol: History You Can See*, The History Press, 2006 / Bristol City Council website / St Mary Redcliffe Church website)

# *May 20th*

**1650:** William Bedloe was born in Chepstow and spent his early years there or in Bristol. He is best known for being an adventurer, informer and fraudster. Throughout the 1670s Bedloe had been in and out of prison for fraud, often impersonating someone of high social standing in his crimes. Bedloe shot to fame following the mysterious death of Sir Edmund Godfrey, claiming that he knew who murdered the London magistrate. He accused the Jesuits, claiming that he had spent four years amongst them, had been in Spain acting as a messenger for them and that he himself had been asked by them to move Godfrey's body from the Queen's residence, Somerset House, by the murderers. Bedloe's initial telling of this story was vague but gradually the story became embellished. However, when he implicated the innocent Samuel Atkins in the murder, Bedloe was not able to recognise him. Similarly it was only after prompting that Bedloe also implicated Miles Prance, a Roman Catholic silversmith. He now styled himself as someone who had infiltrated the Jesuits for the good of Protestant England. In reality, Bedloe was an opportunistic fraud exploiting the hysteria surrounding the Popish plot. He died on August 20th 1680. (*Oxford Dictionary of National Biography*, OUP)

# May 21st

**1753:** Food shortages caused by the previous year's poor harvest led a number of labourers and miners to march to the Council House to demand relief from the Mayor and aldermen and ask that exports of food should be stopped in order to reduce prices. The Mayor declared that this was within his power to do so and the crowd seemed satisfied with the response. However, a group of protesters had attacked a ship bound for Dublin carrying corn. When some of these were arrested, a riot broke out lasting several days. The authorities responded by raising a militia and a number of citizens were enrolled as special constables. The militia was able to disperse the crowd that assembled at Lawford's Gate on May 24th, but not the 900-strong crowd that assembled the next day. The crowd marched straight to the Bridewell in order to free a prisoner who had earlier been arrested in the riots. The rioters were dispersed by a small party of dragoons sent from Gloucester and the fugitives, now scattered in small groups, were followed up by the special constables and a number of petty conflicts took place. During the conflicts four colliers were shot dead and over fifty were wounded. (John Latimer, *Annals of Bristol*, Kingsmead, 1970)

# May 22nd

**1826:** John Latimer records that 'Many thousand persons assembled on the banks of the Avon, near the Hotwell ... in consequence of an announcement of an American named Courtney, that he would take a "flying leap" from St Vincent's rocks to the opposite side of the river. A rope stretched from the highest point of the rocks, above Giant's Cave, was made fast to a tree on the opposite side of the stream; and at the time fixed Courtney appeared, and accomplished the decent of 1,100 feet [330m], in a few seconds to great applause. The feat was repeated on the 5 June with equal success.' (John Latimer, *Annals of Bristol*, Kingsmead, 1970)

———— • ◆ • ————

**1879:** The steam ship *Severn* arrived at Bristol carrying with it three shipwrecked passengers whose boat, the *Firebrick*, had foundered on the North Bishop Rocks, just off St David's Head, in thick fog. The three men had survived on the rock for three days by eating three gull eggs they found whilst trying to signal to passing ships, but the continued fog made this difficult. Captain Mills of the *Severn*, on being alerted to the plight of the men, sent a boat in the charge of the mate to rescue them. (*Bristol Mercury and Daily Post*)

# May 23rd

**1942:** Fred Wedlock, singer, entertainer and broadcaster, was born in Bristol. He was brought up in a pub and it was here that Fred claims he had his first gig, aged 4, earning him *6d*. Later on he discovered that his singing of comic and bawdy songs at youth clubs often attracted girls. After graduating at the University of Swansea he had various jobs, respectively as a Youth Employment Officer, working at Lewis's Department Store and as a teacher in London's East End and his native Bristol. He then changed his career again, becoming a popular performer in folk clubs – consequently Fred Wedlock described himself as having managed without a proper job for thirty years. In 1981 Dave Cousins persuaded Fred to release as a single 'The Oldest Swinger in Town', the title track from an album Fred released a couple of years previously. The single was played by Noel Edmonds on his radio show, helping it to reach No. 6 in the charts. The song was originally written by Ed Pickford but Fred altered the words. Fred continued to perform after his chart success and also turned his hand to broadcasting, particularly on local television and radio. He died on March 4th 2010. (*The Guardian* / *The Times* / www.fredwedlock.com)

# May 24th

**1876:** 'The most extensive fire which had occurred in the city for nearly half a century broke out during the night of 24 May in the premises of Messers Clutterbuck & Griffin, dry-salters, Christmas Street. The flames spread rapidly to the warehouses of Messers Couzens & Co., clothiers; Messers Leonard & Co., drysaleters; Messers Gardner and Thomas, wholesale grocers; and Mr S. Hunt, provision merchant; as well as to the old-established inn, the Old Globe. The destruction of these buildings was in most cases complete, and the entire loss was estimated at £800,000.' (John Latimer, *Annals of Bristol*, Kingsmead, 1970)

———— • ◆ • ————

**1951:** To further research into the nature of cosmic atomic particles, Professor C.F. Powell of Bristol University and his researchers launched an unmanned balloon from the university's grounds at Coombe Dingle. The apparatus on board included photographic plates to record atomic particles and other scientific equipment. Radio contact with the balloon was maintained until it reached 88,000ft (26,800m), when contact was lost. The position of the balloon was tracked using radar until it reached Worcester. The burst balloon, along with its equipment, was later recovered by two researchers from Oak House Farm near Wellington in Shropshire, 100 miles from its starting point. (*The Times*)

# May 25th

**1893:** David Alfred Doudney was born on March 8th 1811 in Portsea. He trained as a printer and moved to London where he had his own business in Holloway. In 1840 Doudney purchased *Gospel Magazine*, which was of strongly Calvinist persuasion, and he became its editor. In 1846 he retired from the printing trade and in November of the same year he went to Ireland to distribute funds raised by the readers of *Gospel Magazine* for the Irish Potato Famine. It was whilst here that he felt the call to take holy orders and was ordained in 1847 by the Bishop of Cashel as licentiate clergyman. Doudney left Ireland in 1859 for Bristol, where he became perpetual curate of St Luke's, Bedminster. Here he continued to edit *Gospel Magazine* and published a number of tracts and devotional works. Whilst at St Luke's he played an active role establishing industrial schools and soup kitchens. He retired from St Luke's in 1890 and moved to Southsea, where he died on 21 April 1893. His funeral took place a few days later on this date. (*Oxford Dictionary of National Biography*, OUP / Reece Winstone, *Victorian and Edwardian Bristol from Old Photographs*, Batsford, 1983)

# May 26th

**1835:** William Edward Godwin, architect and furniture designer, was born in Bristol. After being educated at Exton School in London he went to work for William Armstrong, city surveyor, architect and engineer. Here he seems to have been a self-taught architect and he took over many architectural commissions for the company. However, the lack of recognition of his work by the company led him to set up his own independent business in 1854. His early designs were in gothic and in 1861 he won the contract to build Northampton Town Hall. He was one of the first designers to incorporate Japanese design into their work and this is evidenced by his furniture and wallpaper patterns. However one critic is reported to have said that 'Mr Godwin has gone beyond most people's notions of the boundaries of civilisation and has added Japan.' Back in Bristol Godwin was responsible for the Old Carriage Works at Stokes Croft in a Byzantine style, with repeated rounded arches on the frontages, and additions to Cotham church, including the apse and the tower. He died on October 6th 1886. (www.victorianweb.org / Wikipedia / Nikolaus Pevsner, *The Buildings of England: North Somerset and Bristol*, Penguin, 1958)

# May 27th

**1602:** During Tudor times the beginning of a re-conquest of Ireland took place with troops from mainland Britain going over to Ireland, often passing through the Port of Bristol on their way. One such contingent of 800 troops came to Bristol on the Eve of Whitsun, under the command of Sir William Wingfield. A meeting of the soldiers took place amongst them on May 26th, where they offered 'some abuse to the mayor', William Vawer. Justice was rough and swift for the next day three of these soldiers were sentenced to be 'executed in the High Street upon a gibbet, whither they were bought with constables, and halters about their necks; whereof one of them being mounted had prayed and prepared to die, their pardon was begged and they were released.' (William Adams, *Adams's Chronicle of Bristol*, J.W. Arrowsmith, 1910)

———— ◆ ————

**1873:** 'Some little excitement' was occasioned at Bedminster with the passage of a traction engine, to which was attached four wagons of ore, representing 50 tons of weight. The unusual vehicle was stopped by the police, who expressed the opinion that it would be unwise to travel over Bath Bridge and St Phillip's Bridge as intended owing to the immense weight of the vehicle. (*Bristol Mercury*)

# May 28th

**1827:** A new newspaper was launched entitled *The Bristolian: Daily Local Publication* although its proprietor, John Acland, referred to his publication as a pamphlet. In so doing Acland was avoiding the Stamp Tax levied on all newspapers of the time, instead paying the lower tax applied to pamphlets. This did not fool the authorities for long however, as on June 5th it was decided that Acland's publication was in fact a newspaper. The next day Acland published his newspaper, renaming it *The Bristolian: Daily Literary Publication*, avoiding any items of local interest. Sales suffered and so, in order to generate interest, he reported on the Redding case and was the only reporter in court to do so. Redding was a sailor who imported a 2-gallon keg of whisky bought in Ireland. Since Irish whisky could not be imported into this country, Redding was sentenced to five years compulsory service aboard a king's ship. Acland's report of the case stirred up public emotion and eventually the sentence was overturned. It also landed Acland in trouble with the authorities, as it appeared to them he was avoiding the Stamp Tax again. After only nineteen days as a daily newspaper, Acland announced that there would be no further issues but promised that another pamphlet was to be published twice-weekly. (John Latimer, *Annals of Bristol*, Kingsmead, 1970)

# May 29th

**1946:** The Odeon cinema in Union Street was the scene of a murder. The victim was the manager, Robert Parrington Jackson, who was shot twice in his office. Surprisingly, no one in the cinema heard the fatal shots as they seemed to have coincided with gunshots in the film *The Lights that Failed*. No money was taken from the scene of the crime and no one was ever arrested for the murder. The case remained unsolved until 1989, when Billy Fisher confessed to the murder on his deathbed to his son. He said that he and Dukey Leonard, his accomplice, intended to rob the cinema but panicked when the manager returned to his office. The cinema was first opened on July 16th 1938. The original building was gutted in December 1983 and rebuilt at a cost of £4 milllion and reopened with the new James Bond film *A View to a Kill*. (Dave Stephenson & Jill Willmott, *Bristol Cinemas*, The History Press, 2005)

———◆•———

**1988:** The Tabacco Bond's Building at Canons Marsh was demolished at seven o'clock on a Sunday morning with high explosives. With the building gone construction could start on the new national headquarters of Lloyds Bank. (David J. Eveleigh, *A Century of Bristol*, The History Press, 2007)

# May 30th

**1766:** The Theatre Royal in King Street was opened despite opposition from various religious bodies and difficulty resulting from a 1757 Act of Parliament, which threatened prosecution to anyone acting in an unlicensed theatre as a rogue and vagabond. To avoid the threat of prosecution the opening performance was advertised as *A Concert of Music and Specimen of Rhetorick* – a performance of comedy being introduced between the orchestra's playing. To legalise the theatre an Act of Parliament was required, which was not granted until 1778, allowing George III to grant a Royal Licence. The theatre was designed by the architect James Patey and the foundation stone was laid on November 30th 1764. The auditorium is now semi-circular, where originally it would have been elliptical. Silver tokens were given to those who financially supported the building of the theatre and allowed the bearer of the tokens to view every performance. Today the theatre is better known as the Bristol Old Vic, which takes its name from the Old Vic Theatre Company in London, known for their classical theatre productions, who were invited to the Theatre Royal to set up a resident repertory company in Bristol in 1946. (C.F.W. Denning, *Old Inns of Bristol*, John Wright & Son, 1949 / John Latimer, *Annals of Bristol*, Kingsmead, 1970 / Nikolaus Pevsner, *The Buildings of England: North Somerset and Bristol*, Penguin, 1958 / Bristol Old Vic website)

# May 31st

1910: Elizabeth Blackwell became the first woman doctor to register in this country. She was born on February 3rd 1821 in Bristol, where her father owned a sugar refinery and where she spent much of her early life until 1832, when the refinery burnt down, causing the family to emigrate to America. A chance remark from an ailing friend of her mother, whom Elizabeth was nursing, caused her to change her career. The patient stated that if she could have been treated by a woman then her worst sufferings would have been spared. Despite some setbacks, Elizabeth was eventually accepted at Geneva College in New York. The young male students were apparently unanimous in voting for her entry to the college. She obtained her MD in 1849. Her subsequent career as a doctor was spent mainly in England. In 1859 Parliament legislated for the registration of medical practitioners in this country. Elizabeth applied for registration, which could not be refused, and became the first woman to do so in this country. Unfortunately, whilst attending an infant patient, Elizabeth got some liquid in her eyes and lost the sight in one eye and so had to give up surgery. She spent her final years in Hastings, where she died on this day in 1910. (Marguerite Fedden, *Bristol Vignettes*, Burleigh Press, 1957)

# June 1st

**1630:** A few days previously, Prince Charles, who would later become Charles II, was born between the hours of one and two in the afternoon. He was christened the next day with illustrious godparents, namely the French King, the King of Bohemia and the Queen Mother of France. These were not present at the ceremony itself but deputies were appointed in their place. The news of the royal birth arrived in Bristol five days later, on June 1st. The news 'was accepted with great joy, and expressed in thanksgiving and prayer in all churches for his prosperity. The bells rang all day, and in every street such bonfires that the like of Bristol had never seen.' (William Adams, *Adams's Chronicle of Bristol*, J.W. Arrowsmith, 1910)

---

**1900:** James Knight appeared at Bristol Police Court charged with driving a traction engine through the streets faster than the permitted speed of 2mph. The defendant claimed that he had been trying to accommodate the flow of traffic and not delay tram services. He was fined 10 shillings plus costs. The 2mph speed limit in towns was introduced in the 1865 Locomotive Act and also required a man to walk in front carrying a red flag to warn passers-by of the oncoming vehicle. (*Bristol Mercury and Daily Post*)

# June 2nd

**1515:** John Newland, abbot of St Augustine's, Bristol, died. He became abbot on April 6th 1481 and was a very effective administrator of the abbey and its estates. He kept the offices of treasurer and cellarer for himself so that he could keep tight control of abbey finances. Records show a surplus, despite numerous building works, including the magnificent barn that survives at Ashleworth, Gloucestershire and is currently owned by the National Trust. (*Oxford Dictionary of National Biography*, OUP)

---

**1870:** Gloucestershire County Cricket Club played their first match against Surrey on the Durdham Downs. W.G. Grace was among the players and Gloucestershire won the match by 51 runs. The origins of the club go back to W.G. Grace's father, Henry Mills Grace, who had been responsible for the formation of Mangotsfield Cricket Club in 1844, which, two years later, amalgamated with Coalpit Heath to form the West Gloucestershire County Cricket Club. In 1888 negotiations began to purchase land at Ashley Down, which became the home of Gloucestershire Cricket Club. The first game played there was against Lancashire on July 1st 1889. Club colours were also established in that year. These are fawn, brown, pale grey, dark green, red and navy blue. (Gloucestershire Cricket Club website / Jack Russell, 'Sportsmen of Bristol' in E.V. Thompson et al. *People and Places in Bristol*, Bossiney Books, 1986)

# June 3rd

**1892:** Emily Sturge was born at Cotham, Bristol on April 20th 1847, the eldest of eleven children. For most of her life she campaigned in support of women's suffrage. In 1878 she was made Honorary Secretary of the West of England Brach of the National Society for Women's Suffrage and, from when she first joined in 1872/3 until 1885, she travelled the country attending public meetings, making speeches and campaigning through the Liberal Party. With so few political opportunities open to women at that time, she was elected as Liberal member of the Bristol Schools Board in 1880, where she continued to campaign for equality of access to education and free school meals for the poor. The former aim was partly achieved in 1876 when the University College of Bristol was opened, which admitted students regardless of their gender to most subjects. Sturge was also a member of the Bristol Women's Liberal Association where potential parliamentary and local government candidates were asked to state their position on the issue of women's suffrage. Sturge's life was ended prematurely when, on this date in 1892, she was killed falling from her horse. She is buried at the Quaker burial ground at the Friars Meeting House in Rosemary Street. (*Oxford Dictionary of National Biography*, OUP)

# June 4th

**1874:** The extreme poverty of some of Bristol's inhabitants is illustrated in the diary of Revd Robert Francis Kilvert. On this date he was visiting Bristol and had gone into a confectioner's shop between the Drawbridge and College Green to eat a bun. Here he saw 'a girl lingering about the door, a bare-footed child – a little girl with fair hair, tossed and tangled, with an arch *espiégle*, eager little face and beautiful wild eyes, large and grey, which looked shyly in the shop and at me, with a wistful beseeching smile. She wore a poor, faded, ragged frock, and her shapely limbs and tiny delicate beautiful feet were bare and stained with mud and dust. Still she lingered about the place with her sad, wistful smile and her winning beseeching look, half hiding behind the door.' Moved by her appearance, Revd Kilvert took out a bun and gave it to her. His diary goes on to record, 'I shall never forget the quick, happy and grateful smile which flashed over her face as she took it and began to eat. She said she was very hungry. Poor lamb!' (Marguerite Fedden, *Bristol Vignettes*, Burleigh Press, 1957)

# June 5th

**1793:** Mary Scott, poet, was born in Milbourne Port, Somerset, in 1751 or 1752. Her first publication was *The Female Advocate*, written in her early twenties. In the preface the book suggests that she spent much of her youth as an invalid, having suffered 'years of ill health'. The book was published by Joseph Johnson, who later became a well-known publisher of Protestant dissent. The title page of *The Female Advocate* commended other literary women, especially those of Protestant persuasion and female learning. Mary Scott lived with her parents until her late thirties and then with her brother, Russell Scott, who was a Unitarian minister in Portsmouth in the 1770s. Here she met John Taylor, a student and then tutor at the Daventry Academy for Unitarians. Her mother opposed their marriage and it was not until after her parents had died that the couple married and she moved to Ilminster, where Taylor was minister of a chapel there. She published further poems in *Gentleman's Magazine* and two of her poems 'Dunotter Castle' and 'Verses, on a Day of Prayer, for Success in War' were part of a collection entitled *Poems by the most Eminent Ladies*. She died in Bristol on this date in 1793. (*Oxford Dictionary of National Biography*, OUP)

# June 6th

**1883:** John Morgan appeared at Bristol Police Court charged with embezzling 16 shillings from his employer Mr W. Richards, a timber merchant of Bedminster. Morgan was paid by Mr T.C. Allen, a cashier of Messrs. Arthur & Son, oil merchants for two casks. Although Morgan had received the money for the oil casks he had not passed the money on to his employer, but spent it on drink. In court Morgan's employer, Mr Richards, stated that as John Morgan had been in his employ for a great many years and that this was his first offence, he would be inclined to give Morgan a further chance. The magistrates fined Morgan 21 shillings or twenty-one days' imprisonment telling Mr Richards that he had behaved very kindly and expressed the hope that Mr Morgan would not again abuse his position of trust. (*Bristol Mercury and Daily Post*)

———— • ◆ • ————

**1895:** Sidney Owen, 13, appeared at Lawford's Gate Police Court charged with stealing a tin of salmon to the value of 7*d* from Mr Perry's shop and also with an attempted robbery of the till. As this was Owen's first offence and the boy was previously of good character, he was discharged. (*Bristol Mercury and Daily Post*)

# June 7th

**1896:** On this Sunday evening a young lady 'fashionably dressed in navy blue' was climbing, without the aid of ropes, one of the most precipitous sections of the St Vincent's Cliffs close to the Clifton Suspension Bridge. The feat soon caused crowds to gather on the top of the cliffs on either side of the Avon and they also lined the Suspension Bridge, wondering why she had put herself at such great danger when there were much safer ways to get from the bottom to the top of the cliffs, such as the Clifton Rocks Railway. Her own explanation of why she attempted the feat was that she wanted to have a quiet ramble along the lower part of the cliff. Having ascended some distance she looked back down the cliff and was 'somewhat disgusted' to discover that she was the object of some attention. She did not wish to descend to the bottom lest the crowd should jeer at her so, 'evidently preferring the appearance of the crowd above, she pluckily decided to continue her ascent, which she accomplished with the utmost self-possession, never faltering one step as she gradually neared the buttress of the Clifton Suspension Bridge,' where the police gave her an escort past the crowds. (*Bristol Mercury and Daily Post*)

# June 8th

**1888:** Abbot Newland (d.1515) was responsible for the completion of the transepts and tower of the abbey church and started building work on the nave. However, the work on the nave remained unfinished. By 1542 the abbey became Bristol Cathedral and the half-built nave walls were demolished. It was more than 300 years before the nave would be completed. By 1860 concerns had been expressed regarding the condition of the tower, which needed support at the west end. Rebuilding the nave would give support and enlarge the cathedral, providing the city with a building in keeping with the city's status. George Edmund Street was appointed architect and he designed a nave that harmonised with the existing medieval structure. As Street's son later wrote, 'my father felt that there was really no course open to him but to build on the foundations and on the same lines as the choir and to make the distinction between the old and the new work in the details.' Street also designed the two western nave towers to create more grandeur to the building. Their completion brought the nave project to an end on this date in 1888, when the opening ceremony took place. (Joseph Bettey, *Bristol Cathedral: The Rebuilding of the Nave*, Historical Association, 1993 / Nikolaus Pevsner, *The Buildings of England: North Somerset and Bristol*, Penguin, 1958)

# June 9th

**1790:** At a meeting of the council held on this date a useful improvement was determined upon. The aldermen of the various wards were directed to ensure that the name of each street was set up in a conspicuous place, following criticism in the local press. The work seems to have been completed by the spring of 1791. Of the numerous streets that were named after saints, only one street sign was completed with its full name. This was St John Street, which had recently been opened. (John Latimer, *Annals of Bristol*, Kingsmead, 1970)

---

**1850:** A fire in St James's parish was discovered by a policeman at three o'clock in the morning. The fire occurred in premises on Church Parade belonging to Mr Stone, a silversmith and pawnbroker. The fire spread rapidly owing to the combustible nature of the stock and the part-timber construction of the warehouse. Because of the intensity of the fire, the firemen were not able to save the building, so directed their efforts to saving adjacent premises, including St James's Church. The estimated loss of goods inside the warehouse was £5,000-£10,000. The poor in particular suffered as the fire consumed their pawned possessions and also the loss resulting from the difference between the value of their possessions and the loans they received upon them. (*The Times*)

# June 10th

**1715:** The succession to the English throne after the last Stuart monarch, Queen Anne, who died the previous year, had taken place and George I was now king. Nevertheless, some Bristolians maintained an allegiance to James Francis Edward Stuart, son of James II, who abdicated the English throne in the Glorious Revolution of 1685. Bristolian supporters of the Pretender wore white ribbons on this day, his birthday. A few days previously it had been the birthday of George I, on May 28th. On that day loyal citizens hung out banners whilst Jacobite supporters carried thyme and rue on their coats to signify grief. (John Latimer, *Annals of Bristol*, Kingsmead, 1970)

---

**1849:** A cholera epidemic broke out and lasted until October 16th, with 778 confirmed cases. Of those, 444 people died. The outbreak owed much to the fact that many parts of Bristol were without sewerage, and those sewers that existed drained raw sewage into the harbour. The Froome was an open sewer and a stench existed in summer that was enough to upset weak stomachs. Work on four arterial sewers to divert the sewage from the city's western districts subsequently began in 1855. (John Latimer, *Annals of Bristol*, Kingsmead, 1970)

# June 11th

**1757:** On this date *Felix Farley's Journal* contained the following paragraph: 'We hear that the churchwardens of a considerable parish in this city intend (comfortable to the obligations of their oath) to put laws into force against all those who absented themselves from publick worship on the Lord's Day; and against common swearards, drunkards &c., and it is hoped and much to be wished that an example of this kind would be followed throughout this country.' The fine for not attending church was 1 shilling but systematic non-attendees could expect to be levied £20. Fortunately these proposals do not seem to have gained widespread support and no attempt was ever made to enforce them. (John Latimer, *Annals of Bristol*, Kingsmead, 1970)

———◆———

**1877:** James Cotham was charged with assaulting his lover Elizabeth Powell. Elizabeth was reluctant to testify in court and had to be fetched. The couple had lived together for eight years and James had recently thrown a poker at Elizabeth, injuring her cheek. Two weeks previously he hit her again, reopening the wound. Elizabeth begged that the magistrates did not send Cotham to jail, but they would not listen to her plea, stating that they had a public duty to perform, and sentenced Cotham to two months' imprisonment with hard labour. (*Bristol Mercury*)

# June 12th

**1880:** It was a pleasant summer evening when Cornelius George Bull, 51, went for walk in Leigh Woods at the top of the Avon Gorge. Bull tottered whilst walking and people usually thought that he was drunk, but in Leigh Woods he could be alone. However, whilst walking near the edge he had a paralytic seizure and toppled over the side, falling 30-40ft with only a tree to break his fall. Another man by the name of Robert Bingham, who was out for a walk along the Leigh side of the Avon River, heard groans and found Bull lying on the ground. He summoned a minister who happened to be nearby and ran to get help. Bull was conveyed to the Bristol Infirmary but he died the next day. (*Bristol Mercury*)

———— ◆ ————

**1884:** The success of one of the first thrillers written, *Called Back*, by Bristol-born author Fredrick John Fargus (1847-1885), was celebrated with a banquet hosted by the Mayor of Bristol. Fargus also published a book of poetry, *A Life's Idylls and Other Poems* (1879) and serialisations such as 'The Redhill Mystery', published in the *Yorkshire Post*. A memorial was placed in Bristol Cathedral after his death. (*Oxford Dictionary of National Biography*, OUP)

# *June 13th*

**1788:** The Revd Joseph Easterbrook, vicar of the Temple Church, Bristol, assisted by six Wesleyan preachers and eight 'serious persons', held an unusual service to deliver a man named George Lukins, a tailor of Yatton, from demoniacal possession. At the service Lukins convulsed violently when the exorcists sang a hymn. The voices of these evil spirits proceeded from Lukins's mouth, uttering horrible blasphemies, including a Te Deum to the Devil. However, when the vicar ordered the evil spirits to depart the man, they obeyed, doing so with howling. An account of the exorcism, which had taken two hours, appeared in *Sarah Farley's Journal* of June 21st and gave rise to much controversy. The exorcists were ridiculed by Mr Norman, a surgeon of Yatton, who stated that Lukins was nothing more than a clever ventriloquist who had begun similar acts in 1770, when, during fits of howling and leaping, Lukins had alleged that he was bewitched. On several occasions this act had been used against several elderly and infirm people, whom Lukins claimed were responsible for his apparent torment. The fraud was attributed to Lukins's 'fondness for mystification, stimulated by the simplicity of his dupes'. (John Latimer, *Annals of Bristol*, Kingsmead, 1970)

# June 14th

**1877:** Mary Carpenter, social reformer and educationalist, was born on April 3rd 1817. Seeing the large number of poor children in the Lewin's Mead area of the city, she opened a school there on August 2nd 1846, providing an education for any child that presented itself there. The difficulties of the work presented themselves in her diary on the first day of opening: 'That afternoon I shall never forget. Only thirteen or fourteen boys present; some swearing, some fighting, some crying. One boy struck another's head through the window. I tried to offer up a short prayer, but found it impossible. The boys instead of kneeling began to tumble over one another and sing "Jim Crow".' Undaunted by her experience at Lewin's Mead she turned her attention to the city's juvenile delinquents, believing that rehabilitation was better than retribution and that reformatories should try to promote a family atmosphere. Putting these ideas into practise, she founded a Reformatory School for Boys, which opened in 1852 at Kingswood, followed by the Red Lodge Reformatory for girls in 1854. She remained actively involved with the Red Lodge until her death on this date in 1877. (*Oxford Dictionary of National Biography*, OUP / John Latimer, *Annals of Bristol*, Kingsmead, 1970)

# June 15th

**1861:** The following unusual story appeared in the *Bristol Mercury* on this date. In the St Philip's neighbourhood of Bristol there had been reports of ghostly apparitions in the not too distant past. In order to keep interest in these supernatural apparitions alive, a carpenter living near Stapleton Road thought that he would 'manufacture a phantom'. Accordingly the carpenter made up a figure and placed it outside the window of his sitting room, the puppet being controlled by his son. The carpenter then invited a timid friend to his house and after making excuses to his friend about sitting in the dark they conversed for a while before the carpenter poked the fire rather vigorously, which was the signal for the 'ghostly apparition' to appear. The friend, on seeing the ghastly head, bolted out of the house. Some time later the carpenter invited a baker to his house, who brought with him a friend who had a reputation for being a fire-eater. When the performance of the ghost started, the friend of the baker seized the poker from the fire and, before the carpenter could intervene, went to the window and thrust it at the apparition, severing the mechanism by which the phantom was controlled and so uncovering the fraud. (*Bristol Mercury*)

# June 16th

**1924:** The Corporation of Bristol took over the ownership of the St Anne's Well site at Brislington, preserving the historic and religious site. The well is dedicated to St Anne, who is said to be the mother of the Blessed Virgin Mary. St Anne in medieval England attracted considerable devotion and her feast day, July 26th, has been celebrated in England since 1382. A nearby chapel dedicated to St Anne was built in 1392 but was probably ruined during the Reformation. Evidence of medieval pilgrimage here was uncovered in 1880, when Fr Ignatius Grant of St Mary-on-the-Quay supervised and allowed Henry Jones to excavate the site. Coins were found from the reigns of Edward IV and Henry VII and numerous abbey tokens purchased from Keynsham Abbey, proving that pilgrimages took place here. The movement for the well's preservation began in 1920, led by F.C. Jones, and later a new local newspaper, the *Bristol Adventurer*, took up the cause. This was read by the site's owner, who offered terms. The formal handover took place on this date in 1924, with addresses given by the Lord Mayor Sir John Swaish and Dom Ethelbert Horne. (F.C. Jones, *The Glory that was Bristol*, St Stephen's Bristol Press, 1946 / Marguerite Fedden, *Bristol Vignettes*, Burleigh Press, 1957)

# June 17th

**1862:** John Latimer reports that 'a very brilliant military spectacle took place on Durdham Down'. The day had been chosen for a review of the volunteer corps of Bristol and neighbouring counties, and 6,476 men took part in manoeuvres. Amongst the regiments which had agreed to be present were the Gloucestershire and North Somerset Yeomanry, the Bristol, Gloucester, Newnham, Clevedon, Weston, and Cardiff Artillery, the Bristol and Gloucester Engineers, and the Bristol, Gloucester, Stroud, Tewkesbury, Cirencester, Forest of Dean, Stow, Moreton, Cheltenham, Pershore, Malvern, Evesham, Ombersley, Driotwich, Upton, Bromsgrove, Birmingham, Saltley, Keynsham, Temple Cloud, Taunton, Bridgewater, Wellington, Williton, Stogursey, Wiveliscombe, Yeovil, Crewkerne, Langport, Wells, Burnham, Weston, Frome, Shepton Mallet, Glastonbury, Wincanton, Somerton, Baltonsborough, Wrington, Sailsbury, Swindon, Trowbridge, Chippenham, Bradford, Warminster, Melksham, Wotton Basset, Old Swindon, Highworth, Hereford, Ledbury, Bromyard, Archinfield, Leominster, Kington, Monmouth, Chepstow, Cadoxton, Dorchester, Wareham, Poole, Weymouth, Wimborne and Sherborne Rifles. Owing to the well-ordered preparations, the volunteers reached the ground at the appointed time and in good order: and the review, which was held before Major-General Hutchinson, passed off satisfactorily. A stand, which was capable of seating 5,000 spectators, was well filled, and it was computed that at least 100,000 persons witnessed the manoeuvres. (John Latimer, *Annals of Bristol*, Kingsmead, 1970)

# June 18th

**1618:** 'A fair new ship called the *Jonathan* of Bristoll of the burden of 200 tons and upwards, was launched at the quay.' Disaster, however, beset the ship when, in December 1623, it sank after hitting some rocks, but fortunately no lives were lost. (William Adams, *Adams's Chronicle of Bristol*, J.W. Arrowsmith, 1910)

---

**1849:** George Müller opened the first of his purpose-built orphanages at Ashley Down. These consisted of four rented houses in Wilson Street. However, residents in Wilson Street raised objections to the noise that so many children made, the playgrounds were too small and drainage was a problem. Müller interpreted this as a signal from God that He was leading Müller in a different direction. After praying, he came to the conclusion that larger premises were needed. Thirty-six days later, on December 10th 1845, Müller received a cheque for £1,000. He had solicited no money and relied on the will of God to provide for the charity's needs. Three days later a Christian architect volunteered his services to design and supervise the building of the orphanage. Only when all the money was raised did Müller allow the building work to commence. (A.T. Pierson, *George Müller of Bristol*, Inglis, 1900)

# June 19th

**1903:** Walter Reginald Hammond was born in the royal garrison at Dover Castle. He is best known as a cricketer for England and Gloucestershire County Cricket Club. His talent was recognised at Cirencester Grammar School, where Hammond dominated all sports. His batting average of 57.84 in 1920 led to him being offered a contract for Gloucestershire County Cricket Club. An MCC ruling in 1922 prevented Hammond playing for the club over residency requirements until 1923. Between 1921 and 1924 Hammond occasionally played football for Bristol Rovers, then in the Third Division, but, although Hammond had talent, football was a little too proletarian for his tastes. Highlights at Gloucestershire include the 1928 Cheltenham Festival when he made 360 runs in ten matches. In 1938 Hammond made 1,082 runs for Gloucestershire in eight successive innings, with an average of 180.33. In 1938 he became captain for England. Retiring from cricket, Hammond moved to South Africa, working for a car firm in Durban before becoming the first Sports Administrator at Natal University. He died on July 1st 1965 from a heart attack and was cremated at Durban. (*Oxford Dictionary of National Biography*, OUP)

# June 20th

**1851:** A major colliery accident took place at 11 a.m. at the North Side Coal Pit, Bedminster, belonging to Messrs Goulstone, Garrett & Co. The accident occurred when a coal cart coming up the shaft knocked a supporting timber out of its place. This caused rocks to fall, which knocked other timbers out of place and the mines and the shaft became blocked, trapping forty men and boys below ground. At 9.30 p.m. two men, Mr Knight, proprietor of Aston Vale Colliery and his pit bailiff, John Kew, volunteered to descend into the mine to ascertain if there were any survivors. Two, William Brain and Morgan Phillips, were found first as they were working on an upper seam of coal. No sound was heard from the other men working on a lower seam and the worst was assumed. Because of the 'foul air' in the mine Mr Goulstone acquired a quantity of canvass, which local women stitched together to form a tube and air was blown through it down to the mine. The rescuers were then able to reach the other miners below via another shaft linking the two seams and amazingly found all the men alive. (*Bristol Mercury*)

# June 21st

**1766:** *Felix Farley's Journal* of this date states that a woman who was looking at a pillory exhibition from a window in Wine Street had her eye entirely cut out by a shard of glass when a cabbage stump smashed through the window. (John Latimer, *Annals of Bristol*, Kingsmead, 1970)

———— • ◆ • ————

**1842:** It was reported that three highway robberies had been carried out by the same perpetrators in three days, three of whom wore smockfrocks with Jim Crow hats and two others dressed like navigators with black top hats. Their first attempt on the previous Thursday failed when they heard a carriage approaching but they were successful on the following night, when the men jumped out of bushes on Henleaze Lane; one man pressed a pistol into the victim's mouth whilst two other men pressed their pistols against the victim's left and right temple. The victim, Francis Edwards, was nearly strangled as the thieves tried to get a pocket watch that was still attached to its chain. The following evening four people travelling along Horfield Road in a covered cart were stopped by the men, who demanded money or their lives. Once the robbers had got what they wanted they beat some of their victims with the butt-end of their guns. In a separate incident two labouring men were also robbed. (*The Times*)

# June 22nd

**1728:** *Mist's Journal* reports on the barbarous military punishment meted out on an Irish Roman Catholic soldier who refused to go to church and was whipped in Bristol with the cat of nine tails two days in succession. The punishment was so severe that he begged to be shot or hanged. At around the same time, a sergeant in the Fusiliers was sentenced to receive 2,000 lashes. Following the intervention of several lady citizens of Bristol, the punishment was changed. The sergeant was stripped to his waist and a halter was placed around his neck. He was then dragged through the streets before being driven out of the city. *Read's Weekly Journal* also reports that a solider convicted of drinking to the Pretender's health in Bristol received 1,000 lashes with a cat of nine tails and was thrown out of the army. 'The Pretender' refers to James Francis Edward Stuart, son of James II of England, who was the last Catholic monarch. James II had fled, and thus abdicated the throne after the leading nobles asked William of Orange to launch an invasion of England in what become known as the Glorious Revolution in 1685. Support still existed for James II and his descendents until the middle of the eighteenth century. (John Latimer, *Annals of Bristol*, Kingsmead, 1970)

# June 23rd

**1879:** An article from *The Times* on this date reads: 'As the masons and carpenters, refusing the overtures of the masters, remain on strike, the members of the Bristol Masters Builders' Association have determined to avail themselves of the offers of large bodies of workmen from several towns in the north. If the present foremen continued service with shops full of non-unionists, the men belonging to the unions would decline to work under them in the future. The change of foreman is a serious step for the employers to take; but at a general meeting of the association it was determined upon, and the following resolution was adopted: "That the operatives now on strike having refused the reference to arbitration offered them, this meeting is of opinion that the notice of reduction shall be maintained, that steps shall be immediately taken to fill all shops with men willing to work at the reduced wages, and that the committee of the Bristol Master Builders' Association be a committee for that purpose". A large sum of money was subscribed at the workmen from distant towns. The workmen, on the other had, having posted notices calling upon all operative masons to keep away from Bristol during the dispute, and the struggle bids fair to be very determined on both sides.' (*The Times*)

# June 24th

**1497:** John Cabot stepped ashore on the North American continent, becoming the first European to do so. Cabot set sail a month previously from Bristol in *The Matthew*. It was the only time on the expedition that Cabot and his crew went ashore, Cabot preferring not to 'advance beyond the distance of a crossbow'. *The Matthew* sailed along the coast for about a month before returning to England. (Peter Firstbrook, *The Voyage of the Matthew*, BBC Books, 1997)

———— ◆ ————

**1823:** 'A few days since a person residing a short distance from this city had occasion to employ a labourer in his garden, who undertook to execute the job at a very low price and which proved wholly inadequate to the work. The poor man made an application for some drink, and the lady of the house, in the absence of her husband, compassionating him, very freely gave him cider. When this came to the ears of the worthy individual who hired him, he actually deducted the value of the cider from the amount of the labourer's small pittance. When this was done, the poor fellow turned the tables upon his heartless employer, by laying an information against him for selling cider without a license, and he was accordingly fined the full penalties.' (*The Times*)

# June 25th

**1542:** Paul Bush is consecrated as the first Bishop of Bristol. Born at Dilton, near Westbury around 1489/90, his initial education was at the priory of Edington before going to Oxford, where he was ordained priest. In 1525 he returned as a member of the community at Edington Priory, and wrote numerous theological and devotional works. Later he was appointed royal chaplain. The priory was dissolved on March 31st 1538 and he received a pension of £100. When Bristol diocese was established, he fought hard to uphold the rights of the poorly-endowed bishopric. He was conservative but was happy to go along with the religious changes of the period, including Cranmer's *Book of Common Prayer*, and took advantage of the clergy's new right to marry. However, he had to surrender his bishopric in 1553 with accession to the throne of Queen Mary I as he had broken his vow of clerical celibacy, although his wife by this point had died. He then became rector of Winterbourne, where he died on October 11th 1558. He is buried in Bristol Cathedral. (*Oxford Dictionary of National Biography*, OUP)

# June 26th

**1952:** Architect Charles Fredrick William Denning dies. He was born in Chard in Somerset and in 1901 he went into partnership with Earnest George Rodway. Together they designed buildings that were influenced by the Arts and Crafts style, including 42-48 Downs Park East and the gothic St Alban's Church in Westbury Park. However, as an architect he is better known for his designs in the Georgian Revival style and in 1912 he won a competition in *Country Life* for a cottage in that style. Denning also designed several swimming baths in Bristol during the 1930s, including Bedminster, Shirehampton, Speedwell and Knowle. All were built of brick with stone dressings using principles of Classical architecture. Denning is also known as a painter and during the Second World War painted the devastation following bombing raids. He was Artists' Chairman of the Royal West of England Academy from 1934 and published *Old Inns of Bristol* in 1943, containing his own pen-and-ink sketches. Eustace Button on Denning stated, 'He subscribed to the principle of good manners in architecture. An attitude which felt it was bad form to design a building which flaunted its own individuality.' (Sarah Whittingham, 'C.W.F. Denning: The Reluctant Architect?' in *Bristol Review of Books*)

# June 27th

**1790:** The first Roman Catholic church was opened in Trenchard Street by Fr Robert Plowden. The church was built by the Jesuit order, who had undertaken to serve a mission of Bristol. There are other instances of post-Reformation Roman Catholic worship in the city. During the reign of Charles II Henry Carew secretly acted as a Roman Catholic priest and friar and also held the office of surveyor in the Bristol Custom House. From about 1710 a few assembled for worship in an upper room of Hooke's Mills just outside the city's boundaries. Attempts to prosecute Roman Catholics, whose worship was illegal at this time, were not widely enforced. In 1716 Ward, a gunsmith 'suspected for being a popish priest', was let off after he brought instances of his good behaviour. A Roman Catholic chapel first opened in the city in St James' Back, which could accommodate up to eighty people with a priest named John Scudamore officiating. Many of the worshipers were said to have been Flemings, employed in the spelter works. During the 1745 Jacobite Uprising in Scotland, led by the 'Young Pretender' Charles Francis Stuart, all Roman Catholics were required to take the Oath of Alliance. Only nineteen Roman Catholics in Bristol did so. (John Latimer, *Annals of Bristol*, Kingsmead, 1970)

# June 28th

**1812:** William James Müller, landscape artist, was born at 13 Hillsbridge Place, Bristol. In 1825 he was given a paintbox by anthropologist J.C. Pritchard after he provided illustrations for one of his lectures. Müller also illustrated for W.D. Conybeare's lectures on the fossils found at Lyme Regis, Dorset. An important influence on Müller was his friendship with James Bulwar, curate of St Mary Redcliffe. Together they would sketch different parts of the city and Müller was influenced by Bulwar's collections of James Sell Cotman's drawings, taking from them the warm colouring and Cotman's free technique. Müller also produced a series of watercolour and oil sketches of the Bristol riots, which are currently held in Bristol Museum. He first exhibited at the Royal Academy in 1833 and moved to London in 1839. He visited France in 1840, a trip which provided the basis for his book *Müller's Sketches of the Age of Francis 1st*, published the following year. In 1843 he was invited to join an expedition to Turkey with archaeologist Charles Fellows, where he painted rain-swept landscapes, ruins and people. Exhausted from overwork he returned to Bristol, where he died at the home of his brother on September 8th 1845. (*Oxford Dictionary of National Biography*, OUP)

# June 29th

**1973:** The consecration of Clifton Cathedral took place on the Feast of St Peter and Paul, to which the Cathedral Church is dedicated. The foundation stone had been laid by the then Bishop of Clifton, Joseph Rudderham, in September 1970. It was Bishop Rudderham who had decided that Clifton Cathedral should be reordered and renovated following Vatican II, which had changed the emphasis in Catholic worship. However, the cost of restoring and reordering the interior of the old 'Pro' Cathedral proved costly and the lasting stability of the structure could not be guaranteed. Through some generous benefactors a new cathedral could then be considered. The design was by architects Ronald Weeks, Frederick Jannett and Antoni Poremba of Percy Thomas Partnership, who designed a building where at least 900 people could gather around the high altar. The importance of each area of the cathedral is defined by the height of the roof and the intensity of daylight on each area, which increases with the height of the roof. The roof over the baptistery and the blessed sacrament chapel are 30 feet (9m). The height of the nave rises from 30 feet (9m) at the rear of the nave to 54 feet (16.5m) at the edge of the sanctuary before rising to 90 feet (27m) over the high altar. (Clifton Cathedral website, *Clifton Cathedral Guide Book*)

# June 30th

**1654:** The diarist John Evelyn visited Bristol and describes it as 'a city emulating London, not for its large extent, but manner of building, shops, traffic, exchange, market place &c. The governor showed us its castle of no great concernment. The city wholly mercantile, as standing near the famous Severn, commodiously for Ireland, and the Western World ... But what appeared most stupendous to me was the rock of St Vincent, a little distance from the town, the precipice whereof is equal to anything in nature I have seen in the most confragose cataracts of the Alps, the river gliding between them at an extraordinary depth. Here, we went searching for diamonds and to Hot Wells at its foot. There is also on the side of this horrid Alp a very romantic seat: and so we returned to Bath in the evening.' The diamonds referred to in this extract are known as Bristol Diamonds, but were in fact quartz crystals dug for jewellery and for passing visitors including Celia Fiennes, who visited Bristol in 1698 and acquired 'a piece just as it came out of the rock ... and appeared to me as a cluster of diamonds polish'd and irregularly cut.' (*Diary of John Evelyn* / Celia Fiennes, *Through England on a Side Saddle in the Time of William and Mary*, Cambridge University Press, 2010)

# July 1st

**1967:** The consecration of All Saints' Church, Clifton, took place. The original church was consecrated in June 8th 1868 and was a temporary, brick-built structure. George Edmund Street designed a more permanent replacement to which the nave was constructed in 1872; it was able to hold up to 800 people and all the pews were to be free and un-appropriated. From the beginning the church took on a character that could be described as Anglo-Catholic, with the principal morning service being a Choral Eucharist and full Eucharistic vestments worn by the priest – which at that time was something of a novelty in the Church of England. Within a few years the church had founded a choir school, allowing the church to provide daily choral services and cathedral-style music. The choir school closed in 1962 following pressures on funds. On December 2nd 1940 an incendiary bomb destroyed much of the church. W.H. Randoll Blacking was appointed architect. There was much debate over the reconstruction of the church, but Blacking died before the work could begin. Robert Hare was then appointed architect and produced a more radical design that incorporated the surviving tower, sacristy and narthex, which brought the congregation nearer the altar rather than being separated from it by the choir. (*All Saints' Clifton Guidebook*)

# July 2nd

**1864:** The replacement of Isambard Kingdom Brunel's Hungerford Railway Bridge, which was also a suspension bridge, allowed for the completion of the Clifton Suspension Bridge. The two bridges were of similar length and it was proposed to use the chains of the Hungerford Bridge to complete the Clifton Bridge. A new company was formed in 1860 for this purpose and on June 28th 1861 a second Act of Parliament, authorising the works, had been obtained and granted royal assent. Work to complete the bridge commenced in November 1862, as soon as the chains from the Hungerford Bridge became available. On this date in 1864 the last of the cross girders was fixed to the centre of the bridge and a small party was allowed to pass over the bridge by the resident engineer, Mr Airey. Work then commenced to complete the roadway across the bridge in time for its formal opening on December 8th 1864. (John Latimer, *Annals of Bristol*, Kingsmead, 1970 / G.W. Barnes & Thomas Stevens, *The History of the Clifton Suspension Bridge*, The Clifton Suspension Bridge Trust, 1970)

# July 3rd

**1958:** Arthur Milton (1928-2007) was one of a few men to play at international level in both football and cricket. His career in football began when he played for Arsenal reserve team before being called up for National Service. By 1948 he had made it into the first eleven of Gloucestershire Cricket Club and made his debut against Northamptonshire. At this time he was also playing for Arsenal and, after playing only twelve First Division matches, he was called up to the England squad, replacing an injured Tom Finney, for a match against Austria to be played at Wembley. It was his only international appearance. In February 1955 he transferred to Bristol City for a fee of £3,000 and helped City to reach the top of the division by the end of the season. Finding the demands of playing sport all year round too strenuous, he retired from football in order to concentrate on cricket and made his international debut against New Zealand at Headingly on this date in 1958, scoring 104 runs – the first cricketer to score a century on their England debut since W.G. Grace. He was a well-respected cricketer for Gloucestershire, with a consistent performance on the field. He retired from the sport in 1974. (*Oxford Dictionary of National Biography*, OUP)

# July 4th

**1825:** A riot started on this date between the Bedminster's Irish population and native Bristolians. It was alleged that a number of Irish labourers had been working in Bedminster's tan yards at wages that were considerably lower than that normally paid. It caused a great deal of ill-feeling and animosity from those usually employed in the yards. On Monday July 4th a fight broke out between a young Englishman and a young Irishman, during which it was alleged that the Irish countryman interfered improperly. In consequence more fighting broke out between the two nationalities and the Irishmen sought refuge in houses in Brown Street. The windows of these houses were then smashed by Englishmen. The next evening a large body of Englishmen marched into Bristol from Bedminster and attacked Irish homes in Mann Marsh Street, smashing windows and looting two shops. The arrival of the police, headed by the Mayor, eventually restored order. Seven Englishmen and two Irishmen required treatment in the Bristol Infirmary. On Wednesday evening, 3,000 people congregated in Corn Street, Clare Street and Marsh Street. No trouble broke out on this occasion owing to the presence of the city's constables and a squadron of the 10th Hussars were standing by ready to act if needed. (*The Times*)

# July 5th

**1970:** The SS *Great Britain* returned to Bristol with tens of thousands of people lining the banks of the Avon to welcome home the ship that first set sail from the city almost 127 years previously. Crowds cheered as the 3,300-ton ship, towed by two tugs, was moved up the Avon towards the Cumberland Basin. The *Great Britain*, after her life as a ship, was used as a storage vessel at Port Stanley on the Falkland Islands. By 1937 the vessel was no longer watertight so she was towed a short distance from Port Stanley and the hull breached. In 1970 businessman Jack Hayward put up £150,000 to pay for her return to Bristol. The ship was secured on a huge pontoon to make the journey across the Atlantic. Bad weather made the journey hazardous and a huge crack in her hull added to the difficulties. The Avonmouth Dock Authorities were anxious to get the ship on her way because of the fragile condition of her hull and the next suitable tide would have been in two weeks' time. The most difficult aspect of the journey up the Avon was passing the horseshoe bend, reckoned to have been something of a squeeze for the 322 foot ship. (*The Times* / www.ssgreatbritain.org)

# July 6th

**1886:** At Bristol Police Court Melvin Parker (54), an American sailor recently discharged from his ship, was charged with shooting John Mayo with intent to do him grievous bodily harm. The prisoner boarded the 3.20 p.m. train from Bristol to Cardiff on June 26th as a third class passenger. John Mayo, a railway official, was checking the tickets when, seeing that Parker had a double-barrelled shotgun by his side, asked what he found to shoot at sea. Without provocation Parker replied, 'To shoot fellows such as you!' Parker then drew a revolver and discharged it at Mayo, the bullet entering the upper part of his arm. Stephen Roberts, a porter, then dashed into the carriage, seizing both the revolver and shotgun from Parker and securing him, despite Parker's threats to shoot anyone who molested him. Mayo was taken to a hospital to have the bullet removed under anaesthetic. Parker was committed for trial at the next Bristol Assizes, which was held the following month. He was found guilty of unlawful wounding and sentenced to seven months' hard labour. (*The Times*)

# July 7th

**1904:** On this date an issue of the *Era* carried a report of Walford Bodie's show held at the Bristol People's Palace Music Hall during a three-week run, where it was claimed that Bodie cured up to fifty patients with incurable conditions from the Bristol Infirmary and General Hospital. His methods could be described as a mix of hypnotism, muscular manipulation and faith healing. Bodie started out as a music hall entertainer and his success built on a reputation established through these healings, which made him a thorn in the side of the medical establishment and it was not uncommon for medical students to heckle during his performances. Bodie was also known for his ventriloquism and as a stage hypnotist. Bodie was a striking individual with a large, pointed and somewhat dramatic moustache and undoubtedly had much stage presence. Some of Bodie's secrets were revealed in a successful 1909 court case brought against him by a former assistant. Here it was revealed that Bodie carefully selected his 'patients' and that their symptoms were often exaggerated. (*Oxford Dictionary of National Biography*, OUP)

# July 8th

**1781:** Tom Cribb was born in Hanham, Bristol. He became was one of the most successful pugilistic fighters of his day. Aged 13, he moved to London, working successively as a bell hanger, coal porter, and sailor. His work as a coal porter gained him the nickname the Black Diamond. His first public contest was against George Maddox, on January 7th 1805, whom he beat in seventy-six rounds in 2 hours 10 minutes. On July 20th 1805, he was defeated for the only time in his career by George Nicholls. In 1807 he was trained by Captain Barclay for a fight against Jem Belcher. Barclay staked 200 guineas on Cribb and the fight took place on July 8th. Cribb was the victor after forty-one rounds. In a fight against Bob Gregson on October 25th, Gregson was, in the twenty-third round, unable to rise, and so Cribb won just before he himself passed out. Belcher challenged Cribb to a rematch on Epsom Downs on February 1st 1809, which Belcher again lost. Another challenge came from Thomas Molineaux, a black American. He was twice beaten by Cribb, who won the second fight in just 20 minutes, disappointing spectators. He retired as a publican and died on May 11th 1848. (*Oxford Dictionary of National Biography*, OUP)

# July 9th

**1947:** After the Second World War, the Bristol Aeroplane Company found itself with spare capacity and the company, under the leadership of Sir George White, turned part of the business to small-scale car production and so Bristol Cars was born. By the middle of 1947 the time had come to launch the first car and so a series of full-page adverts were taken in *The Motor*, the first appearing in the issue of July 9th 1947. The first model, the 400, was based on the pre-war BMW 328 and shared its engine and some styling features. The adverts described the Bristol as 'A new car ... with pedigree ... bringing to motoring the cumulative benefits of the Bristol Aeroplane Company's long experience in high craftsmanship and precision engineering.' Development continued on the car throughout 1947 and early 1948, so that when *The Motor* tested it in May 1948, the car was considerably modified from when *Autocar* had tested it earlier in January 1948. The acceleration from 0-70mph in May was 8 seconds quicker than it had been in January. Bristol Cars are still manufactured at Filton, while the only showroom is located in Kensington, London. (Christopher Balfour, *Bristol Cars: A Very British Story*, Haynes, 2009 / Chris Horton (ed.), *The Encyclopedia of Cars*, Troddy Books, 1990)

# July 10th

**2000:** In 1943 brothers Aldo and Frank Berni bought their first licensed restaurant in Bristol. It was called 'Horts' and specialised in oyster soup and Dover sole. Gradually the brothers added more restaurants to their chain, which became known as Berni Inns. When food rationing was ended in 1954 the inns became well known for their set menu, including in the 7s 6d meals of steak and chips with peas, bread and butter, followed by pudding or cheese. This limited menu meant that no trained chef was needed and the cooking facilities were simply a grill and a deep fryer. The brothers also replaced tablecloths with placemats and apparently managed to save £700,000 each year in laundry bills. Quality control was maintained by issuing a set of detailed instructions for every step of the operation. The Berni Inn concept grew until it comprised of 147 hotels and restaurants. In 1990 the chain was sold to Whitbread and many of the restaurants were re-branded Beefeater. Aldo continued to live in Bristol until his death on October 12th 1997, whilst Frank retired to Jersey and died on this date in 2000. (*Oxford Dictionary of National Biography*, OUP)

# July 11th

**1836:** Bristol Zoo was opened by the Bristol and Clifton Zoological Society. The aims of the society were given a year earlier when Dr Henry Riley, at a meeting of the society, motioned that 'this meeting being persuaded that a Zoological Society in Bristol and Clifton will tend to promote knowledge by facilitating observation of the habits, form and structure of the animal kingdom, as well as affording rational amusement to the neighbourhood.' (John Latimer, *Annals of Bristol*, Kingsmead, 1970 / A.N.H. Green-Armytage, *Bristol Zoo 1835-1965*, Arrowsmith, 1965)

———◆———

**1920:** Charles George Stephens, a hairdresser from Bedminster, was killed whilst trying to shoot Niagara Falls in a 6ft (2m) barrel, which plunged over the 158ft (48m) drop. His attempt was watched by Mrs Anne Edison Taylor and Bobby Leach, who had both attempted the feat before and survived. The barrel was said to have 'cracked like an eggball on the rocks'. Attempts were made to locate the body but only his arm was recovered. Stephens was already something of a daredevil, being an experienced parachutist and having kissed lions in their den, even shaving some of his customers whilst lions were prowling around. He was survived by his wife and nine children. (*The Times*)

# July 12th

**1696:** Thomas Goldney, Bristol merchant, was born. He was educated in a Quaker household before joining his father's business. In 1717 he went to work in Coalbrookdale, Shropshire, where his family had mining interests and where he served as a clerk collecting money and taking orders. He took over the family business when his father died in 1731. During the 1740s he extended his interests with shares in the Warmley Brass Company, the Bristol Lead Company, ships and mines in Devon and Cornwall. The declaration of war with Spain in 1739 allowed him to develop a trade in guns. He also had substantial land interests, inheriting Elberton Mansion House, a few miles to the north of Bristol. He also had a townhouse at College Green, and a house at Clifton. In 1752 he helped establish a Quaker bank. Although a Quaker, he was not a particularly active member and although he supported the Whigs when he voted he took no active role in politics. After his death, his Clifton residence passed to his elder sister, Hannah Ball, in 1768 and then to Gabriel his younger brother, who died in 1796. The last Goldney to live at the house was Ann. Goldney House is now owned by the University of Bristol. (Bristol University website / *Oxford Dictionary of National Biography*, OUP)

# July 13th

**1539:** According to *Adams's Chronicle of Bristol*, on May 15th 1539 George Wisard, a preacher from Scotland, gave a sermon at St Nicholas's Church that was considered to be blasphemous and was said to lead many of the city's population into error. Sadly the details of what the heresy Wisard is alleged to have preached were omitted by the chronicler, although we know that his accuser was the Dean of the diocese, John Kearney. Wisard was taken to the Archbishop of Canterbury before whom, along with the Bishops of Bath, Norwich and Chester and other doctor's of the Church, he was examined, convicted and condemned. He was sent back to Bristol where, on this day in 1539, he had to 'bear a faggot' in St Nicolas's Church and about the parish and again a week later on July 20th in Christ Church and about the parish there. To 'bear a faggot' in this context refers to the bundles of sticks used to burn heretics alive. Since Wisard recanted his heresy he was made to bear the sign of a faggot by being made to wear an embroidered emblem of sticks that would have been used to burn him on his sleeve. (William Adams, *Adams's Chronicle of Bristol*, J.W. Arrowsmith, 1910 / *Oxford English Dictionary*)

# July 14th

**1951:** John Atyeo signs for Bristol City Football Club aged 19, becoming Bristol City's chief goal scorer and remaining with the club throughout his professional career. His contract stated that he should always be on top wages (which then amounted to £12 per week) and that he should be allowed to stay at home in Dilton Marsh to enable him to complete an apprenticeship as a quantity surveyor. Further conditions included a £100 donation to his amateur club Westbury United. Atyeo made an impact in the first match he played for his new club ,which was against Newport County and watched by 28,426 people at Ashton Gate. Atyeo set up two goals for other players and headed in a goal himself. Atyeo would soon go on to play for England. He could be described as a country boy at heart and kept chickens at his home, supplying a great many of the Bristol City staff with eggs. Atyeo's last and 645th game took place on May 10th 1965, against Ipswich Town at Ashton Gate. In that game he managed to pass the 350-goal barrier scored in league and cup games with a 4–1 win. On retiring from football Atyeo pursued a career in teaching. (Peter Godsiff, *Bristol City: The Complete History of the Club*, Wensum Books, 1979)

# July 15th

**1854:** Henry Werrett, a farmer of Coalpit Heath, was infuriated by a fox that took his hens in broad daylight. When he saw the fox he loaded his gun and balanced himself on a manger in order to get a clear view of the fox. Unfortunately he slipped and as he fell to the ground the gun went off, injuring him in the chest. His last words were said to be 'I'm a dead man', before he collapsed and died. At the subsequent inquest the coroner recorded a verdict of accidental death. (Nicola Sly, *A Grim Almanac of Bristol*, The History Press, 2011)

———— • ◆ • ————

**1878:** At Lawford's Gate Petty Session it was reported that 'two lads, named William Bryant and Richard Schutz, pleaded guilty to stealing potatoes from the garden of Mr Thomas Barratt. Bryant, who had been previously convicted, was committed for six weeks imprisonment, and Schutz was fined 15s 6d and costs, or, in default 14 days' imprisonment.' (*Bristol Mercury and Daily Post*)

# July 16th

**1878:** Thomas Ricks, a quay porter, was charged at Bristol Police Court with stealing a goose from the steamship *Hancott*. Ricks was unloading the ship and attempted to hide the goose under his coat, but it was noticed by the third engineer. It was evident that the bird had only recently been killed. In his defence Ricks stated that he found the bird dead amongst a consignment of barley. Although no one had witnessed Ricks killing the bird, the magistrates did not believe him and he was sentenced to a month's imprisonment with hard labour. (*Bristol Mercury and Daily Post*)

---

**1992:** Rioting started on the Hartcliffe Estate after two men, Shaun Star and Keith Buck, died in a police chase after the men stole an unmarked police motorbike. The stolen motorbike collided with an unmarked police car. The subsequent rioting lasted three days after some locals blamed police for the deaths of the two men. Masked gangs went around armed with clubs, iron bars, bricks and petrol bombs. After the first night of the disturbances sixty-five people were arrested, fifteen police officers were injured, ten cars were set alight and twenty shops were damaged. The library was also damaged after 'Murderers' was daubed in huge letters on the wall. (*Western Daily Press*)

# July 17th

**1545:** *Adams's Chronicle of Bristol* states that 'here was a marvellous great thunder, lasting from eight of the clock until four in the morning, at which instant Mr Abbington died and the thunder ceased.' (William Adams, *Adams's Chronicle of Bristol*, J.W. Arrowsmith, 1910)

---◆---

**1768:** John Slack, pugilist, died in Bristol. He was born around the year 1721 in Norfolk and his trade was originally that of butcher. At his debut fight on October 12th 1743 in London he beat John James, and remained unbeaten until twice beaten by Thomas Smallwood. His fame was gained after beating a seemingly invincible John Broughton, one of the foremost fighters of his day. The fight against Broughton took place on April 11th 1750 where, despite the fact Broughton was the favourite, Slack beat his opponent in 14 minutes. Slack's other notable victory was against Pettit, who walked off the stage after 25 minutes, browbeaten by his indomitable opponent. In Bristol Slack triumphed over brothers John and Cornelius Harris on February 6th and March 6th 1755 respectively. John was apparently beaten in 6 minutes. (*Oxford Dictionary of National Biography*, OUP)

# July 18th

**1848:** William Gilbert Grace was born at Downend on the outskirts of Bristol. He was a colossal figure in the game of cricket with performances that would be remarkable today. In first class cricket his scores over his lifetime amounted to 56,896 runs, including 126 centuries, and 2,864 wickets. His family was devoted to the game and Grace describes that: 'By the time I was nine years old I had got over the elementary stage of stopping the ball, and was slowly acquiring power in meeting it firmly and playing it away.' Grace had an unusual batting style, hitting almost every ball that was bowled in the middle of the bat. Once, in 1884, when Australia came to play England, the tourists complained that the English bats were wider than they ought to have been. Consequently, when some of the English players carefully measured and even planed the edges of their bats, W.G. Grace laughed, claiming that he didn't care how much they shaved off his bat, 'All I want is the middle'. He died on 23 October 1915. (Trevor Bailey, *A History of Cricket*, Allen & Unwin, 1979 / A.A. Thompson, 'W.G. Grace' / *A Penguin Cricketer's Companion*, Penguin, 1979 / Gloucestershire County Cricket Club website)

# July 19th

**1843:** A special train arrived from London carrying the Prince Consort and Isambard Kingdom Brunel. At Bristol Temple Meads they were greeted by the band of the Life Guards and cheering crowds. After a banquet they assembled to launch the SS *Great Britain*. After the success of the SS *Great Western*, Brunel wanted to advance the design of shipbuilding further. He initially planned a wooden hull of 2,000 tons but soon realised that this would not be strong enough to cope with Atlantic conditions. An idea came to him in October 1838 when he saw the iron-hulled paddle steamer *Rainbow* come into the Floating Harbour. He gained permission to sail in the vessel to test its seaworthiness. Suitably impressed, he designed an iron-hulled ship of over 3,000 tons. When the SS *Archimedes* came to Bristol dock he found that it had a screw propeller patented by Charles Pettit. Brunel soon adopted the idea with some enthusiasm for the SS *Great Britain*. (Adrian Vaughn, *Isambard Kingdom Brunel*, John Murray, 1991)

———— • ◆ • ————

**1970:** The SS *Great Britain* finally entered the Floating Harbour. It had been in the Cumberland Basin after being towed up the Avon on July 5th, waiting for a high enough tide to enable the ship to pass through the locks into the harbour and the Great Western Dock. (Wikipedia / Adrian Ball & Diana Wright, *SS Great Britain*, David & Charles, 1981)

# July 20th

**1796:** Edward Hodges, organist and composer, was born in Bristol. His first appointment was as organist at Clifton parish church before becoming organist of St James Church in 1819 and then St Nicholas' Church in 1821. Around this time Hodges began to compose anthems and service settings. In 1825 he was awarded the degree of doctor from Sydney Sussex College, Cambridge. Throughout his life he continued to publish literature on music, contributing regularly to *Quarterly Musical Magazine* and *Musical World*. In 1838 he moved with his family to America and became organist of St John's Episcopal Church, New York. In 1846 he became organist of Trinity Church and had the organ built to his own specification. Hodges still continued to compose music for the Church, a collection of which was published under the title *The Trinity Collection of Church Music*. Examples of his music include the hymn tune 'Gloucester', commonly set to Arthur J. Mason's hymn 'Look Down on us God of Grace', and the hymn tune 'Habakkuk'. Hodges returned to England after becoming ill in 1863 and died on September 1st 1867 at Clifton. (*Oxford Dictionary of National Biography*, OUP / www.cyberhymnal.org)

# July 21st

**1733:** A council meeting was held to petition the removal of the High Cross, which stood at the corner of Wine Street and High Street. The cross was erected in 1373 when Bristol gained county status, and it served to mark the place of the market. A representation from those desiring the removal of the Cross claimed that, 'It hath been insinuated by some that this Cross, on account of its antiquity ought to be lookt upon as something sacred. But when we consider that we are Protestants, and that Popery ought effectively to be guarded against this nation, we make our request to you to consider: If the opening of a passage to the four of the principal streets in this city not to outweigh anything that can be said of this superstitious Relick, which is at present a public nuisance.' John Vaughn, a goldsmith and banker whose shop stood by the cross, offered to swear that his life and his property were endangered by the weather-worn cross, especially during high winds. It was taken down a month later. The cross now stands in the gardens of Stourhead, Wiltshire. Crosses in other towns were taken down for similar reasons. (John Latimer, *Annals of Bristol*, Kingsmead, 1970)

# July 22nd

**1850:** Bristol historian John Latimer records that: 'In the summer of 1849 a small vessel commenced to ply as a passenger boat between the Drawbridge and Cumberland Basin; when the novelty and cheapness of the mode of transit caused the enterprise to be very profitable, and naturally brought competitors into the field. In the summer of 1850, seven additional steamers were provided for carrying on the traffic, which had heavily increased. On the evening of 22nd July, one of the vessels, the *Red Rover*, which was said to have carried a thousand passengers during the day, was starting on her concluding voyage from the Cumberland Basin, with about fifty passengers on board, when the boiler exploded, scattering death and destruction around. Fifteen individuals were either instantly killed or died from their injuries; several others were seriously maimed. The verdict given at the first coroner's inquest was, "that the deceased had met with his death in consequence of the bursting of a boiler which at that time was in an unfit state to use."' (John Latimer, *Annals of Bristol*, Kingsmead, 1970)

# July 23rd

**1926:** Reginald Dyer, who spent his final years living in Long Aston, Bristol, died. Dyer was a former army General and is a controversial figure who polarises opinion: either he was a brilliant man who prevented a potential uprising, or he callously ordered his troops to fire into a crowd, killing 379 innocent people. The Punjab was experiencing civil disorder when Dyer arrived in Amritsar on April 10th 1919 amidst rioting following the arrest of several nationalist leaders. The deputy commissioner R.B. Becket, realising the worsening situation, relinquished control, allowing Dyer to impose martial law. Dyer ordered that no one should enter or leave the city, set up a curfew and banned public meetings, which could be broken up by force if required. On April 13th news reached Dyer of an unauthorised assembly at the Jallianwalla Bagh, a walled-enclosure near the Golden Temple. To disperse them he ordered his troops to fire into the 20,000-strong crowd without warning, killing 379 people and injuring many more, who did not receive medical attention. When news of the Amritsar Massacre reached Britain it caused widespread uproar and a subsequent investigation was highly critical of Dyer actions. In 1920 Dyer resigned from the army and retired to Bristol. (*Oxford Dictionary of National Biography*, OUP)

# July 24th

**1885:** An unusual and remarkable swimming feat took place on the Avon when Minna Wookey, aged just 11, swam half a mile from Bath Bridge to Bedminster Bridge with her feet and hands tied. The announcement that Minna would undertake the feat had the effect of lining the banks of the river with thousands of spectators. Mr G.M. Longney, secretary of the Leander Swimming Club, first tied Minna's wrists together and then her legs just above the ankles. 'Diving from the boat, she commenced her task in an earnest manner, and principally with a powerful stroke she made good headway, soon reaching the footbridge. The applause of the spectators seemed to give her fresh energy, not that she seemed at all fatigued, and again resorting to the side-stroke, she eventually completed the distance. Being lifted into the boat at Bedminster Bridge she was greeted with loud cheers, and the bandages having been cut, she again dived into the river and swam to a point opposite to Bathurst Basin, where she got out and was carried into the van waiting for her.' Minna was presented with a bouquet of flowers by a member of the Leander Swimming Club. (*Bristol Mercury and Daily Press*)

# July 25th

**1565:** The feast of St James in Bristol was marked by a fair and 700 soldiers travelling to Ireland passed through the city. Unfavourable winds kept the soldiers in the city for six weeks as they could not sail. A brawl started and Captain Rendall, on hearing of it, tried to execute martial law on the troublemakers. A gibbet was erected in the High Street and all soldiers were commanded to see the execution of the offenders, but on hearing if their penitence Rendell spared them the death penalty. (William Adams, *Adams's Chronicle of Bristol*, J.W. Arrowsmith, 1910)

---

**1887:** As part of Queen Victoria's Jubilee celebrations, a display involving 4,000 troops on Durdham Down was planned. However, it had to be abandoned owing to the conduct of the spectators. Staging had been erected for reserved ticket-holders only, which was resented by a crowd of 50,000 and led to unrest. (John Latimer, *Annals of Bristol*, Kingsmead, 1970)

---

**1888:** A statue of Queen Victoria, which still stands on the edge of College Green, was unveiled by Prince Albert Victor, Duke of Clarence and grandson to the monarch. The statue is 8 feet 6 inches high and weighs 4 tons and was sculpted by Joseph Edgar Boehm. It was erected to celebrate the Queen's Golden Jubilee the previous year. (www.about-bristol.co.uk)

# July 26th

**1643:** Royalist forces seized Bristol. Nathaniel Fiennes, the Parliamentarian Governor, had refused to surrender to Prince Rupert two days previously. Edward Hyde, Earl of Clarendon, records the fierce battle that ensued with heavy losses on the Royalist side, noting that 'all men were cast down to see so little gotten with so great a loss.' Once Royalist forces were able to enter the town, Fiennes surrendered and was promised a safe passage away from the city. Despite such assurances Nehemiah Wallington, a Puritan, notes in an exaggerated fashion how the defeated Parliamentarians were harassed as they left of the city: 'The Cavaliers fell upon us in a most furious and barbarous manner, plundering and rifling all sorts of persons sparing neither age nor sex, but took away our horses, cloaks, bags, monies ... searching the women in a most uncivil manner for money, presenting their swards and pistols at such as did any that deny them, and when we alleged the terms of our agreement, they would not acknowledge any at all, beside other villainies.' (Tristram Hunt, *The English Civil War At First Hand*, Phoenix, 2003)

# July 27th

**1770:** Clifton parish church contained numerous tablets and memorials to naval and military men until a bombing raid destroyed much of the building in November 1940. One tablet located at the entrance to the church did survive – that of Robert Dinwiddie, who died on this date in 1770. Dinwiddie was born in Germiston near Glasgow in 1693, the son of a merchant, and became involved with colonial affairs, being made a Customs Collector in Bermuda in 1730 earning £30 per year. In 1738 he was made Surveyor-General for the southern part of America. When he visited Barbados he uncovered many frauds carried out by the plantation owners, which did not make him very popular. In 1753 he was appointed Governor of Virginia. The French were also making incursions into the Ohio region by building a fort and threatening to cut the English off from the entire western region of America, and so Dinwiddie sent a young solider along with 100 men on a dangerous mission to demand that the French withdraw. That young solider was George Washington, who would later become the first President of the United States. This developed into the Seven Years' War, when Britain and France fought for supremacy in America. (Marguerite Fedden, *Bristol Vignettes*, Burleigh Press, 1957)

# July 28th

**1399:** Bristol Castle fell into the hands of Henry Bolingbrook (later Henry IV) during his conquest of England, where he fought against the unpopular king Richard II. The castle was defended by William Scrope, who loyally served Richard II throughout his reign and had been created Earl of Wiltshire by him. Entrusted to look after Queen Isobel at Wallingford Castle, who was just 11 years old at this time, he had retired to Bristol when Bolingbrook invaded England. When he was captured by Henry Bolingbrook he was summarily tried and beheaded the next day, along with two other councillors of Richard II – Sir John Bussy and Henry Green. (*Oxford Dictionary of National Biography*, OUP)

**1876:** A railway accident occurred near Long Ashton. It involved the express train known as *The Flying Dutchman*, which left the rails whilst journeying towards Bristol. The two men on the footplate of the engine were killed and several of the passengers were severely injured. The cause of the accident was blamed on the defective condition of the track and blame was passed on those officials deemed responsible for the fault. (John Latimer, *Annals of Bristol*, Kingsmead, 1970)

# July 29th

**1857:** An unusual case appeared before Bristol magistrates when an elderly man named Mr Skinnier, residing at St Philip's, was charged with assault on a man named Finch. It appeared that on Sunday evening he asked to talk with Finch at his house. Finch went round but was struck on the head by Skinner with his walking stick. Skinner is reported to have said, 'You ****, see what you have put on me.' Under cross-examination, Finch eventually admitted that he and two other men named McCullock and Brown had persuaded Skinner that he was suffering from witchcraft and that they could increase his afflictions at their will, being skilled in the 'black arts'. The men had persuaded Skinner to purchase a heart and stick pins, in it saying that when it was roasted it would cure Skinner's ailments. His wife, however, would not allow the procedure to take place. It was also clear from the demeanour of Mr Skinner that he was verging on lunacy and so he was merely fined the cost of the summons. Finch was cautioned that pursuing these alleged practices could make him liable to be committed as a rogue and vagabond. (John Latimer, *Annals of Bristol*, Kingsmead, 1970)

# July 30th

**1816:** Deborah Castle was born in Bristol. She was brought up as a Unitarian. Her marriage to Sir John Bowring and her subsequent move to Exeter, on November 8th 1860, allowed her to get involved in local philanthropy, supporting the education of young women and the university extension movement. As a prominent Unitarian in Exeter she put the case for practical Christianity. She also became involved in the Bristol and West of England Society for Women's Suffrage and became one of its vice-presidents, a position she held until her death on July 28th 1902. (*Oxford Dictionary of National Biography*, OUP)

———◆———

**1928:** Regent cinema in Castle Street opened. It was designed by W.H. Watkins and a large crush hall at the front of the cinema allowed 1,000 people to wait under cover. It also featured a Wurlitzer organ which rose from beneath the stage. Frank Williams was the organist. The cinema was bombed during an air raid on November 24th 1940. Fortunately the raid occurred on a Sunday and so no one was in the building. Matters would have been different had the air raid occurred a week later, when the government was due to lift the ban on Sunday opening. (Dave Stephenson & Jill Willmott, *Bristol Cinemas*, The History Press, 2005)

# July 31st

**1743:** Richard Savage (1697/8-1743), poet and playwright, claimed to be the illegitimate son of Richard Savage, the 4th Earl Rivers. He became best known for works such as *The Bastard*, a satire on illegitimacy, *The Wanderer*, and *The Progress of the Divine*, which is considered by some to be one of the best satires written of its time. He came to Bristol in September 1742 in order to stage a revised version of his play *Sir Thomas Overbury*. On January 10th 1743 Savage was arrested for debt of £8, which he owed to a Mrs Read, or 'Madam Wolfbitch' as Savage called her. Here he remained for the last six months of his life, carefully concealing his imprisonment and his illness. He was looked after by the keeper of the prison, Abel Dagge, who also tried to get Savage released. On July 25th, Savage, complaining of back pain, lapsed into a coma. On July 31st he said his final words to Dagge, 'I have something to say to you.' He was unable to remember what it was and continued with, ''Tis gone'. He died the following morning and was buried at Dagge's expense in St Peter's churchyard in Bristol. (*Oxford Dictionary of National Biography*, OUP)

# August 1st

**1750:** The first banking company was established in Bristol with the proprietors opening the offices in Broad Street. The company had five partners, namely Issac Elton, Harford Lloyd, William Miller, Thomas Knox and Matthew Hale. It was one of the few banking houses outside of London. Private bankers could be found in the city before this date although banking was not, unlike this new venture, their sole occupation. These include John Vaughan, a goldsmith who lived at the intersection of Wine Street and High Street, and James Wood, a prosperous draper who also operated as a banker in the city from 1716. (John Latimer, *Annals of Bristol*, Kingsmead, 1970)

———— ◆ ————

**1832:** The parish of St George's was created. Its parish church, designed by Robert Smirke, was opened as a chapel-of-ease to St Augustine's in 1823. By the 1960s, however, the church was in urgent need of repairs and threatened with closure. However, when the popular vicar Canon Percy Gay appealed for £5,000 for urgent repairs, three times that amount was raised and the church soon reopened. After Canon Gay's death during the 1970s, the church was declared redundant following dwindling attendances. It is now a concert hall where a wide variety of music is showcased. (St George's website / Maurice Fells, *Bristol: History You Can See*, The History Press, 2006)

# August 2nd

**1714:** 'A cooper living in Baldwin Street had invited some friends to spend the afternoon with him, and proposed that they should smoke in the summer house of the "pretty large garden" attached to his house. The pavilion was said to have been a rendezvous of the Bristolians concerned with the Rye House plot, and to commemorate the circumstance, a wooden crown surmounting a globe and been suspended from the roof.' The Rye House Plot concerned a planned attempt to assassinate Charles II because of his pro-Catholic policies. The plot gained its name from Rye House in Hertfordshire where the plans were laid. Charles II avoided assassination by travelling along the road early before an attempt on his life could be made. Back in Bristol the revellers on entering the building 'were horrified by observing that that the ornament was hidden by an enormous cobweb, measuring 3½ feet in length. The cooper averred that the place had been swept during the previous week. The phenomenon was regarded as an awful portent, and multitudes flocked to witness it.' (John Latimer, *Annals of Bristol*, Kingsmead, 1970)

---

**1784:** The first mail coach ran between Bristol and London and took 16 hours to complete the trip. (John Latimer, *Annals of Bristol*, Kingsmead, 1970)

# *August 3rd*

**1590:** 'Richard Ferres a wherry man of London, upon a wager came thence by water to Bristoll: he set to sea on midsummer day and landed at the Backe into the afternoon at half ebb; and brought his wherry upon men's shoulders to the Towlsey.' (William Adams, *Adams's Chronicle of Bristol*, J.W. Arrowsmith, 1910)

———— ◆ ————

**1760:** The boy-poet Thomas Chatterton enters Colston's School, a charity school for poor boys. It was not the first time that Chatterton had been schooled, for when he was five he was dismissed from school for 'being a dull boy incapable of improvement'. On leaving Colston's in 1767 he gained a covetous apprenticeship as a legal scrivener. In his spare time he wrote poetry but made his name by passing off his work as someone else's. Through family connections he accessed the archives of St Mary Redcliffe Church, where he claimed to discover the poetry of a fifteenth-century monk named Thomas Rowley. Experts praised the poems, that is, until they were discovered to be the work of Chatterton himself. Later he moved to London to try to make a living from his poetry but he died, in poverty, from an accidental overdose of arsenic and opium on August 24th 1774. He was just 17. (*Oxford Dictionary of National Biography*, OUP)

# August 4th

1700: Mrs Pugsley dies aged 80. Her funeral was reminiscent of a wedding. She was carried on a bier with a wedding dress as a shroud. It was preceded by a violinist playing a merry tune and two girls strewing flowers and sweet herbs. St Nicholas's Church bells rang without being muffled to give the impression of being rung for a celebration rather than for a funeral. Mrs Pugsley was the widow of an officer killed during the siege of Bristol in 1645, who, on the orders of Thomas Fairfax, Commander-in-Chief of the Parliamentarian Army, was buried in a field next to Nine-Tree Hill with full military honours. Mrs Pugsley had only been married to her husband a short time and visited his grave every day until she died and was buried next to him. The place where her husband was buried gave the name to a field and a well located within it. Pugsley's Well in medieval times was dedicated to the Blessed Virgin Mary and consisted of two basins by two springs. The larger of the two was used for drinking and the smaller basin was reputed to have healing properties, especially for eye conditions. (John Latimer, *Annals of Bristol*, Kingsmead, 1970 / Marguerite Fedden, *Bristol Vignettes*, Burleigh Press, 1957 / F.C. Jones, *The Glory that was Bristol*, St Stephen's Bristol Press, 1946)

# August 5th

1830: The General Election following the death of George IV was fiercely fought in Bristol. The Whigs, or Liberals as they were increasing known, were hopelessly divided on the issue of slavery and put up two candidates. The West Indies interest was represented by James Evan Baillie, whilst the anti-slavery candidate was Edward Protheroe, son of a former city MP. The Tories put up Richard Hart-Davis. Polling in Queen's Square for the first time was conducted in booths and voting was spread over five days. During that time the election was marred by considerable violence. John Temple, a Liberal supporter, had his windows smashed by a pro-slavery mob whilst some friends of Protheroe were set upon by men on horseback armed with bludgeons. After one of the many street affrays at the election, twenty-seven people required treatment in the Bristol Infirmary. Over 1,500 people were placed on the register of freemen by the rival parties to increase their support. Polling closed on August 5th and the results duly announced. Hart-Davis won the election, receiving 5,012 votes, whilst Baillie received 3,377 votes and Protheroe 2,840 votes. This election contest was a costly one, with upwards of £34,000 being spent by all parties and Baillie's share alone amounting to £18,000. (John Latimer, *Annals of Bristol*, Kingsmead, 1970)

# August 6th

**1492:** The will of John Forster arranged for the maintenance of the Bristol Almshouse and the attached fifteenth-century chapel, 'The Three Kings of Cologne', which was built in 1504. Accommodation for eight poor men and four or five poor women was available and inmates had small gardens in order to grow vegetables. (Marguerite Fedden, *Bristol Vignettes*, Burleigh Press, 1957)

———— ◆ ————

**1497:** John Cabot returned to Bristol from his journey to North America. He was the first European to set foot on the mainland of that continent. He was granted an audience with Henry VII on August 10th so Cabot wasted very little time in travelling to see the king once he landed at Bristol. Given the state of the roads it is likely the journey took him three days. The king was pleased with Cabot's success and granted him an annual pension of £20. It was not a huge amount and was to be granted out of customs passing through Bristol rather than from the king's own purse. With Cabot's fame at an all-time high he wanted the king to finance another voyage across the Atlantic and in due course Henry granted the necessary letters patent on February 3rd 1498. (Peter Firstbrook, *The Voyage of the Matthew*, BBC Books, 1997)

# August 7th

**1855:** Edward Mills Grace was born on November 28th 1841 at Downend. Like his famous younger brother, W.G. Grace, he became a first class cricketer whose interest in the game was fostered by his father and maternal uncle when the family practiced in the orchard of their home. On this date, aged just 13, E.M. Grace was included in the twenty-two-man West Gloucestershire cricket team to play against the England All Elevens. The England All Elevens was a travelling side formed to play against the odds, that is, to place against teams of more than eleven players. E.M. Grace made his first Lord's appearance in July 1861. Like his brothers, E.M. Grace studied medicine and had a practice in Thornbury. He also helped to establish Gloucestershire Cricket Club as a first class side, helping them to win the county championship in 1876 and 1877. He was a somewhat autocratic secretary of Gloucestershire Cricket Club between 1871 and 1909 and one committee minute simply read 'Present: E.M. Grace and that's all.' He died on May 20th 1911 and is buried in Downend parish churchyard. (*Oxford Dictionary of National Biography*, OUP)

# August 8th

**1373:** A charter from Edward III granting that 'the said town of Bristol with its suburbs and the precinct of the same according to the limits and bounds, as they are limited, shall be henceforth be separated from the said Counties of Gloucester and Somerset equally and in all things exempt, as well by land as by water, and that it shall be a County by itself and [be] called the County of Bristol forever.' (Quoted in J.H. Bettey, *Bristol Observed*, Redcliffe, 1986)

---

**1850:** Smugglers were captured in the Bristol Channel owing to the efforts of Mr Davis, Bristol's revenue officer. Previously Davis had seized some tobacco at Cook's Coal Yard in Hotwells Road, which he suspected of being run in a boat called the *Wave* of Abertham. Davis took his own boat and sailed out on the Bristol Channel and at about 3 o'clock in the morning found the *Wave* in Limpett Bay. Davis boarded her, and finding tobacco on board, she was seized. Placing the *Wave* in the charge of his own crew he went further down the Bristol Channel and seized the *Henri*, a French vessel, and found bales of tobacco and deck stone sinkers for the purposes of sinking them. (*The Times*)

# August 9th

**1875:** The first horse-drawn trams started operating in Bristol, running from Colston Street to Blackboy Hill. At the opening ceremony were the Lord Mayor, officials from the Tramways Company and members of the public. The route was lined with flags and bunting whilst St Michael's Church bells rang out a peal in celebration. The press noted that many passengers were impressed with the speed of the trams, which ran every 8 minutes, and 2*d* allowed you to travel along the line of 1 mile 62 chains. Work began on the line on July 29th 1873 but met with strong resistance the following year. Objections to the tramway came from a number of parties; the first from affluent Clifton, where many feared an influx of the lower orders of society, spoiling amenities in the area. Other objections followed from the Sunday Observance and Temperance Societies, whose leaders thought that the trams would rush even more people to sin. More objections came from shopkeepers who feared a loss of trade to the larger shops of the city centre. Consequently the lines were left unused for a year until parliament granted approval. (John B. Appleby, *Bristol's Trams Remembered*, J.B. Appleby, 1969)

# August 10th

**1241:** Eleanor of Brittany (1182/4-1241) was the eldest daughter of Geoffrey Duke of Brittany and Constance, Duchess of Brittany, and sister to her younger brother Arthur. For most of her life she was held under protective custody by King John, her uncle. She came to England in 1203 and was imprisoned in various castles, including Corfe Castle, Dorest; Burgh Castle, Westmorland; and Bowes Castle, Yorkshire. Despite appeals from Philip Augustus she was never released and remained a pawn of the English Crown. She was kept at Bristol Castle between 1224 and 1234 and 1238 or 1239, until her death. Surviving records at Bristol give a glimpse of what life was like for her. She was visited at least once a week by the bailiffs and four leading citizens to ensure her welfare. She had access to serving ladies and chaplains and enjoyed a protein-rich diet typical of many aristocrats. Her food consisted of fresh water and sea fish and meat. Her main beverages seem to have been milk and ale. Eleanor never married and she died on this date in 1241 and was buried at St James's Priory, Bristol. However, in accordance with the wishes given in her will, her body was later re-interred at Amesbury Convent. (*Oxford Dictionary of National Biography*, OUP)

# August 11th

**1817:** Mr Penny and Mr Brigstock were returning in a gig through Ashton when a footpad demanded their money and watches. Penny handed 5s, stating that it was 'all he deserved'. The footpad then relieved Brigstock of his purse, which contained just 6d. Penny tried to hit the thief with his stick but the robber pulled out a pistol. However, he got away with very little, calling his victims 'illiberal stingy fellows'. (*The Times*)

———— • ◆ • ————

**1853:** 'Shortly before 1 o'clock, an accident of a very serious character occurred at the Zoological gardens, Clifton, near this city. It appears that Mr Gyngell, the pryotechnist, who has a shed in the gardens for the manufacture of the fireworks used at the galas, had been for some days engaged in manufacturing a quantity of rocket, and other fireworks, to be let off at a gala on Monday next. This afternoon, as some persons were engaged in ramming the composition into the rocket case, by some accident the materials ignited, and the result was an explosion which destroyed the shed and the whole of the fireworks which had been manufactured. Two of the assistants were also seriously injured – one of them so much that he had to be at once conveyed to the Bristol Royal Infirmary.' (*The Times*)

# August 12th

**1774:** Robert Southey, poet, historian and reviewer, was born in Wine Street. He was educated at Westminster School and gained entry to Oxford University. His radical streak showed itself in a periodical produced by himself and his friends, which included an attack on corporal punishment, branding it the devil's work. It earned his expulsion from school and nearly cost him his place at Oxford, as the headmaster wrote to the university of his undesirable behaviour. In December 1795 he visited Spain and later published *Letters Written During a Short Residence in Spain and Portugal*, a collection of prose and verse which was sufficiently popular to run to a second edition. On his return to England the poet Coleridge invited him to stay in Keswick, where he remained for over forty years. Throughout his career he divided his time between his family and writing epic poetry such as *Joan of Arc*, which had many favourable reviews, and *Thalaba the Destroyer*, which was set in Arabia. His histories include *History of Brazil* and *History of the Peninsular War*. In 1813 he became the Poet Laureate, which he saw as an opportunity to promote the good order of the country. He died on March 21st 1843. (*Oxford Dictionary of National Biography*, OUP)

# August 13th

**1574:** Gunpowder stored at the Pelican Inn blew up, killing five people instantly. A further five people died from their injuries over the subsequent eight days. The explosion occurred the day before Queen Elizabeth I was due to visit the city. (William Adams, *Adams's Chronicle of Bristol*, J.W. Arrowsmith, 1910)

**1829:** *The Times* reported the death of a fashion-conscious young woman from Bristol, who died after 'the folly and fatal effects of following, for the sake of appearances only, the fashion of the day' for repeatedly lacing her corset so tightly that she was unable to stoop in the normal way. She often loosed her stays when she returned home because of the discomfort that she suffered. This habit brought on a cough, violent palpitations and other diseases of the heart and she consequently died. Her age was reported as being about twenty. The article goes into considerable detail about the subsequent autopsy, revealing that the chest cavity was reduced in size and other internal injuries contributing to the ill-health of the young woman. (*The Times*)

# August 14th

**1574:** Queen Elizabeth I visited Bristol and was met by the Mayor and the common council. She also visited Bristol Grammar School, where the boys' poetical recitations were cut short as their orations were so lengthy. The Queen remained in the city for a week. (John Latimer, *Annals of Bristol*, Kingsmead, 1970)

———— ◆ ————

**1899:** Joseph Croot, the last town crier of Bristol, died. He was appointed by the Corporation in 1855, when the office of crier was very profitable. He claimed to earn up to £150 per year in addition to the £4 paid by the council, who provided him with a new uniform each year. He wore a black livery coat with brass buttons, tricorn hat, blue velvet breaches and gaiters complete with a bunch of flowers attached across his chest. He attended all civic ceremonies. Business for the crier was particularly profitable in the poorer districts, where he used to 'cry' runaway wives for disconsolate husbands and often acted as arbitrator between the two parties. On market day he would go and 'cry' against thieves. His office declined from the 1870s as cheaper newspapers became more common. His last duty was in 1893, to announce a forthcoming auction sale. (*Bristol Mercury and Daily Post* / Reece Winstone, *Victorian and Edwardian Bristol from Old Photographs*, Batsford, 1983)

# August 15th

**1348:** Geoffrey le Baker, a chronicler at Oxford, states that on this date plague, known as the Black Death, reached Bristol. However, the only contemporary reference to the plague in Bristol comes from a Patent Roll dated April 15th 1349, where the Crown granted to the good men and parishioners of St Cross of the Temple a pardon for having acquired from the Prior of St John of Jerusalem (England) half an acre of land adjacent to the churchyard, which had been filled up with burials resulting from the pestilence. Analysis of Bristol's population suggests that the death rate in Bristol was around 35-40 per cent. Bristol's unhygienic conditions may have played a role in the high death toll with much of the population drawing their water from wells, which were easily contaminated from nearby cesspits. Efforts to improve the water supply came in 1376, when an official was appointed by Mayor Walter Derbe to look after three of the conduits bringing water into the city. Bristol seems to have quickly recovered from the Black Death, as evidenced from church building in the fourteenth and early fifteenth centuries. (Charles E. Boucher, 'The Black Death in Bristol' / *Transactions of the Bristol and Gloucestershire Archaeological Society Vol. 60*)

# August 16th

**1876:** Between 11 p.m. and midnight a fire broke out in the premises of Mr Thomas Skinner, a manufacturer of 29 Castle Street. The fire started in the factory at the back of the shop and spread through warehouses and workrooms. At this stage nobody noticed the presence of the fire. At the front of the premises were apartments in which lived Mr and Mrs Skinner and their two children, who at the time were sleeping on the first floor. Also in the building was Mr Skinner's nephew, a man named Hewlett, who had a small room over the second floor. Hewlett was about to extinguish his lamp for the night when he heard Mrs Skinner give alarm of a fire. They managed to escape through an attic window on to the roof. However, the other family members remained trapped inside the building. A man named George Rubrey, who had gained access to the roof in order to help rescue those inside, was unable to do so owing to the smoke. The fire brigade were not able to get a main water hose on the blaze for half an hour and Mr Skinner and his children perished, probably from the effects of the smoke. (*Illustrated Police News*)

# August 17th

**1817:** A tale of heroism was reported in *The Times* on August 21st 1817, a few days after the event: 'On Sunday, as two children were playing upon the Quay at Bristol, they unfortunately precipitated themselves into the river just at the time that the tide was at the highest; the little innocents sank, and many persons who say the accident, and were rendering all assistance in their power to rescue the children in vain, had given them up for lost, when a sailor lad, belonging to one of the vessels in the harbour, plunged in and brought up one of the children, which he fastened to a rope thrown out for the purpose and dived three times after the other before his laudable exertions were crowned with success, and he came on shore nearly exhausted, to behold the happiness and receive the caresses of the agonized parents, who were eye-witnesses to the accident. The age of the lad was only fourteen years. An immediate trifling subscription was entered into to reward him.' (*The Times*)

# August 18th

**1855:** Charles Loxton and Richard Badham appeared at the Council House charged with assaulting George Briggs, footman to the Mayor. Briggs's face bore recent signs that he had been attacked. The assault was said to have taken place near the entrance to Tyndall's Park, when the prisoners were alleged to have asked Briggs when he had his hair 'whitewashed' last. Briggs replied that it was none of their business and that if the abuse continued he would find means to have it stopped. Loxton apparently then struck Briggs in the left eye, causing his hat to fall off. The two continued to assault Briggs until the arrival of a Mr Bolt and his brother. One of the defendants then threatened Mr Bolt for interfering. A policeman arrived on the scene and took the names of all concerned. In court Loxton and Badham were positively identified by the policeman as being the men he interviewed on the night, but the Bolt brothers were not so sure. Both Loxton and Badham claimed that they were elsewhere on the night and were able to produce witnesses to confirm their stories. Consequently the charges were dropped. (*Bristol Mercury*)

# August 19th

**1718:** *The Historical Register* reported that Sir Edward Longville was killed on Durdham Down in a racing accident. It was also the first record of such an annual meeting held on the Down. (John Latimer, *Annals of Bristol*, Kingsmead, 1970)

———— ◆ ————

**1755:** A case of rough justice was reported in the *Bristol Journal* when a soldier, court-marshalled for stealing a shirt, was sentenced to 1,000 lashes. The convict then attempted suicide by trying to cut his throat. On the partial recovery of the poor man the authorities ordered 200 lashes and that he be discharged from the regiment. (John Latimer, *Annals of Bristol*, Kingsmead, 1970)

———— ◆ ————

**1775:** An advert for umbrellas appeared on this date in a local newspaper – a first in Bristol. At the time the umbrella was a novelty item. Indeed, during the second half the seventeenth century those of ventured out onto the streets of Bristol with an umbrella were subject to much ridicule. Even in 1778, a footman who bought one in Paris was jeered by the London populace when he tried to use it there. In 1785, £1 14s was paid for an umbrella for the use of Bristol's Council House. (John Latimer, *Annals of Bristol*, Kingsmead, 1970)

# August 20th

**1791:** The British obsession with the weather has been part of our national psyche for some time, with unusual effects of the weather over Bristol being reported nationally in *The Times*: 'On Monday last, this city and its neighbourhood experienced one of the worst thunderstorms ever remembered. It began between three and four o'clock p.m. and continued with little intermission until about two o'clock the following morning. During Monday the atmosphere was so darkened, and the claps of thunder so tremendously loud as to appal the stoutest heart and the lightening was vivid beyond description, so that we fear numerous accounts will reach us of its destructive effects. We have already heard of a man, who, driving a cart on Coalpit Heath, was riding on the shaft, from which he was struck by lightening, and the cart wheel going over him, he was brought to our infirmary so much hurt that he expired soon afterwards. A man on the Bridlington-road was also struck down and left in a senseless state, but happily soon recovered. The bed curtains at a house in Temple Cloud, on the Wells-road, were set on fire by the lightening, but timely exertions prevented any further material damage.' (*The Times*)

# August 21st

**1731:** The manufacture of chocolate in the city can be traced to this date with an advert in *Farley's Bristol Newspaper* stating: 'His Majesty having been pleased to grant to Walter Churchman, of Bristol, Letters Patent for the sole use of an Engine by him invented for the expeditious, fine, and clean making of Chocolate to greater perfection than by any other method in use, the patentee purposes to sell his Chocolate at the common prices ...' (John Latimer, *Annals of Bristol*, Kingsmead, 1970)

---

**1851:** Newspaper reports emerge of a highway robbery that took place in the carriage road near Redland Court. Mr Godwin, 75, had been out for a walk for the benefit of his health when he was attacked from behind. Although Mr Godwin did not see his attacker a witness ran to his aid and was able to give the police a description. Later a constable, on entering the Boars Head in Lamb Street, scared the fugitive, who ran off with the officer in pursuit, even chasing him across the roofs of several houses. The robber took refuge in a house but, stumbling over an item of furniture, he fell and was easily captured by the constable. (*Daily News / Morning Chronicle*)

# August 22nd

**1594:** Despite the victory of Sir Francis Drake over the Spanish Armada in 1588, the threat posed was still a real one for some time to come, as this chronicle extract hints: 'Our Queene's storehouse for powder and cordage of the navy was burned [on this date] ... no doubt by some that expected a new invasion.' (William Adams, *Adams's Chronicle of Bristol*, J.W. Arrowsmith, 1910)

———•◆•———

**1797:** 'A fatal accident happened to a man named Hickes, who was a common carrier between this city and Thornbury for many years – A whiskey with two men in it, having been run away with by the horse, one of them was thrown out of it, but the other keeping his feet, cried out for assistance near the public house at Felton, when Hickes ran across the road to stop the furious animal, in which attempt, the shaft of the whiskey, entered his body with such violence as to cause his death the next day.' (*The Times*)

———•◆•———

**1882:** Louisa Roberts, 13, was sentenced to a week in prison after stealing a blanket and four shirts to the value of £2. Her mother, knowing the property to be stolen, was sentenced to six weeks for receiving stolen goods, as the magistrates considered that she should have known better. (*Bristol Mercury and Daily Post*)

# August 23rd

**1783:** William Tierney Clark, civil engineer, was born in Bristol in 1783. His father died when he was young, leading to a loss of education, and so he was apprenticed to a Bristol millwright. After he finished his apprenticeship Clarke went to Coalbrookdale Ironworks, where he was able to learn about cast and wrought-iron applications. John Rennie noticed Clark's talent during a visit to Coalbrookdale and invited him to take a post with more responsibility at his own ironworks in Blackfriars. In 1811 Clark took the post of engineer at the West Middlesex Waterworks, which he retained until his death. He increased the reservoir capacity of the plant from 6.16 to 40 million gallons, installed a water mains across the Thames at Hammersmith and reservoir filter beds at Hammersmith. In 1818 he undertook consultancy work and was responsible for a number of projects, including the Thames and Medway Canal, Hammersmith Suspension Bridge, Gravesend Town Pier and the suspension bridge linking the cities of Buda and Pest over the Danube. Clark was one of the earliest members of the Institution of Civil Engineers. He died in Hammersmith on September 22nd 1852. (*Oxford Dictionary of National Biography*, OUP)

# August 24th

**1535:** The following is an extract from a letter by Richard Layton, a commissionaire collecting information on the wealth of monasteries, to Thomas Cromwell. Layton did not have a good opinion of monastic houses and writes this dispatch from the Priory of St Augustine in Bristol: 'Please your mastership to understand, that yersternight we came from Glastonburie to Bristow to Saint Austins where we begin this morning intending to dispatche both this house here, being but xiii canons ... I send yowe reliques, first two flowers wrapped in white and blacke sarcenet that on Christmas eve ... will spring, burgen [buds] and bere blossoms ... Ye shall also receive a bag of reliques, wherein you shall see strange things ... as God's cote, our Ladie's smock, part of Gode's supper ... The scripture of everything shall declare unto you all; and all these of Maiden Bradley, where there is a holy Father prior and hath vi children, and but one daughter married yet of the goodes of the monasterie, trusting shortly to marry the reste. His sonnes be tall men waiting upon him, and thankes Gode he never meddled with married women, but with maidens the fairest that could be gottyn, and always married them right well. The pope considering his fragilitie gave hym licence to keep a whore.' (Quoted in J.H. Bettey, *Bristol Observed*, Redcliffe, 1986)

# August 25th

**2009:** A mysterious sign was found at the Coral Café at Bristol Zoo dedicated to 'one of the world's most widespread species' – humans. The sign, the work of pranksters, and in the style of Bristol Zoo's animal information boards, stated that 'after a gestation period of nine months, the young usually live in the parents' nest for around sixteen years ... In adolescence the offspring adopt a more nocturnal lifestyle and engage in ritualised activities of drinking fermented liquids and dancing to rhythmical sound, which scientists believe may help them to find a mate. Humans usually pair for life, retiring from most social activities and moving into brick or concrete nests once a partner is found.' Furthermore 'the human diet is very adaptable to regional crop varieties and personal taste, with some groups able to survive on chipped potatoes and sugary drinks. Groups of humans are often fed by unrelated individuals in exchange for tokens made of paper, metal and plastic – behaviour which can frequently be seen in this enclosure.' The zoo's director stated that, 'We think it's a great sign and have no intention of removing it, however I think that one is probably enough.' (Bristol Zoo website)

# August 26th

**1871:** An 'extraordinary accident on the Great Western Railway' was reported in the *Bristol Mercury* on this date. The accident occurred just outside Bristol Temple Meads station on the bridge across the Floating Harbour and involved the 3.15 p.m. New Passage to Temple Meads service, which had nearly reached its destination when the locomotive, *Vixen*, suddenly left the rails, dragging the tender and two carriages. The locomotive went across the tracks and hit the masonry of the bridge with tremendous violence, making a breach of the wall 8-9 yards in length. Fortunately no one was hurt in the accident and since the train was so near the platform the 200-300 passengers aboard the train were able to leave their carriages and walk up to the platform. The locomotive projected 2-3 feet over the parapet and was only stopped by a piece of stone masonry that was too large for the engine to surmount. It was also fortunate that the dislodged masonry did not strike some lads who were bathing near the bridge. The locomotive was salvageable and the line was repaired and reopened in two hours. (*Bristol Mercury*)

# August 27th

**1836**: Initial funding for what became the Clifton Suspension Bridge was given by an alderman named William Wick, who left £1,000 in 1753 to be invested until £10,000 had been raised. In 1829 a committee was formed to hold a competition inviting designs for the bridge, with Thomas Telford judging. Telford, on examining the designs, rejected all of them, including Brunel's, believing that the proposed spans were too long. Telford proposed his own design with tall gothic towers supporting the roadway of the suspension bridge. Writing in response to Telford's proposals, Brunel stated that his proposed spans were 'within the limits to which suspension bridges might be carried, the idea of going to the bottom of the valley for the purpose at great expense, two intermediate supporters, hardly occurred to me...what a reflection such timidity will cast on the state of the Arts today.' Brunel agreed to reduce the spans to 630ft (192m), resulting in an arguably unnecessary abutment for the suspension bridge on the Leigh side of the gorge, whose foundation stone was laid by the Marquis of Northampton on this date in 1836. (Adrian Vaughn, *Isambard Kingdom Brunel*, John Murray, 1991 / L.T.C. Rolt, *Isambard Kingdom Brunel*, Book Club Associates, 1972 / G.W. Barnes & Thomas Stevens, *The History of the Clifton Suspension Bridge*, The Clifton Suspension Bridge Trust, 1970)

# August 28th

**1963:** Inspired by the bus boycotts in Alabama, similar action was taken in Bristol with the black populous refusing to travel on Bristol's buses. To this end, Paul Stephens, a youth worker, phoned the Bristol Bus Company enquiring if there were any vacancies for a worker said to be of above average education and training to be a Boys' Brigade officer. The Bus Company was interested and said it would arrange an interview. When it was mentioned that the candidate was coloured, Stephens was told that an interview would be out of the question and that he should tell his potential candidate that there were no vacancies at the company. It was the justification needed for activists to launch a boycott on April 29th 1963. This situation sparked much comment in the local press. The General Manager of the Bus Company, Ian Patey, defended the company's position, stating that, 'We don't employ a mixed labour force as ... we have found from observing other bus companies the labour supply gets worse, not better'. After much attention in the local press regarding the boycott and public opposition to the colour bar, the ban was overturned on this date in 1963. (*Bristol Evening Post / The Times*)

# August 29th

**1896:** Minnie Baker, a young girl, was charged with stealing a sheet from Bridget Baxter of 54 Milk Street. The sheet was pledged at a local pawnbroker's shop. The sheet was taken from the house of Mrs Coles, where it had been brought to be mangled and where Minnie lived. It was believed that Minnie had also been guilty of several petty thefts from her relatives, but not prosecuted. She was sentenced by the magistrates to be taken to the Red Lodge Reformatory for five years.

———— • ◆ • ————

**1857:** An inquest was held at The Ship, Redcliff Hill, to determine the facts surrounding the death of labourer Edward Robbs, 22, at his place of work the previous day. The accident occurred when Robbs, relaxing during his dinner hour, was lying down by a stack of planks around 20 feet high. A heavily laden wagon was being driven past and the vibrations from the passing cart caused the stack to fall. Although his colleagues shouted a warning, it was of no avail and the stack collapsed on the unfortunate Robbs, who left a wife and three children. (Nicola Sly, *A Grim Almanac of Bristol*, The History Press, 2011)

# August 30th

**1736:** Among several prisoners tried at the Guildhall was one 'Long Jack' Vernon, who was charged with robbery from a house in St Michael's Hill. At his trial Vernon refused to enter a plea for his crime. Because of this he was told that he would be pressed to death. The unfortunate victim would be place between two boards and weights would be added until the prisoner was crushed to death. Fear of the punishment caused Vernon to reconsider and for his crimes he was sentenced to death by hanging. On hearing his sentence Vernon is reported to have said, 'Damn it, I don't value my life as a halfpenny.' (Nicola Sly, *A Grim Almanac of Bristol*, The History Press, 2011)

———— • ◆ • ————

**1984:** An Intercity 125 train consisting of two power cars and five carriages completed a record-breaking run between London Paddington and Bristol Temple Meads. The train reached speeds of 130mph and completed the journey in 62 minutes 33 seconds – 5 minutes and 2 seconds faster than the previous record, which had been set in 1977. The average speed over the journey was 112.8mph. (Rex Kennedy, *Ian Allan's 50 Years of Railways 1942-1992*, Ian Allan, 1992)

# August 31st

**1752:** Bristol historian John Latimer writes that 'Cricket had few local votaries in the middle of the eighteenth century. It is never mentioned in the newspapers except as offering, like pugilism, racing, and cockfighting, an opportunity for gambling.' Hence this early reference to the game in *Felix Farley's Journal* of August 29th, which contained an advertisement for a cricket match to be played on Durdham Down between eleven men of London and eleven men of Bristol for the prize of 20 guineas. The match may have also kick-started the professional game in the area where local businessmen would sponsor 'challenge matches' played between professional sportsmen. Sadly, the result of the match has not been recorded. (Jack Russell 'Sportsmen of Bristol' in E.V Thompson et al. *People and Places in Bristol*, Bossiney Books, 1986 / John Latimer, *Annals of Bristol*, Kingsmead, 1970)

---

**1840:** The first train to depart Bristol Temple Meads station bound for Bath left the unfinished station building, just a few minutes behind schedule. It had been due to leave at 8 a.m. and the rails into Brunel's original station had only been laid a few hours previously. The first train was hauled by *Fireball* and was decorated with flags. Church bells also rang out in celebration of the event. The train was made up of three first class and five second class carriages. Through trains to London did not start until the following year, on June 30th 1841, when the Box Tunnel was completed. (Mike Oakley, *Bristol Suburban: Temple Meads, Local Stations, Halts and Platforms 1840-1990*, Redcliffe, 1990)

# September 1st

**1843:** A police constable was told by a young boy that a man and two women had been murdered in a cottage on Gloucester Road. After summoning a colleague, the two constables entered the isolated cottage to find three inhabitants severely wounded. They were John Maddox, a milkman of 21, his wife Mary Maddox and her sister Mary Ann Priest. All three had deep lacerations and those of John Maddox were described as having penetrated to the bone. The surgeon was immediately summoned and the victims were conveyed to the infirmary with little hope of survival. The person responsible for this crime was named as John Clarke, who, not having employment, had been taken in by the Maddox household. It seems that Mary Maddox let slip that she was to be paid a considerable sum that was indebted to her. Clarke afterwards made enquires about this sum in order to steal it. At 4.30 on the morning of the crime she awoke to find Maddox beating her with a poker. The commotion woke Mary Priest who, mistaking Clarke for the husband, cried out 'Good God Maddox, what are you doing?' and in consequence received several blows to the head. Clarke then made his escape with about 13 shillings stolen from the property. (*Bristol Mercury*)

# September 2nd

**1843:** The first of a series of articles known as the 'Churchgoer articles' appeared in the *Bristol Times*. The articles typically reported on the shortcomings of the parish, its church, its parishioners and the quality of the sermon. Initially these articles looked at churches in Bristol. 'Churchgoer' was in fact *Bristol Times* editor Joseph Leech. The first article concerned Bristol Cathedral, where he was critical of the warden who initially failed to show him to a free pew until this is pointed out to the warden by another parishioner. Leech also describes the 'cathedral congregation is as ever a motley one; the only *invariable* and legitimate attendance being, I may so speak, those antiquated young urchins who look as if, like Rip Van Winkle, they had risen from sleep of hundred years in the dress of that period ... The other portions of the congregation are composed of persons who have quarrelled with their own parish authorities about pews, or their own parish ministers about opinions – persons who are fond of music, or fancy that they can sing chants; and persons who have gone there so long that they forget the cause of their first visit, and have never missed a Sunday for thirty years.' (Joseph Leech, *Rural Rides of the Bristol Churchgoer*, Alan Sutton, 1982 / *Bristol Times*)

# September 3rd

**1702:** Queen Anne visits Bristol, the royal party being greeted by Mayor John Hawkins at Lawford's Gate. The Queen passed through the city amid much cheering and proceeded to the home of Sir Thomas Day, where she dined, knighted the Mayor and permitted the Mayoress and other dignitaries to kiss her hand. (John Latimer, *Annals of Bristol*, Kingsmead, 1970)

———— • ◆ • ————

**1736:** Two convicts were 'taken to the gallows field at St Michael's Hill ... The careless manner in which the executions were then conducted ... was strikingly manifest on this occasion'. After the men were hung for the usual time their bodies were taken down, yet when the men were being placed in the coffins they both showed signs of life. One the men, John Vernham, convicted of burglary and who had refused to enter any plea at the time of his trial, recovered consciousness enough to be able to speak to bystanders, but died the following night. The other man, named Harding, was bled before regaining consciousness when many people were allowed to visit him. Harding, convicted of shoplifting, was said to 'always have been defective in his intellects' and so it was decided that he should not be hanged again but to be taken care of in an almshouse. (John Latimer, *Annals of Bristol*, Kingsmead, 1970)

# September 4th

**1818:** A novel use for umbrellas was found, as this article from *The Times* newspaper of this date shows: 'the Bristol coach, on its way to town was unfortunately overturned on the off side, near Marlborough forest. In the inside were eight passengers, including two children, and on the outside twelve, with the driver. Some of the individuals sustained injuries from bruises, but no serious accidents occurred beyond them and the fright occasioned by such a disaster. The person riding by the coachman alighted on his feet in an upright position; which no doubt, was occasioned by the buoyancy of the umbrella he was holding over his head (it raining fast at the time) with a firm grasp, and thereby rendering his descent gradual. This confirms the propriety of using an umbrella as a fire-escape, as suggested by one of our correspondents lately.' The correspondent in question did indeed make the suggestion in *The Times* on August 25th 1818, stating that 'if an umbrella could be procured when a person found it necessary to leap out of [a] window, by holding it extended, the violence of the descent would be very considerably checked, and the danger consequently lessened.' (*The Times*)

# September 5th

**1930:** Alfred the Gorilla arrived at Bristol Zoo and became one of the zoo's most popular attractions. Two years previously, Alfred had been filmed playing in the streets by an American expedition filming in central Africa. It transpired that his parents had both been shot when they raided a crop for food and Alfred was suckled by a local woman. Alfred proved a popular attraction at Bristol Zoo, where he was regularly walked around by his keepers often in woolly jumpers, and the date of Alfred's arrival at the zoo was celebrated as his birthday. He had a distinctive personality and was said to have disliked bearded men, double-decker buses and aeroplanes. He was also in the habit of throwing things at visitors. Because of these personality traits he became known as the 'dictator of the zoo' during the 1940s but also, perhaps, as a way of deriding Hitler. Alfred died in 1948 after suffering from tuberculosis. Alfred the Gorilla underwent the process of taxidermy, undertaken by Rowland Ward of London, then a famous firm of taxidermists. He was exhibited at Bristol Museum, where he remains today. (*Author's field notes*)

# September 6th

**1898:** The formal opening of the Cabot Tower on Brandon Hill by the Marquess of Dufferin and Ava took place. The Marquess had also laid the foundation stone on June 26th 1897, in the year of Queen Victoria's Jubilee. Costing £3,250, it was built to commemorate the journey of John Cabot to North America in 1497. There are 199 steps to the top, which is 105ft (32m) high. It was designed by W.V. Gough and is constructed from pink sandstone with limestone dressings. The hill on which the tower is situated has a long and interesting history. The hill takes its name from an Irish saint, Brendan (484-577), who built a chapel on the hilltop and who is most famous for setting out across the sea in search of the Promised Land. Later, a hermitage was set up near the field of St Brendan, for in 1351 Lucy de Newchurch repeatedly asked to shut herself away from the world at the site. The hermitage and chapel were abolished during the Reformation. Later Mr Read sets up a windmill in its place, in 1565, and in 1625 the Corporation of Bristol acquired the land. (John Latimer, *Annals of Bristol*, Kingsmead, 1970 / Marguerite Fedden, *Bristol Bypaths*, Rankin, 1954 / Andrew Foyle, *Pevsner Architectural Guides: Bristol*, Yale University Press, 2004)

# September 7th

**1979:** The first Bristol International Balloon Festival was held at Ashton Court over the weekend of 7-9 September. The origins of the Balloon Festival start with one man, Don Cameron. Cameron came to Bristol during the 1960s to work for the Bristol Aeroplane Company at Filton. In his spare time he enjoyed gliding at the Bristol Gliding Club at Nympsfield and it was here that he was introduced to a new form of ballooning. Seven members of the group then built the *Bristol Belle*, the first modern balloon produced in Britain. Cameron Balloons was subsequently formed in 1970 to build these modern balloons. Throughout the 1970s Don was flying balloons in all sorts of locations, from the Sahara to across the Alps. In 1978 he tried to cross the Atlantic in a balloon but failed, landing in the sea 100 miles from France. After giving a talk to the Bristol Junior Chamber, the idea of a festival emerged. During the first balloon festival, spectators were treated to a mass ascent of twenty-seven balloons. By 2010, over 100 balloons took part. (Bristol Balloon Fiesta website)

# September 8th

**1806:** Patrick Cotter O'Brien, otherwise known as the Irish or Bristol Giant, dies. He was over 8 feet tall. Born in County Cork in Ireland he later added O'Brien to his surname, claiming to be a descendent of Brian Boru (926-1014), an Irish king. In November 1779 he came to Bristol and was leased to a Bristol showman. After a dispute over a fictitious debt he was thrown into a debtors' prison, but was subsequently released and moved to London. Simply being very tall earned Patrick an average of £10 per day. He drove his own carriage, specially modified to accommodate his legs, and slept on two double beds pushed together. Later he returned to Bristol, staying in the home of Joseph Francis Mardyke in Hotwell Road, where he died aged 46. He left particular instructions for the burial of his body, to stop it getting into the hands of surgeons. He was buried in the former Roman Catholic chapel in Trenchard Street, in a grave 12ft deep, carved into rock, and secured by iron bars to deter grave robbers. His body was exhumed in 1972, when his height was verified at 8 feet 1 inch (2.46m). (John Latimer, *Annals of Bristol*, Kingsmead, 1970 / Marguerite Fedden, *Bristol Bypaths*, Rankin, 1954)

# September 9th

**1995:** Twenty thousand people lined Redcliffe Quay for the official launch of *The Matthew*, a replica of the ship Cabot used on his first voyage to America. The ribbon was cut by Lady Wills, wife of the Lord Lieutenant of Avon and launched with, rather appropriately, a blue bottle of Bristol Sherry. Only a limited amount of information was known about the original *Matthew* as no customs records for Bristol exist between 1493 and 1503 and no ship of that name for Bristol is in the records for 1492-3. It may suggest that *The Matthew* was a relatively new ship. Work on the replica ship began in February 1994, undertaken by a team of shipwrights experienced in building wooden boats and headed by project manager Mike Blackwell. The original ship was built of oak, although the replica used African opepe for the keel as suitable English oak long enough for the keel to be made using a single piece of wood could not be found. Even with modern power tools the replica ship took two years to complete. After the official launch, *The Matthew* was hauled out of the water so that the interior could be fitted out. (Peter Firstbrook, *The Voyage of the Matthew*, BBC Books, 1997)

# September 10th

**1645:** Parliamentarian forces led by Sir Thomas Fairfax and Oliver Cromwell launch an attack on Bristol beginning at 1 a.m. Bristol was defended by Prince Rupert, nephew to Charles I. Prince Rupert was cut off from other Royalist forces and was outnumbered. He consequently surrendered, was given reasonable terms by the Parliamentarians and the next day Prince Rupert and his forces were allowed to leave Bristol peaceably. The loss of Bristol was a major blow to the King's cause in the West Country. Charles I was furious with his nephew, writing the following letter to him a few days later, 'Though the loss of Bristoll be a blow to me, yet your surrendering it as you did is so much of an affliction to me ... My conclusion is to seek your subsistence ... somewhere beyond these seas, to which end I send you a pass; and pray God to make you sensible of your present condition, and give you means to redeem what you have lost.' Oliver Crowell was elated at the outcome, detecting God's handiwork, as shown by his letter to William Lenthill, House of Commons Speaker: 'they that have been employed in this service know that faith and prayer obtained this city for you.' (Quotes from J.H. Bettey, *Bristol Observed*, Redcliffe, 1986)

# September 11th

**1817:** 'Edwin Thrackston RN exhibited, before Mr Alderman Daniel and a number of merchants and ship-owners of Bristol, the buoyant properties of his newly-invented life-boat, which we are happy to say, exceeded the most sanguine expectations of himself and all who beheld it. Its other peculiar qualities and advantages are to be tried in a few days in Kingroad. The extreme length of the boat exhibited is 24 feet, beam 6 feet 6 inches; and it is rowed with ten oars, double-backed. It is constructed with canvass ... in lieu of plank; and has cork bilge-floats, which may be applied as life-buoys, to throw out in cases where men may be washed overboard from any wreck, with a large fender round the boat, which from its elasticity is capable of repelling any violent concussion. She took on board 30 persons when filled with water up to the valves, and had 28 standing in one gunwale without the least danger of upsetting. Upon an emergency 60 persons might be stowed within her. She rows well and light on the oars when thus filled, and turns with great rapidity in her length. Boats may be built on a similar construction of any shape or form.' (*The Times*)

# September 12th

**1651:** Charles II, after the Battle of Worcester, was forced to flee from the Parliamentarians and passed through Bristol disguised as a servant to a Mrs Lane. It is likely that Charles II approached Bristol via Chipping Sodbury, Winterbourne and Stapleton, entering the city by Lawford's Gate. Charles crossed the River Avon by ferry at Rownham, rather than cross Bristol Bridge, which would have been dangerous, and he arrived at Leigh Court during the evening of September 12th. Whilst there, Charles overheard a conversation given by Pope, the butler, who was at the Battle of Worcester and on the side of the King. The King asked of Pope, 'What kind of man was he?' Pope answers by describing the king exactly, but stated that the King was three fingers taller than the disguised Charles. Later the King draws Pope into his confidence telling him his identity and gets Pope to seek ships sailing to France or Spain from Bristol. With no sailings within a month Charles made his way to the south coast making his escape near Brighton in Sussex on October 15th 1651. His sailed only a few hours before Parliamentarian troops came to arrest him. (John Latimer, *Annals of Bristol*, Kingsmead, 1970 / J. Hughes (ed.) *The Boscobel Tracts: Relating to the Escape of Charles The Second after the Battle of Worcester and his Subsequent Adventures*, William Blackwood, 1857)

# September 13th

**1890:** William Davis, described as a middle-aged man, appeared before Bristol Police Court charged with possession of four stolen hammers. The day before he was spotted by PC Lawrence, who at the time was in plain clothes, when he saw Davis offer the hammers for sale to the proprietor of a second-hand tool shop. Lawrence arrested Davis shortly afterwards. Davis tried to claim that the hammers were his but subsequent enquiries proved that the hammers had been stolen. Since Davis had no criminal record he was fined 21 shillings or in default twenty-one days' imprisonment for the crime. The magistrates commended Constable Lawrence, remarking that he had done his job remarkably well. (*Bristol Mercury and Daily Post*)

---

**1914:** Robert and Margery Bush, owners of Bishop's Knoll, a large house with its own grounds in Stoke Bishop, converted the house into a wartime hospital at their own expense. The first patients arrived on this day in 1914 and it was the only privately-run hospital to receive wounded soldiers from the front line. (David J. Eveleigh, *Bristol In Old Photographs 1850-1919*, Sutton Publishing, 1999)

# September 14th

**1852:** John Latimer in *Annals of Bristol* writes that 'the rapid development of telegraphic business brought into increased prominence the troublesome question of "local time", still registered by the parish clocks, messages from London being received at the Bristol office about ten minutes before the time at which the purported to be dispatched. At a meeting of the Council on the 14 September, 1852, it was resolved – three inveterate admirers of the ancient ways protesting against the innovation – to regulate clocks by Greenwich time.' The telegraph companies were not the only ones affected by the fact that local time was kept in different parts of the country. It caused problems for the railways in producing timetables for their trains. The Great Western Railway decided that London Time would be used at all of its stations as early as November 1840. Other railway companies soon followed, including the North Western Railway, which introduced London Time at their stations in Liverpool and London in January 1846. In 1845 the Liverpool and Manchester Railway Company had unsuccessfully petitioned parliament to set a standardised time. It was not until August 2nd 1880 that the Statutes (Definition of Time) Bill was made law, which introduced a standardised time across Britain. (John Latimer, *Annals of Bristol*, Kingsmead, 1970 / http://greenwichmeantime.asia/info/railway.htm)

# September 15th

**1855:** The *Bristol Mirror* reported that workmen who were digging sewers in Stapleton Road found two or three human skeletons. An inquest was later held at the Coach and Horses, which concluded that the bones were buried in a piece of ground that was formerly a ditch. The newspaper, presumably keen to provide a fuller explanation, states that a highwayman named Groves lived in the neighbourhood and that the place where the bodies was found was a ditch surrounding his residence. The remains therefore were some of the notorious highwayman's numerous victims. Another story of the action of highwaymen in the Stapleton area in the first half of the nineteenth century concerns the story of a farm labourer who was robbed coming from the direction of Bell Hill, when he was stopped by two highwaymen. The poor labourer handed over five shillings, his weeks' pay, to the men. Realising that he had nothing to feed his wife and children he feel to his knees, begging that the highwaymen might hand back some of the money. Touched by the man's plea, one of the men scattered a few coins on the ground before galloping away. The labourer picked up the coins and found them to be eight Georgian guineas in all! (F.C. Jones, *The Glory that was Bristol*, St Stephen's Bristol Press, 1946)

# September 16th

**1932:** Cyril Unwins, chief test pilot for the Bristol Aeroplane Company, flew a Vickers Vespa biplane fitted with a supercharged Bristol Pegasus radial air-cooled engine and achieved a new record altitude of 43,976ft (13,404m). The new height exceeded the previous record of 31,181ft (13,158m), achieved by Lieutenant A. Soucek of the United States Navy. The flight was made over the Severn Valley and the pilot was equipped with oxygen supplies and electronically-heated clothing. The flight was started just after one o'clock. To make the assent Unwins climbed in wide circles. In total Unwins was in the air for 2 hours. The information gained on this flight made possible a pair of Westland biplanes fitted with similar engines to fly over Mount Everest for the first time in 1933. Bristol engines continued to be used to break altitude records when, in 1934, Italian pilot Renato Donati flew a Pegasus-engined Caproni biplane to 47,360ft (14,433m). On June 30th 1938, Flt-Lt M.J. Adam succeed in flying a Bristol 138A to an altitude of 51,937ft (16,440m), landing at Farnborough 2¼ hours after take off. Of the nine occasions since 1928 when the altitude record was broken, five of these attempts had used a Bristol-built Pegasus engine. (*The Times* / C.H. Barnes, *Bristol Aircraft Since 1910*, Putnam, 1970)

# September 17th

**1881:** Two policemen on patrol at the Floating Harbour noticed a fire in the Albion Wharf Cooperage. Since they could not get hold of the key to the buildings, they broke down the door and saw that the roof of a shed had caught fire. They quickly procured a bucket and threw water on the flames until the fire brigade arrived with a hand-pump to put out the rest of the blaze. The fire was started when workmen left some rubbish burning. Fortunately the damage was light. (*Bristol Mercury and Daily Post*)

---

**1896:** The only two people known to have been thrown over the Clifton Suspension Bridge with murderous intent were Ruby Brown, aged 12 and her sister Elsie, aged 3. The act was perpetrated by their father, a tradesman from Birmingham, who was said to have been suffering from 'temporary derangement'. Their survival from the 245ft (76m)-high bridge was, it seems, owed to their light weight and the high tide which broke their fall. They were rescued from the Avon by a passing pilot boat and taken to the Bristol Infirmary. (John Latimer, *Annals of Bristol*, Kingsmead, 1970 / G.W. Barnes & Thomas Stevens, *A History of the Clifton Suspension Bridge*, The Clifton Suspension Bridge Trust, 1970)

# September 18th

**1556:** The reign of Mary I in Britain led to the death of many Protestants and one such martyr was William Saxton, a weaver of Bristol. He was condemned for his belief that there was no physical presence of Christ in the bread and wine of the Eucharist after the words of consecration. His execution is described in *Foxe's Book of Martyrs*: 'As he went to the stake he sang psalms. The sheriff, John Griffith, had prepared green wood to burn him; but one master John Pikes, pitying the man, caused divers [many] to go with him to Ridland [Redland], half a mile off, who brought a good store of helme-sheaves [bundles of straw], which indeed make good dispatch with little pain in comparison with that he should have suffered with green wood. In that mean space, whilst they went for the sheaves, the said Saxton made good exhortations to the people, and after died constantly and patiently with great joyfulness.' (John Foxe, *The Acts and Monuments of the Church*)

———•—•———

**1967:** The call stand system, whereby Avonmouth's 1,200 dockers were hired on a daily basis, ended. It was the end of a forty-seven-year campaign to gain permanent employment for the dockers. (Reece Winstone, *Bristol As It Was 1963-1975*, 1990 / *Bristol Evening Post*)

# September 19th

**1921:** Hotwells railway station, located beneath the Clifton Suspension Bridge, and southern terminus of the Bristol & Port Railway Company's line to Avonmouth, is closed in order to make way for the Portway Road to Avonmouth. The line opened on March 6th 1865, but the railway company did not release the timetable until a few minutes before services commenced, fearing that the locomotive would not be able to cope with so many passengers. The railway's importance soon declined when the line to Avonmouth was linked to the main line following construction of the Clifton Tunnel. Hotwells station was lined by two tunnels: the 73-yard long Portway No.1 and the longer 175-yard No. 2 tunnel. After the railway's closure the tunnels were next used during the Second World War. The No.1 tunnel was used as a store for the council and the museum whilst the No.2 became an air-raid shelter, with passes issued to prevent overcrowding. There had previously been disturbances when 3,000 people turned up seeking shelter. In January 1941 the BBC attempted to install an emergency studio but angry locals staged a sit-in protest, forcing the technicians to move on. The No.2 tunnel is currently being in-filled to prevent it collapsing. (www.forgottenrelics.co.uk)

# September 20th

**1867:** Colston Hall opened, becoming Bristol's main venue of musical acts. The site of the hall had originally been a thirteenth-century friary, which was replaced by a Tudor mansion known as the Great House. This house became Colston's Boys' School in 1707, founded by the Bristolian merchant philanthropist Edward Colston (1636-1721). The school was on the site until 1857 and in 1861 the site was purchased by the Colston Hall Company, who demolished the mansion and erected the hall. On September 1st 1898 a fire broke out in the nearby Clark's Clothing Factory and spread to the hall, gutting the place. A second hall was built in 1901 and the site was purchased by the City Council, who have managed the place ever since. In the 1920s the famous Russian pianist and composer Racmaninov is said to have performed at the venue. Remodelling of the hall took place in 1935 and the third Colston Hall opened in December 1936. The hall survived the Bristol Blitz but a discarded cigarette destroyed the building on February 5th 1945. A replacement building was erected to mark the Festival of Britain in 1951. Other famous performers here include *The Beatles*, who debuted on March 15th 1963. (Colston Hall website)

# September 21st

**1756:** John Macadam was born in Ayrshire and is best known for his method of road construction, which he pioneered on Bristol's turnpike trust roads. As a child Macadam is reputed to have constructed a cross-section of road in Maybole, where he attended school. He settled in Bristol in 1801 and quickly established himself in civic society, becoming freeman of the city in 1805 and helping to establish Bristol Commercial Rooms in 1811. In the early nineteenth century the quality of road construction was variable and in 1810 evidence was asked for by parliament to facilitate improvement. Macadam contributed to this inquiry proposing his own method of road construction, namely that roads should be constructed by preparing a well-drained subsoil and using much smaller stones which were compressed to give an impermeable surface. This construction later gave rise to the term Macadamisation. He put these methods into practice becoming General Surveyor to the Bristol Turnpike Trust. As his reputation increased he acted as a consultant to other turnpike trusts, much to the annoyance of the Bristol Turnpike trustees, who disliked his absences from Bristol, leading to Macadam's resignation from the trust in 1825. Macadam died on November 26th 1836 whilst returning from a trip to his native Ayrshire. (*Oxford Dictionary of National Biography*, OUP)

# September 22nd

**1757:** Although many captured African slaves went to work on plantations in the New World a few were sent to Britain to work, often in stately homes as domestic servants. Occasionally the slaves ran away from their masters and advertisements for their return appear in contemporary newspapers. The *Bristol Journal* of March 12th 1757 published the elopement of a slave called Starling, who 'blows the French horn very well'. Starling's owner offers one guinea for his capture. On September 22nd the same year an advert appeared for Captain Ezekiel Nash's black servant, offering a reward to the person giving information as to his whereabouts and threatening persecution to those who might conceal him. The same newspapers also contained adverts for the sale of slaves in this country, including this example from *Felix Farley's Bristol Newspaper,* where Captain John Gwythem offers for sale 'a Negro man about 20 years old, well limb'd, fit to serve a gentleman or to be instructed in a trade.' *Felix Farley's Journal* of August 2nd 1760 contains this pithy advertisement: 'To be sold, a Negroe Boy about ten years old. He has had the small pox.' (John Latimer, *Annals of Bristol*, Kingsmead, 1970)

# September 23rd

**1880:** Three children appeared at Bristol Police Court. George Butt (6), William Butt (8), and a boy names Anstey (13), were charged with stealing a number of brass door plates. A constable arrested the two younger boys, who were attempting to wrench the brass plate protecting the keyhole of Messrs Osborne, Ward & Co., and took them into custody. Anstey was arrested by another officer on suspicion of theft and was found to have brass plate about his person and a number of keyhole protectors. All of the youngsters claimed that they were going to sell the brass to a marine dealer's on the Broad Plain. Indignation was expressed by magistrates at any person purchasing brass from such small boys. Anstey was sentenced to ten days' imprisonment and five years' detention in a Protestant Reformatory. The younger boys were handed over to their fathers owing to their age. (*Bristol Mercury and Daily Post*)

———— • ◆ • ————

**1905:** During a tour of the northern hemisphere the New Zealand All Blacks play Bristol to a crowd of 6,500 spectators. The All Blacks were victors, winning 41-0. (Bristol RFC website / All Blacks website)

# September 24th

**1810:** A great many Bristolians flocked to Stokes Croft to see the ascent of Mr Sadler's balloon, which was to be raised by hydrogen gas. The balloon ascended with its two aeronauts, Mr Sadler and Mr Clayfield, amidst applause and shouts of wishes for their safe return. The balloon went down near Woodspring Priory and then westwards over the Bristol Channel, towards Cardiff, and then back across the Channel towards Devon. However, an escape of air caused the balloon to descend rapidly and it landed in the water 4 miles from the coast. Fortunately, the men were rescued by a boat from Lynmouth. (*The Times* / John Latimer, *Annals of Bristol*, Kingsmead, 1970)

---

**1921:** The Memorial Stadium, home to Bristol RFC, is opened by G.B. Britten, the Lord Mayor of Bristol. Bristol RFC was formed in 1888 after the Carlton Club invited rival clubs Redland Park and Westbury Park to form a city team. The Memorial Ground was given the name in memory of local rugby players who fell during the First World War. In the opening match Bristol were the victors, defeating Cardiff 19-3. Since August 1996 the grounds have been shared with Bristol Rovers Football Club. (Bristol RFC website / Bristol Rovers website / Wikipedia)

# September 25th

**1575:** A Bristol chronicle records the fate of some pirates: 'This year was certain pirates taken in Crokandpill in an Irish bark, that robbed the barks that came to St James Fair. They left the bark in Wales, and 4 of them were taken and brought to Bristoll.' On this day 'they were arraigned, whereof 3 were condemned and hanged on a new gibbet in Cannell's Marsh near the river's mouth over against Gibtailer (where was then a house which since was burned by on James Young negligently in tarring of ropes); the other pirate was saved.' (William Adams, *Adams's Chronicle of Bristol*, J.W. Arrowsmith, 1910)

---

**1885:** H.F. Cooper left Bristol with the intention of riding his bicycle 220 miles in twenty-four hours. He started at ten minutes past midnight and twelve hours later he reached Hounslow, 110 miles away. He set back towards Bristol and succeeded in riding as far as the twenty-seventh milestone from Bristol. Cooper claimed that he would have reached Bristol had heavy rain not led to the deterioration of the road from Marlborough. Nevertheless, Cooper managed a total distance of 202 miles, which is still an impressive performance. (*Bristol Mercury and Daily Post*)

# September 26th

**1837:** Born on September 20th 1777 in Mangotsfield, Francis Greenway later established himself as an architect with premises in Limekiln Lane. In 1806 he designed the Assembly Rooms, Clifton. However, on March 23rd 1809, Greenway was sentenced to transportation after pleading guilty to forgery over a building contract. In Australia Greenway established himself again as an architect and designed numerous public buildings, including the Hyde Park Convict Barracks and St James's Church, Sydney. He was buried in East Maitland Cemetery on this date in 1837. (*Oxford Dictionary of National Biography*, OUP)

———— ◆ ————

**1932:** The first public air service between Bristol and Cardiff was established. The first passengers to use the service were 'two Bristol ladies who spent some time shopping in the Welsh city and returned home by air. An experimental service between the two cities was conducted by Captain C.D. Barnard in July, but the present service, established by Mr Norman Edgar, of Bristol, is to be a permanent one and is intended mainly for the use of business men having urgent business to transact. The journey occupies about 20 minutes. The service is limited to two trips each way daily, the fares being 12s 6d single and 22s 6d return. At each end passengers are conveyed by motor-cars from the city centres to the aerodromes.' (*The Times*)

# September 27th

**1940:** Wartime reporting was subject to government censor and as such, newspapers, following an air raid in Bristol, could only inform their readers that the bombing of a 'west town' had taken place. Only after a few days had elapsed would it be mentioned that Bristol had been affected. The following is an extract from the *Western Daily Press* on bombing raids at Filton. The article formed a series detailing air raids in the city in the Second World War which were published in 1946 ans which used the diary of George H. Gibbs, deputy to the city's ARP Controller: 'On this day, two days after the devastating attacks on the Aeroplane Works, the Germans came over with the same intentions. At about 11.30 a force of about nine bombers, accompanied by fighters, came over the city, but a squadron of Hurricanes was waiting for them. A.A. guns were in actions as well, and the formation was dispersed before it could reach its target. Regardless of the danger crowds of people came out in the streets to watch the "dog fights" taking place in the city.' (*Western Daily Press* / Reece Winstone, *Bristol in the 1940s*, 1961 / Helen Reid, *Bristol Blitz: The Untold Story*, Redcliffe Press, 1988)

# September 28th

**1834:** Robert Gray was born in London on September 11th 1762 and was educated at Eton and St Mary Hall, Oxford. At Oxford he took holy orders. In 1790 he published *Key to the Old Testament and the Apocrypha*, which analysed the history of the Old Testament. He was appointed to a stall at Durham Cathedral in 1804 and a year later he became rector of Bishopwearmouth, Sunderland. Gray showed a concern for his parishioners and whilst there he founded a school and hospital. In 1827 he became Bishop of Bristol, reputed to be the poorest see in England. Because of this he was allowed to keep the stall at Durham Cathedral as Bristol gave him a comparatively small income of £1,700 each year. Gray also held firm to his principles, opposing both Catholic emancipation and parliamentary reform. When reform was prevented in 1831 and riots broke out in Bristol and Gray was asked to stop worship at Bristol Cathedral. He refused to do so and the service went ahead with him preaching. During the riots the bishop's palace was burnt down with 6,000 books destroyed or stolen. Gray's losses were estimated at £10,000 after the riots. He died at his home in Clifton on this date in 1834. (*Oxford Dictionary of National Biography*, OUP)

# September 29th

**1873:** James Phelps, landlord of the Jolly Nailors' pub in West Street, St Philip's, was caught by John Clarke, inspector of weights and measures, for selling beer in an earthenware cup. Since the cup did not have the measure marked, it meant that he was liable to be fined the sum of £10. It was the inspector's job to stamp cups but he refused to stamp earthenware cups as he knew that the stamp affixed to such cups was easily shifted and put on a smaller vessel, although the un-stamped jug in this case contained liquid of an appropriate measure. Phelps also claimed that the beer had been measured out in a stamped pewter tankard and then poured into the earthenware jug. The magistrate gave him the benefit of doubt and acquitted him of all charges, although the defendant had to pay his own costs. (*Bristol Mercury*)

———— • ◆ • ————

**1881:** It was reported that the Bristol ship *Essex* was found abandoned in the Gulf of Mexico and without her mast. Her decks were completely swept and her stern washed away. The *Essex* left Pensacola for Cardiff on August 13th with twenty-three crew members and a cargo of pinewood. (*Bristol Mercury and Daily Post*)

# September 30th

**Until 1973:** Pie Poudre Courts were established during Norman times as temporary courts to deal with felons on the occasion of a fair or market. The name *pie poudre* originates from the old French meaning 'dusty feet', as justice was able to be met swiftly as not to allow miscreants enough time to shake the dust of off their feet and leave. Each year on September 30th, beside the Stag and Hounds in Old Market Street, a proclamation would be read declaring the Pie Poudre Court open. The court originally took place out in the open under an oak tree but soon moved indoors to the Stag and Hounds public house. The court was in session to 1870 when, owing to the amount of liquor consumed, the court was wound up. The tradition to open the court ceremonially continued until 1973, when the town crier invited all those who had legal business with the court to come forward. The court was then immediately adjourned to other quarters. In 1973 Bristol's Pie Poudre Courts were legally abolished and the tradition came to an end. The panelled room used for the court can still be seen at the Stag and Hounds as can the Jacobean staircase leading to it. (C.F.W. Denning, *Old Inns of Bristol*, John Wright & Son, 1949 / Maurice Fells, *Bristol: History You Can See*, The History Press, 2006)

# October 1st

**1906:** The first regular passenger service starts at Ashton Gate railway station. It would become Bristol's most opened and closed station. It was initially opened as a simple wooden platform to serve football fans at the Ashton Gate Stadium. The first train had in fact arrived on September 15th for football fans at the nearby Ashton Gate Stadium. In 1917 the station closed on account of wartime austerity. The station was rebuilt and reopened on May 26th 1926 to encourage passenger traffic on the Portishead Branch. The greatest use came for football specials, where the signalmen on the line were often recruited to collect tickets on match days. After carrying out their duties they too would go and watch the match. Football specials decreased after the Second World War, as did regular passenger traffic, and under Dr Beaching the line closed to passengers for good on September 7th 1964, though remained open for freight. However, Ashton Gate station opened again for football specials on September 29th 1970, when the first such train arrived from Birmingham, and the service continued until 1977. The last use of the station came during Billy Graham's Mission England Campaign held at Ashton Gate Stadium, when the station was reopened temporarily between the 12th and 19th of May 1984. (Mike Oakley, *Bristol Suburban: Temple Meads, Local Stations, Halts and Platforms 1840-1990*, Redcliffe, 1990)

# October 2nd

**1715:** Jacobite support was to be found in different parts of the country during this period and from time to time the threat of a rebellion surfaced. The principal support at this time for the pretender, James III, to the throne was from the Duke of Beufort, Lord Lieutenant of Bristol. He died young, just a few weeks before the death of Queen Anne, and left only a 7-year-old heir. In September 1715, a group of rebels assembled at nearby Bath on the pretext of drinking the waters. On this date in 1715 the authorities got wind of a plot to seize Bristol by Somerset Jacobites and promptly ordered that the city gates were shut and cannon mounted at Redcliffe and Temple, and a militia was organised to defend the city from attack. Several prominent Jacobites were arrested, who were described by their opponents as 'a set of rakehells, who kept a drunken club to carry on treasonable designs.' One of these was Mr Hart, a merchant who was charged with having 'a great quantity of war-like stores for the use of the disaffected.' The hope of the rebels was quickly dashed by the arrival of a large body of troops to Bath and Bristol. (John Latimer, *Annals of Bristol*, Kingsmead, 1970)

# October 3rd

**2008:** The contract was signed allowing Abels Shipbuilders, based at the Albion Dockyard, Bristol to rebuild the hull of the *Medway Queen*, the last surviving estuary paddle steamer in the United Kingdom. The ship was built on the River Clyde, Scotland in 1924 and worked mainly on the River Thames and River Medway. During the Second World War she was requisitioned to work as a minesweeper and later as a training vessel in Scotland. In 1940 the *Medway Queen* became one of the most famous 'little ships' of Dunkirk, making seven crossings across the English Channel in seven days to evacuate troops. The ship became known as the 'Heroine of Dunkirk'. After the war she continued to be used as a paddle steamer on the Thames and Medway until 1963. Afterwards she became a marina clubhouse and nightclub on the Isle of Wight. In 1984 she was salvaged and brought back to Chatham in Kent. In 1985 the Medway Queen Preservation Society was formed in order to restore the ship to her former glory. The rebuilding of the hull at Bristol was made possible by a £1.86 million grant from the Heritage Lottery Fund in 2006. This work is ongoing at the time of writing. (BBC News website / Medway Queen Preservation Society website)

# October 4th

1906: Ashton swing road/rail bridge was opened by the Lady Mayoress, Mrs A.J. Smith, and linked Long Ashton to Hotwells. Trains passed on a lower level whilst a road was constructed above. A high cabin above the road section controlled the swing bridge. The bridge was constructed by John Lysaght & Co. The cost of the original bridge was estimated at £36,000, which was to be shared jointly between the Corporation and the Great Western Railway. However, the costs escalated to more than twice the original estimate and most of the cost was born by the Corporation. During the early years of operation the bridge was swung at least ten times per day, but traffic on the Avon soon declined and the bridge was swung for the last time in 1936, and was fixed in 1951. The roadway and control cabin were removed in 1965, and the railway was singled in 1976. The tracks remain in-situ but are disconnected from the main railway network. A cycleway/footpath now also crosses the bridge. (www.transportheritage.com / www.bristishlistedbuildings.co.uk)

———◆———

1976: InterCity 125 trains are introduced between Bristol and London, with five journeys in each direction per day. Journey times are reduced by 15 minutes. (Rex Kennedy, *Ian Allan's 50 Years of Railways 1942-1992*, Ian Allan, 1992)

# October 5th

**1856:** In the autumn the Prince of Wales made an incognito tour of the West of England and visited Bristol on this date in 1856. Here he attended a service at Bristol Cathedral, where, as no fee was forthcoming, the sub-sacrist led the stranger to a bench in one of the aisles, instead of one of the better pews, where the heir to the throne remained throughout the service. Bristol historian John Latimer states the 'greediness of the Cathedral underlings has always been notorious and states the case of a Bristol sub-sacrist who was said to have hoarded £20,000 died whilst Sydney Smith was one of the prebendaries. Smith had a reputation as a witty cleric and wryly commented that now he understood the full force of the text 'I'd rather be a doorkeeper in the house of my God, than to dwell in the tents of the wicked' (Psalm 84: 10). The same text was inscribed on a tomb of a Salisbury Cathedral verger. Similarly an Anglican bishop who visited Bristol Cathedral around the time was treated with indignity for having presumed to look at some of the monuments without having been guided by an official. (John Latimer, *Annals of Bristol*, Kingsmead, 1970)

# October 6th

**1808:** The Prince of Wales, accompanied by the Duke of Sussex, having arrived at Berkeley Castle, accepted an invitation from Bristol Corporation to visit the city, where His Royal Highness was presented with the Freedom of the City in a gold box. His entrance into the city greatly disappointed onlookers as it was made in a closed carriage – the choice of which was owing to the Prince suffering from a swollen face. Afterwards he inspected the guard and a banquet in his honour took place in Mansion House. He stayed in the city for about four hours before returning to Berkeley Castle. (John Latimer, *Annals of Bristol*, Kingsmead, 1970)

———— ◆ ————

**1847:** A tragic accident took place when a young woman went over the edge of the Avon Gorge at St Vincent Rocks and was 'dashed literally to pieces', after falling over 300ft (91m). Miss Welsh had been in the habit of coming to the Downs for air and exercise. She had been observed by several people sitting on a dangerous projection near the Giant's Cave. Miss Welsh had earlier been warned by a police officer about her position. She thanked him but did not move away. It seems likely that the cause of her fall was slipping on short grass. (*The Times*)

# October 7th

**1564:** The link between the natural phenomenon of the aurora borealis and coming disaster was often made, as this extract from a chronicle shows: 'This year the 7th October here was seen in the element red beams in length like a pole, and also fire like a furnace: whereof that here followed a very great plague, which endured a whole year; whereof here died 2,500 people.' (William Adams, *Adams's Chronicle of Bristol*, J.W. Arrowsmith, 1910)

———— • ◆ • ————

**1791:** Born on November 6th 1743, Richard Champion became a leading porcelain manufacturer of Bristol. He formed a partnership with fellow Quaker William Cookworthy, who patented a process for the production of hard paste porcelain and in 1768 opened a factory at Plymouth. Production transferred to Bristol at Castle Green in 1770 and in 1773 Cookworthy sold his patent to Champion. Champion, who had no practical experience of porcelain manufacture, nevertheless used his managerial skills to improve the quality of the products, and was granted an extension to the patent in 1775, despite opposition from Josiah Wedgewood. The high costs of porcelain production and the decline of the American trade brought the company close to bankruptcy in 1778 but production continued until 1781. Three years later his family emigrated to South Carolina, where Champion died on this date in 1791. (*Oxford Dictionary of National Biography*, OUP)

# October 8th

**1811:** *The Times* reported on this date that during the previous week 'a hair-dresser of Bath undertook to run from the Old Bridge, Bath, to the first house in Temple-street, Bristol, and return to Bath (above 24 miles) in 4 hours and 56 minutes, which wonderful task he performed in 3 hours 51 minutes.' (*The Times*)

———— ◆ ————

**1864:** The *Bristol Times* reported a 'water famine' in Clifton, stating that 'several housekeepers have been driven to such straights that in some cases we have actually seen Paterfamilias start in a fly with an empty barrel by the side of the driver, and go in search of a supply to the nearest spring which in some cases is a mile off.' A water supply was only available for a few hours each day to conserve supplies. The year 1864 had been particularly dry, with only 6½ inches falling in the first five months. Further rainfall was not sufficient to replenish the reservoirs. By December of that year the water company insisted on the full rates payable for that year and further increases in the water rates were planned for the following year despite the lack of water supply. This left customers less than impressed. (John Latimer, *Annals of Bristol*, Kingsmead, 1970)

# October 9th

**1906:** The Merchant Venturers Technical College in Unity Street burned down. The fire brigade were quickly on the scene but were unable to stop the fire and concentrated their efforts on saving surrounding historic buildings. All available men were called in to fight the blaze. Water was pumped from the fire brigade's fireboat *Fire Queen*, which was moored at Broad Quay. The fire started in a laboratory on the upper floor and spread to the floors below. Fortunately no one was killed in the blaze and the building was fully insured. Contemporary newspapers describe the brightness of the fire as 'being like a sunrise'. The severity of the fire prompted an increase in the number of firemen in the city. The Merchant Venturers had been involved with education in Bristol since 1595, when they ran a school for the children of mariners. By the eighteenth century the school was known as Bristol Trade School before being renamed as the Merchant Venturers School and then finally as the Merchant Venturers Technical College. The college became part of the engineering department when the University of Bristol was created in 1909. (Dennis Hill, *Firefighting in Bristol 1877-1974*, The History Press, 2007 / Nicola Sly, *A Grim Almanac of Bristol*, The History Press, 2011 / Merchant Venturers website)

# October 10th

**2005:** At 5.30 a.m. a fire broke out at the warehouses of Aardman Animations, destroying over thirty years of props and models. The flames were said to have reached 100ft (30m) and it took fifty firefighters to put out the blaze. Although many of the models were in metal cases, the heat of the fire simply melted the plasticine models. Aardman Animations are well known for their plasticine characters, including Morph, Wallace and Gromit, Shaun the Sheep, and the film *Chicken Run*. Aardman Animations has been located in Bristol since 1976 and was founded by Peter Lord and David Sproxton in 1972. The company first came to prominence with the plasticine character Morph, which was made for the BBC's *Take Heart* programme. Animator Nick Park joined the company in 1986 and was responsible for the Wallace and Gromit animations. These animations continue to win BAFTAs since the series of films started with *A Grand Day Out* in 1989. Park was philosophical about the blaze, stating that, 'Even though it is a precious and nostalgic collection and valuable to the company, in light of other tragedies, today isn't a big deal.' (*The Independent* / BBC News website / Aardman Animations website)

# October 11th

**1979:** A Boeing 707 with 58 tons of fuel on board went through a hedgerow boundary at Bristol's Lulsgate Airport whilst taking off. The plane then crossed the A38 and caused £5,000 worth of damage to the approach-lighting system. Staff in the control tower reported that the 707 became airborne right at the end of the runway. By that time one of the controllers had pressed a switch to turn the traffic lights on the A38 to red. A piece of the aircraft's trailing edge also broke away as it struck the hedge and landing lights. Those on board the plane were told what had happened but elected to continue their flight. The plane subsequently landed at Kuwait, where repairs were made before it flew on to Bombay. The incident was later written up by the Accidents Investigation Branch Department of Trade and concerns was expressed that an aircraft was able to take off with no checks made on its weight and condition. The Accident Investigation department also had difficulty in tracking down the owners of the aircraft, with doubt expressed about the authenticity of the plane's Zaire registration. (*The Times*)

# October 12th

**1864:** The fourth Annual (Anglican) Church Congress took place in the city, presided over by the Bishop of Bristol. Joseph Lynne, a cleric in deacon's orders, made a startling appearance in monk's attire, styling himself as Brother Ignatius. He professed to have founded a monastic system according to the Order of St Benedict within the Church of England. In the evening he gave lectures to crowds of around 2,000 people at the Athenæum and Rifle-Drill Hall. His followers had already established a community in Bristol, which Ignatius gave pastoral oversight, but it was difficult to maintain the fledgling community. When the order moved to Trenchard Street their unusual practices often caused crowds to assemble and led to disturbances where the police had to be called. These practices included a procession held on the Feast of the Assumption (August 15th), which took place at 2 a.m. In another incident two drunken monks were expelled from the community for refusing to obey their prior. Several such incidents led to Ignatius expelling the prior, who called himself Br Cyprian and he went off to establish his own community in Montpellier. Several supporters from Trenchard Street went with him, which ceased after Cyprian's expulsion by Ignatius. (John Latimer, *Annals of Bristol*, Kingsmead, 1970 / *Bristol Mercury*)

# October 13th

**1860:** A man was shot by a dog. John Hodges, 21, a cowherd employed by Martha Rudall, went to ferret for rats in the hedgerows with Robert Green. Hodges was armed with a gun and accompanied by a sheepdog, which, according to the local populace, would kill anything from a hare to a rat. The ferret had gone into one of the mows and brought out a rat and Hodges was standing up, hoping to 'choke it off' whilst at the same time hugging the muzzle of a loaded shotgun. The butt-end of the gun was resting on the ground. The dog, keen to get at the rat, started to jump up and down near to where the gun was resting, whereupon a paw came in contact with the hammer of the gun and pulled it back so that when it rebounded it fell on the cap and the gun went off. The charge shot off part of Hodges's coat collar and entered the left side of his neck, severing the jugular vein, and finally lodged in his head. Hodges died a few minutes later from his injuries. (*Bristol Mercury*)

# October 14th

**1899:** William Ellis Metford died at his home, Redland Villa, in Bristol. He was born in Taunton on October 4th 1824 and studied at Sherborne School, where he showed an interest in mechanics and rifle shooting. After marrying on February 12th 1857, he took an appointment as an engineer to the East Indian Railway. However, the couple were caught up in the fighting of the Indian Mutiny at Monghyr. Until British troops arrived, Metford organised a defence force and manufactured bullets for the rifles. The episode contributed to the failure of his health and so he returned to England. Metford was particularly interested in ballistics engineering and in 1856 he invented an explosive bullet. These bullets were later declared illegal by the St Petersburg Convention in 1868. Nevertheless, Metford was awarded £1,000 plus expenses for the work. He developed the rifle using deep grooves and lead bullets and in 1870 he began production of a breech-loading rifle. In 1888 the War Office selected the design to be used on British rifles, using Metford's bore with the bolt action and detachable magazine invented by James Lee. The rifle became known as the Lee-Metford rifle and was long in use. (*Oxford Dictionary of National Biography*, OUP)

# October 15th

**1809:** Samuel Morley was born. He would later become a businessman, philanthropist and MP for Bristol between 1868 and 1885. His father was a manufacturer of hosiery with premises in London. From his father Morley also inherited a belief in evangelical dissent and believed that everyone had the right to interpret the Bible in their own way. As an employer he was particularly benevolent by the standards of the day, giving high wages to his workers, ensuring that they worked in light and bright conditions and giving generous pensions. In politics he largely agreed with Gladstone's Liberalism. He even declined a peerage from Prime Minister William Gladstone to the House of Lords in 1885 as he disapproved of the chamber. Ill heath affected him through 1886 and he died on September 5th 1886. As MP for Bristol he was a popular figure and an inscription on the base of a commemorative statue erected after his death reads: 'To preserve for their children [of Bristol] the memory of the face and form of one who was an example of justice, generosity and spirit. This statue was given by 5,000 citizens.' The statue is located on a traffic island between Lewins Mead and Rupert Street. (*Oxford Dictionary of National Biography*, OUP / *Author's field notes*)

# October 16th

**1987:** The first house to be built in Bradley Stoke was occupied. The home was built on the John Foxwood development, which is now part of the Stean Bridge Road area. There was little publicity for the event but on October 16th 1987, Ideal Homes organised a civic reception for the first new residents of the Branson Court Development, an area now known as Pye Croft. The first plans for Bradley Stoke were published in 1982, with land mainly set aside for housing, but also for some light industry in the north of the town, schools and 163 acres of open space. In March 1987 Sir John Cope, MP for Northavon, cut the first sod of earth with a JCB digger rather than the traditional spade. The name Bradley Stoke was chosen from the two brooks, the Bradley Brook and the Stoke Brook, which pass through the area. From its inception, the Bradley Stoke Community Association has lobbied for the formation of a parish council. The first councillors were elected on March 19th 1992. Soon afterwards the parish council became a town council, allowing the chair to designate themselves as Mayor. (David Chandler, 'A History of Bradley Stoke' on www.bradleystokematters.co.uk / BBC News website)

# October 17th

**1891:** 'On Saturday, about one o'clock, a pig kept in the rear of the premises occupied by Mr Withers, butcher, East Street, accidentally got into the old Malago stream, which runs through the back yard. The animal lost its footing, and was carried away by the force of the "fresh" water through the archway under the main road to the rear of the New Inn; from thence under Southville, and ultimately, after being in the stream for hours, found its way beneath the "flap" which conveys the water into the river Avon. When in the river it struck out for Bedminster Bridge, but before reaching that structure it was observed by some onlookers, one of whom descended by the chains attached to the bridge and fortunately succeeded in grasping the pig by the ear. The animal was then placed in a sack and conveyed to the Bedminster police station, and subsequently restored to Mr Withers, apparently none the worse for its extraordinary swim.' (*Bristol Mercury and Daily Post*)

# October 18th

**1891:** Gronow Davis, who was awarded the Victoria Cross, died at his Bristol residence and was buried at Arnos Vale Cemetery on October 23rd. He was born in Clifton on May 8th 1828 and joined the Royal Artillery in June 1847, becoming a Lieutenant in 1848. In 1855 he was made Captain and served in the Crimean War from July 6th 1855, taking part in the siege and fall of Sebastopol and the Battle of Tehernaya. It was during the Crimean War that Gronow Davis was awarded the Victoria Cross, for his 'great coolness and gallantry' in the attack on the Redan on September 8th 1855, on which occasion he commanded the spiking party and saved the life of Lieutenant Sanders of the 30th Foot Regiment by jumping over the parapet of a sap and crossing open ground under the enemy's 'murderous fire' to assist in conveying Sanders, whose leg was broken and was severely wounded. He continued to do the same for several other wounded soldiers. After Crimea, Gronow Davis continued to rise through the ranks, finally becoming a Major General in 1881. (*Morning Chronicle / Bristol Mercury and Daily Post*)

# October 19th

**1868:** A branch line that was being constructed from Bristol Temple Meads to the Floating Harbour revealed the existence of a network of subterranean passages running underneath Redcliffe parish. On this date, an exploration of these passages was made to the Floating Harbour by a 'party of half a dozen gentlemen' and architect Mr W. Rice made a plan of the passages. The caves were man-made and the largest cavern is 45ft in diameter and 7ft high, with a roof supported on eight columns. The caves are thought to have been excavated between the fifteenth and eighteenth centuries. The extracted red sandstone may have been turned into sand and used for Bristol's glass-making and pottery industries, which once flourished around the Redcliffe and Temple areas of the city. In later years the caves were used as storage space and to dispose waste from the glassworks and from William Watts' lead shot tower, which stood on Redcliffe Hill. During early excavations it was suggested that slaves were kept in chains and that smugglers stored contraband here, but no evidence has come to light to suggest that this was ever the case. (*Daily News* / Maurice Fells, *Bristol: History You Can See*, The History Press, 2006)

# October 20th

**1873:** The inquest opened into the singular death of Herbert Phipps Jones, 17, who was killed by the ignition of phosphorous contained in a bottle in Jones's trouser pocket. Jones was employed by Mr Rawlings of Denmark Street, who had recently purchased some bottles from Mr Parson, a dentist of Great George Street, and it was the job of the deceased to wash out these bottles. Bridget Murphy, a domestic servant employed by Mr Rawlings, said that about six weeks prior to the tragedy Jones was again employed cleaning the bottles. The contents were emptied into an ash barrel before being washed. However, a particular combination caused the contents of the barrel to ignite. Bridget Murphy ran to get a pail of water but when she threw the water over the barrel the contents exploded, filling the house with smoke. On the day of the tragedy, Jones was once again washing the bottles in the yard when Bridget, taking him a cup of tea, discovered Jones engulfed in blue flames. She ran to fetch water whilst another man named Clements tore off Jones' trousers to stop the burning. It was of no avail and Jones later died. (*Bristol Mercury*)

# October 21st

**1781:** Matthew Wasbrough, steam engine engineer and inventor, died. He was born at 3 Narrow Wine Street, Bristol. Here his father jointly-owned a brass founding and clock-making business. On March 10th 1779 he was granted a patent for his invention, which turned the reciprocal motion generated by the steam engines of the time into rotary movement using a series of pulleys and wheels. He was the first engineer to get this type of power from a steam engine as up until now the only practical application of steam engines was for pumping. He hoped that the application would prove useful to power shipping but for now he used his invention in his father's workshop. Another engine was also provided for John Pickard's Mill located in Snow Hill, Birmingham. However, the design proved unreliable until a crank was substituted and a subsequent patent was granted to Pickard on August 23rd 1780. (John Latimer, *Annals of Bristol*, Kingsmead, 1970 / *Oxford Dictionary of National Biography*, OUP)

———◆———

**1843:** The last four-horse stagecoach ran between London and Bristol. The demise of the service reflected the coming of the railway to Bristol, which provided a quicker means of travel to and from London. (John Latimer, *Annals of Bristol*, Kingsmead, 1970 / C.F.W. Denning, *Old Inns of Bristol*, John Wright & Son, 1949)

# October 22nd

**1817:** The night steamer *William and Mary* left Bristol for Waterford with sixty people on board. The vessel struck a rock near Flat Holm in the Bristol Channel and sank. Only twenty-three people survived. The night was clear and blame for the accident rested with the ship's mate, who had been left in charge by the captain. The mate saved himself by forcing some ladies to leave the only lifeboat. (John Latimer, *Annals of Bristol*, Kingsmead, 1970)

———— • ◆ • ————

**1937:** *The Times* on this date reports that 'thirteen young Spaniards who had escaped Spain in a commandeered trawler from a fishing village near Gijon sailed up the River Avon at Bristol last night after being towed by the Liverpool steamer *Etrib* over 500 miles. They described how they fled to the mountains when Franco's army swept over their homesteads and lived for three months in hiding, feeding on scraps of food and birds which they killed with stones. Finally reduced to the verge of starvation, they stole through Franco's lines by night and, reaching a fishing village a few miles west of Gijon, they overpowered the owners of a trawler and made them put to sea. For a day they drifted in the Channel, with little food and no fuel, until they were eventually picked up by the *Etrib*.' (*The Times*)

# October 23rd

**1816:** The weathercock of St Nicholas's steeple was 'replaced by the person who removed it; his name is Hutchings, a native of Bridgewater, aged 38. An immense concourse of people assembled to view the apparently hazardous undertaking. Hutchings says, he could ascend to the weathercock without any assistance of ladder of scaffolding.' (*The Times*)

———◆———

**1882:** Upwards of 3 inches of rain fell during forty-eight hours on October 22nd and 23rd, causing severe flooding in parts of Bristol. By evening a section of Stapleton Road was 4ft (1.2m) underwater. At the Black Swan Inn in Stapleton Road, the water rose to the level of the signboard over the entrance to the premises. Boats were needed to help those stranded in their homes. The effect on the poor was disastrous with many practically ruined. A fund was raised on their behalf. Nevertheless, because of the dampness of their dwellings, the poor experienced illness over the next winter. It also emerged that unscrupulous speculative property builders built on land that was known to flood each year. On September 28th 1886 the council applied to parliament to allow them to build a culvert from the Froom near Broadweir to the Floating Harbour, with a view to prevent similar inundations. (John Latimer, *Annals of Bristol*, Kingsmead, 1970)

# October 24th

**1873:** Robert Francis Kilvert led a relatively unexciting life as a Victorian clergyman, yet his diaries make for fascinating reading. After his first curacy in Clyro, Breconshire, in 1865, he moved back to Wiltshire for a short time, making frequent visits to Bristol. Often he travelled on market day in order to take advantage of the cheap railway tickets. On October 24th 1873, he arrived by the 9.20 train for the music festival. Arriving at the Trenchard Street entrance of Colston Hall for the unsecured tickets, he came across a crowd that had been waiting for some time. 'Directly the doors were thrown open at noon a dreadful struggle began. People got wedged in the doorway and were shot like canon balls from the terrible pressure from behind.' In the end 'we were forced asunder in the fight.' Evidently people did not queue in 1873! In October 1874 he visited St Mary Redcliffe, which 'is still under repair – the roof of the nave is now being restored. The verger said that the church had been under the workmen's hands for the last forty-five years.' Kilvert strikes the sounding pillars, but 'they do not ring as they did formerly.' (Marguerite Fedden, *Bristol Vignettes*, Burleigh Press, 1957)

# October 25th

**1771:** Robert Lovell, poet, was born in Thomas Street, the son of a wealthy Quaker. He married Edith Bourne (1741-1781) and followed in his father's business as a pin manufacturer. However, he does not seem to have been entirely happy with his profession, as can be evidenced from his volume of satire *Bristoliad*. He later collaborated with Southey, producing a volume of poetry entitled *Poems by Bion and Moschus*. His second marriage to Mary Fricker in 1794 caused him to become estranged from his family, as Mary was both a non-Quaker and had become an actress after her father's bankruptcy. Lovell died in Bristol on May 3rd 1796 after a bout of fever he caught at Salisbury. Lovell's father refused any help to his daughter-in-law and infant son, also called Robert, and the family was maintained by fellow poet Southey. The younger Robert Lovell became a London printer in 1824 and a few years later went on a tour of Europe. However, he did not return to Britain and seems to have mysteriously disappeared without trace, having last been seen at Marseilles. Foreign Office enquires and journeys by Henry and Nelson Coleridge in search of him yielded nothing. (*Oxford Dictionary of National Biography*, OUP)

# October 26th

**1822:** The *Bristol Journal* reported on the activities of the 'resurrection men' when a body of a young woman was stolen from St Augustine's churchyard and conveyed to a dissecting chamber situated in the cathedral precincts. A quarrel is said to have started between the 'resurrection men' and the surgeons, causing a crowd to gather outside. When the door was forced the crime was discovered. The *Bristol Mercury*, however, states that the 'dissecting chamber' was situated above the shop of the greengrocer and the lady owner, on seeing a 'resurrection man' with a large sack, was suspicious and attempted to stop the man but was not successful. Alerting her neighbours to the incident, a crowd soon gathered outside the shop, one of whom was the husband of the dead woman. After checking her gravesite and finding that the body had been taken, he went to the shop and climbed a ladder to gain access to the upstairs room. Several friends also followed. On seeing the body of his wife a scuffle ensued and the body was carried off by the widower. The surgeon was pursued from the scene by the crowd, narrowly escaping with his life. (John Latimer, *Annals of Bristol*, Kingsmead, 1970 / *Bristol Mercury*)

# October 27th

**2008:** A Bristol University student spent a night in jail after crashing his £10,000 silver Mini into a flight of steps, causing extensive frontal damage to the car. The impact caused damage to the radiator, the two front tyres burst and both the driver and passenger airbags went off. Six security staff, two police cars and a police helicopter were sent to the scene in order to arrest the 18 year old at 1 a.m. The driver was subsequently arrested for drink-driving and was found to be over the limit. Witnesses stated that the car was driven around the university grounds over paths and grass at speeds of around 30mph before the accident. Many contemporary reports in the press stated that the student was trying to recreate the scenes from the *Italian Job*, a 1969 film starring Michael Caine where a gang of robbers escape using Minis through the backstreets of Turin. The car had only been given to the student by his parents the day before. (*The Telegraph / The Mail / The Sun / The Evening Standard*)

# October 28th

**1822:** 'The following most awful instance of the uncertainty of human life took place at the house of Abraham Davis, a Jew, dealer in Marine Stores, 97, Old Gravel Lane, Ratcliff highway:- On Sunday Mrs Davis complained of being unwell, and asked her husband for something she fancied. He said she was always longing for something, and wished she was stiff in her grave. He no sooner repeated these words than he was seized with a shivering – he became speechless, and he was a corpse before twelve o'clock, having been previously in perfect health. Mrs Davis was so shocked at the circumstance that she took to her bed, and was a corpse less than six hours afterwards. Many persons out of curiosity were round the house yesterday making enquires.' (*Bristol Mercury*)

———— • ◆ • ————

**1850:** A case of burglary was brought before Bristol magistrates when 'on Sunday evening during the temporary absence of the family, the house of Mr W. Turtle, Old Park, Bristol, was burglariously entered, and a large quantity of wearing apparel and other property was taken off. The police suspected a man named Haynes, whom they captured, and in whose room they found all the property, with other stolen articles, and a complete set of burglars' implements.' (*The Times*)

# October 29th

**1831:** Sir Charles Weatherell, Recorder of Bristol, was an opponent of electoral reform because it gave voting rights to Catholics, and claimed in the spring of 1831 that the citizens of Bristol were indifferent to reform, resulting in popular demonstrations of disapproval. The middle class in particular supported reform as it would establish a fairer distribution of seats and end the so-called 'rotten borough', whilst the lower orders hoped for better living standards. However, the House of Lords voted against it on October 8th, creating a simmering resentment in the populace. On October 29th, Sir Charles Weatherall's carriage made its way through the crowds of demonstrators to open the assize court before adjourning to Mansion House, where civic celebrations continued. A minority of special constables over-reacted against the crowd by beating some of them up when missiles had started to be thrown. At four o'clock in the afternoon a renewed attempt was made to storm the Mansion House, devastating the downstairs rooms. Sir Charles made his escape over the roof to the window of the adjoining house and swapping his clothes with a postillion in some stables at the back. The riots lasted a total of three days. (John Latimer, *Annals of Bristol*, Kingsmead, 1970 / Geoffrey Amey, *City Under Fire*, Lutterworth Press, 1979)

# October 30th

**1777:** A windmill known as the snuff-mill on Clifton Down was destroyed by fire. Although not interesting in itself it allowed some years later, in April 1828, for the Society of Merchants to allow William West, an artist, to rent the ruins of the building at a nominal rate. William West rebuilt the structure, turning it into a house, and restored the tower. A year later he fitted the tower with a telescope and a camera obscura, turning the place into an observatory. A few years later he excavated a passageway through the rock to the 'Giant's Cave', giving commanding views out over the Avon Gorge. The cave is also known at St Vincent's Cave or Ghyston's Cave. West was a photographic pioneer using an early process known as the photogenic process, whereby a negative image could be formed when an object was placed on photographic paper and exposed to light for a short period. He achieved a certain degree of sophistication, prompting the *Bristol Mercury* to state that 'Our talented fellow citizen Mr West, of the Clifton Observatory has succeeded in producing a beautiful photogenic medallion-likeness of Queen Victoria.' (John Latimer, *Annals of Bristol*, Kingsmead, 1970 / *Bristol Mercury*)

# October 31st

**1147:** Robert, Earl of Gloucester, was born around 1100, the illegitimate son of Henry I. He became a leader of one of the dominant factions at his father's court. He was married to Mabel, an heiress to lands in the West Country and Glamorgan. Following his father's death, he did not immediately support his half-sister Empress Matilda's claim to the throne, but equally was no great supporter of King Stephen either. From 1137 it became apparent that there were major differences between himself and the king and his support switched to the Empress Matilda. His first major battle in support of the Empress was a siege on Worcester, which was sacked on November 7th 1137. The Empress's forces advanced, and Robert aided an attempted siege of Winchester in 1141. However, the King's forces were stronger than expected and whilst leading a rearguard action to cover the Empress's safe retreat to Devizes, Robert was captured by Flemish mercenaries at Stockbridge. He was released following a series of complex hostage negotiations. Towards the end of 1147 he fell ill with fever and died on this date in 1147 in Bristol. He was buried at St James's Priory Church, which he founded as a priory of Tewkesbury Abbey. (*Oxford Dictionary of National Biography*, OUP)

# November 1st

**1755:** Strange natural phenomena with no apparent explanation were witnessed. This included the ebbing tide on the Avon suddenly reversing and flowing back upriver, water in deep wells becoming discoloured and undrinkable, and the water in Hotwells turning blood red. The local populace hurried to church to offer prayers to God to avert their own destruction and that of the world. The water remained foul for some time. The phenomena was not, however, caused by supernatural forces. Several hundred miles away, Lisbon in Portugal had suffered a massive earthquake, later estimated at 9 on the Richter scale, which resulted in a tsunami whose effects were widespread throughout Europe. (John Latimer, *Annals of Bristol*, Kingsmead, 1970)

———— ◆ ————

**1867:** All turnpikes in Bristol were abolished. Since the receipts from the tolls had managed to pay off all mortgages it was decided at a meeting of the Bristol Turnpike trustees that the tolls should cease. The motion was duly carried, albeit by a small majority. Objections included those from Bristol trustees, who alleged a £2,000 bill to maintain the 18 miles of turnpike roads in the city. (John Latimer, *Annals of Bristol*, Kingsmead, 1970)

# November 2nd

**1636:** Edward Colston, merchant and philanthropist, was born in Temple Street, Bristol. In 1654 he was apprenticed to the London's Mercer's Company and later made his fortune in the mercantile business. By 1689 he resided in Mortlake, Surrey, where he lived for the rest of his life. From the 1690s Colson became heavily involved with philanthropy and the majority of his donations benefitted Bristol. These include founding almshouses in King Street and on St Michael's Hill, endowing Queen Elizabeth's Hospital and assisting the Merchant Venturers to found Colston's Boys' School in 1710. In 1712 Temple Parish received finds to clothe and educate forty poor boys. Churches also benefited, including Temple, St Mary Redcliffe, St Werburgh, All Saints' and Bristol Cathedral, where Colston attended daily services whenever he stayed in the city. Colston was a high churchman opposing both Catholicism and dissent. Consequently Colston ensured that children from his schools were brought up as Anglicans and were given apprenticeships. Colston died on October 11th 1721. Strict instructions were given for his funeral: His body was to be carried in a hearse from London to Bristol, and then those who benefited from his charitable works were to process with the coffin to All Saints' Church, where he was buried. (*Oxford Dictionary of National Biography*, OUP)

# November 3rd

**1855:** A letter from the Bishop of Bristol addressed to his clergy appeared in *The Times* regarding the consecration of St John the Baptist, Bedminster. The new church was designed by John Norton and replaced an earlier medieval church. The interior of the new church was richly decorated, including carved foliage and a three-bayed carved reredos at the east end. This reredos had concerned a great number of people, who considered it too Catholic. Demonstrations both in favour and against the reredos occurred and in his letter the bishop was pleased that no clergy had taken part in these protests. The bishop stated that he was 'influenced by the constant desire to appease strife, unite all clergymen in works of piety and love' and that he 'endeavoured to procure the removal of the reredos by means calculated to give triumph for neither party.' The bishop expressed surprise that his request was refused but consecrated the church anyway on October 30th, in order that a large a populous parish of over 1,000 souls should not go without a church. St John the Baptist's Church survived until November 24th 1940, when it was damaged by bombing. The ruins were demolished twenty-seven years later. (*The Times* / www.churchcrawler.pwp. blueyonder.co.uk – a website devoted to Bristol's churches)

# November 4th

**1828:** *The Times* newspaper on this date contained the following article: 'At the Bristol Sessions, which ended last week John and Margaret Shipp were found guilty of manslaughter and sentenced to twelve months imprisonment. A fellow lodger being troubled with an asthma, which terribly annoyed them, they determined to get rid of him, and employed a sweep to stop up the flue of the chimney communicating to the fireplace in his bedroom, which caused such a density of smoke, that he was suffocated. The wife went to see how their scheme succeeded, and finding the poor fellow in a dying state dragged him out of the room, but it was too late, as he expired immediately.' (*The Times*)

———— • ◆ • ————

**1880:** A 'Grand Demonstration' was held in Colston Hall organised by the Bristol and West of England National Society for Women's Suffrage in support of the Women's Disabilities Removal Bill. The meeting attracted more than could be held by the 3,000 capacity of Colston Hall and so another hall was also used. The society was formed in 1868 and its first public meeting was held in January 1870, when none of the speakers was a woman. (Elizabeth Crawford, *The Women's Suffrage Movement: A Reference Guide, 1866-1928*, Routledge, 2004)

# November 5th

**1828:** Sydney Smith was the prebendary of Bristol Cathedral whose duties included preaching a sermon held annually on Guy Fawkes' Day in front of local dignitaries. Normally the sermon was full of anti-Catholic sentiment. Smith, however, preached toleration, arguing that civil restrictions because of a man's religion should be removed. This included Roman Catholics, who were denied emancipation at this time. In the sermon he called on his hearers to 'annihilate the phantoms that terrify weak minds, and which have no better foundation in *Foxe's Book of Martyrs* or the plot of Guy Fawkes.' It was too much for some hearers, for at the subsequent banquet Smith noticed that certain members of the Corporation looked 'as though they could not keep the turtle on their stomachs'. The controversy spilled over into the newspapers. *Felix Farley's Journal* thought that Smith had gone too far whilst the *Bristol Mercury* took the side of the prelate, reprinting much of the controversial sermon and decrying their rival. Before coming to Bristol, Smith had helped to start the *Edinburgh Review* in 1802, contributing some articles, and said of Scotsmen that, 'it requires a surgical operation to get a joke into a Scottish understanding.' He was later made a canon of St Paul's. (Marguerite Fedden, *Bristol Bypaths*, Rankin, 1954 / *Bristol Mercury*)

# November 6th

1898: A brawl took place in St Simon's Church, Baptist Mills, Bristol. During the 11 a.m. celebration of Holy Communion, whilst the congregation were still kneeling, Mr E.J. Castle stood up and stated, 'I protest against idolatry.' The churchwarden, Mr Bristow, told him to leave the church but he refused, continuing to shout and cause a disturbance. Castle was protesting against the ritualistic practices that took place, including the use of incense and the elevation of the sacraments. Such practices formed part of the Catholic revival in the Church of England and were considered by some to be too close to Roman Catholic practice. 'Considerable commotion' was caused amongst the congregation and Castle was eventually forcibly ejected by the churchwarden. He was later fined 40 shillings. (*The Times*)

———— • ◆ • ————

1957: A fifteen-strong crew of a prototype 301 Bristol Britannia aircraft died when their plane crashed during a test flight. The plane crashed into a wood at Downend, just before midday on its return to the Bristol Aeroplane Company at Filton. Parts of the aeroplane crashed into several nearby houses but fortunately no one on the ground was killed. (*The Times*)

# *November 7th*

**1831:** Sir Nathaniel William Wraxall was born in Queen's Square on April 8th 1751. In 1769 he was sent to Bombay, representing the East India Company. However, in 1772, for reasons unknown, he abandoned his career and returned to England. His first tour of Europe took place in 1774-5 and he started travel writing. His first book, entitled *Cursory Remarks Made in a Tour Through Some Northern Parts of Europe*, was published in 1775. He returned to England in 1780 and, using his connections, he secured the constituency of Hindon, Wiltshire in 1781. Horace Walpole complained of him 'popping into every spot where he can make himself talked of, by talking of himself; but I hear he will come to an untimely beginning in the House of Commons.' Wraxall, in fact, remained an MP for fourteen years. His most widely read publication was published in 1815, entitled *Historical Memoirs of My Own Time*. This publication led to him being sued for libel by the Russian diplomat Count Vorontsov, for suggesting that Catherine the Great had been responsible for the death of the German Princess of Württemburgand. He was sentenced to imprisonment for six months, of which he served three. (*Oxford Dictionary of National Biography*, OUP)

# November 8th

**1743:** The *Gloucester Journal* of this date contains an article by a Bristol correspondent on what he believed to have been a disturbing case of witchcraft. A cobbler living in Horse Street says that he called a woman 'an old witch'. In retaliation she sent a cat to his house, which seized his finger whilst the man attempted to drive the animal out. The cat would not loosen its grip on the man until it was squeezed to death. The man was dipped in salt water at Sea Mills, but this counter-charm was unsuccessful and it is said that the man died in great agony. (John Latimer, *Annals of Bristol*, Kingsmead, 1970)

---

**1880:** A French steamer, the *S.B. Say*, arrived in Bristol from Nantes, France. On board were eleven Capuchin monks. They had been forced to flee France following the activities of an anti-clerical government, which at the time was expelling many religious congregations. The Brothers were on their way to Ireland, to stay with a community of their Order at Roach's Town, County Cork, and study in peace in order to become priests. (*Bristol Times and Daily Post*)

# November 9th

**1790:** 'The Bristol Mail Coach was overturned by a gang on Tuesday night at Longford, close by the bridge, the near side of the body was broke in pieces, and the passengers very much hurt. The coachman is so terribly bruised that he lies dangerously ill at the Kings Arms, Tywford.' (*The Times*)

***

**1857:** James Freeston escaped charges of being drunk at the magistrates' court after being arrested at Thomas Street the previous day. Freeston claimed that, whilst returning to Bristol from Cathay, he had been attacked by someone who thrust a handkerchief over his face and had attempted to force him to drink something. Although Freeston could not remember any details of the alleged incident, he claims that he was robbed of his watch, chain and wallet. When police arrested him they ignored his claims that he had been robbed. The magistrates, on inquiring as to the place where Freeston had been arrested, learned that it was an area full of brothels. Consequently they decided to believe Freeston's story and acquitted him of all charges. They also ordered the police to investigate the alleged crime. (Nicola Sly, *A Grim Almanac of Bristol*, The History Press, 2011)

# November 10th

**1851:** The SS *Demerara* was being towed down the River Avon by powerful tugs. The ship had been built by the firm of William Patterson (who also built the SS *Great Britain*) and was en-route to the Clyde, where engines were due to be fitted. After passing underneath the Clifton Suspension Bridge the ship became stranded upon some rocks. An attempt was made to re-float the vessel on the night tide but this failed and the ship continued to block the river. Eventually the vessel was towed back to Patterson's yard and written-off with a value of £15,000. It had cost £48,000 to build her. (Maurice Fells, *Bristol: History You Can See*, The History Press, 2006)

───── ◆ ─────

**1964:** The Beatles played at Colston Hall – the last gig of their UK tour. The band finished 'If I fell' and were about to begin their final song when flour was thrown at them from the roof. Four students had gained access to the lighting gantries to drop the flour. An eyewitness records that Ringo Starr was the most covered and just stood there. John Lennon looked at Paul McCartney and they both stated laughing before carrying on regardless. (Colston Hall website)

# November 11th

**1891:** The boiler house chimneystack of the Feeder Road Saw Mills crashed to the ground after being blown down in a strong gale. It killed Benjamin Smith, a wood-chopper, who was standing in front of the boiler house, which was covered only by a light timber roof. He was killed instantly. The stack also injured two men, William Ford, who suffered a broken arm and bruises to his head, and George Cantle, who also suffered bruises to his head. Sixteen other men who were working close by had a remarkable escape from the falling stack. The accident occurred during the men's lunch hour and an unfortunate circumstance also played a role in the death of Benjamin Smith. Normally Smith went home for his lunch and usually returned to the mill with only a few minutes to spare before the resumption of work at 2 o'clock. However, on this day Smith arrived early with at least ten minutes to spare. On his return he commented on the rough weather outside and it was at that point the chimneystack fell upon him. (*Bristol Mercury and Daily Post* / Nicola Sly, *A Grim Almanac of Bristol*, The History Press, 2011)

# November 12th

**1636:** 'About 9 of the clock, the south-west wind blowing very hard upon a full spring tide, caused a great inundation of waters to flow, as all the shops and cellars on the Backe and quay were filled therewith, and received much loss by that sudden and unexpected storm. The storm caused much damage to the low-lying ground surrounding the Severn and parts of Bristol by the quay also flooded. The author of *Adams's Chronicle* compares this inundation to a similar flood that occurred on January 20th 1607, claiming that 'this flood in my judgement, and by the judgement of others that set marks for both, do affirm, that it was not so high by a foot as in the last great flood.' (William Adams, *Adams's Chronicle of Bristol*, J.W. Arrowsmith, 1910)

**1851:** An amateur company of comedians gave a performance at the Victorian Rooms for the benefit of the Guild of Literature and Art. The pieces included a performance of *Mr Nightingale's Diary* by Charles Dickens and Mark Lemon. Charles Dickens was also manager of the troop and was one of the chief performers. Every available seat had sold out several days before and following several appeals the performance was repeated two days later. (John Latimer, *Annals of Bristol*, Kingsmead, 1970)

# November 13th

**1909:** Winston Churchill arrived in Bristol to speak at the Anchor Society banquet. His visit attracted protests from suffragettes campaigning for equal franchise. Churchill was surrounded by a cordon of policemen, whilst others kept the crowds at bay. Despite these precautions, Miss Teresa Garnett managed to strike Churchill on his cheek with a whip, shouting, 'Take that you brute!' The police were already alert to suffragette disturbances as the day before, a stone had been thrown though a window of the Liberal Club in Bristol. Around the stone was a piece of paper, which read, 'Protest against inviting Cabinet Ministers to speak in Bristol whilst women are being force-fed in prison.' Two women were arrested for throwing stones that night, namely Miss Vera Wentworth and Miss Witman. Further arrests were made that weekend for stone-throwing, including Effie Lawes, Helen Pickford and Mary Allen. The women refused to pay their fines so they were sent to prison. Two of the women, Vera Wentworth and Mary Allen, went on hunger strike and had to be force-fed, whilst Teresa Garnett set fire to her cell and was sent to the punishment block. (*The Times* / Nicola Sly, *A Grim Almanac of Bristol*, The History Press, 2011)

# November 14th

**1822:** A well-dressed man, en-route to Exeter from London, stopped off at the Talbot Inn and made enquires of connecting coaches. He stayed the night at the inn and the next morning, after breakfast, he was presented with his bill of 7s, whereupon he declared that he had no money. With no friends or relatives in Bristol, he offered to leave some part of his dress as payment, promising to redeem them on his return from Exeter. He took off his pantaloons and, since 'he had a frock coat, and a good pair of drawers', he 'did not appear to feel the loss of his pantaloons.' Afterwards he went to another Bristol inn, The Bush, where again he made enquires to a coach that he intended to take the following day and ordered his dinner. The next day he rang his bell hurriedly and exclaimed that he had been robbed of his pantaloons, containing £10 10s. Concerned about the respectability of his inn, the landlord refunded the man his money and sent for a tailor to bring some replacement pantaloons. On receiving the money the man took himself off. The con was only discovered when the two innkeepers later met in the market place. (*The Times*)

# November 15th

**1821:** *The Times* reported that the year 1821 had been a notable one for the large numbers of slugs and snails. The Gloucestershire village of Tockington, on the outskirts of Bristol, was particularly affected. In a small, dry field, inhabited by the snail species *helix virgata*, the numbers were said to have increased very rapidly, giving rise to 'the most ridiculous and extravagant' explanations. In the words of the newspaper: 'any trifling occurrence varying from the everyday sights of life becomes a wonder to a common mind, it was immediately concluded (and some had the impudence to declare they had witnessed it) that these snails fell in the form of a heavy shower from the clouds, predicting private and public misfortune, and all the calamities that a heated fancy or a weak mind could suggest! One man at Bristol actually circulated a paper, considerably to his emolument, announcing this event as a sign of the latter day, and the coming of the Messiah!' Despite the predictions of calamity owing to the presence of these snails, it was later reported that when autumn came and the snails returned to their holes in the banks, the owner of the field was very much alive and well. (*The Times / Anthenaeum and Literary Chronicle No. 73, March 18 1829*)

# November 16th

**2000:** Russ Conway, real name Trevor Herbert Stanford, died. He is best known as a composer and pianist with number one hits *Side Saddle* and *Roulette* in 1959. He was born at 71 Coronation Road, Bedminster on September 2nd 1925. He claimed that he had had only one piano lesson in his life, preferring to spend the money for lessons on trips to the cinema. He was conscripted into the navy in 1942 and was awarded the Distinguished Services Medal for minesweeping in Greece. It was whilst serving in the navy that he lost one of his fingers, not in action, but in a bread slicer. During the 1950s Conway moved to London, gaining work as a relief pianist in a club, as a rehearsal pianist, and undertook some composition work. His first composition, *Primera*, was conducted on television by Eric Robson. Eventually he got the opportunity to produce his own records, but his name was not thought suitable because of the lively style of music that he played. He chose the name Russ Conway, which were the names of two other well-known performers – namely Russ Henderson of the Russ Henderson Trinidad Steel Band and singer Steve Conway. Russ Conway went on to make thirty-two recordings between 1957 and 1967. (*Oxford Dictionary of National Biography*, OUP)

# November 17th

**1577:** The government at this period did not issue any coins that were below the value of a single penny. Consequently local tradesmen stepped in to fill the gap with tokens that were made of lead, tin or mixed metal, and were essentially valueless, leading to widespread discontent. The Privy Council minutes of November 17th 1577 order a letter to be sent to Mr Hannam, the Recorder of Bristol, who was then practicing in the Westminster courts, to describe the problem and enclose samples of the coins. The Recorder recommended that the city councillors should introduce a general stamp. Acting on this advice, £30 worth of official tokens were minted the following year. Subsequent batches were issued throughout the reign of Queen Elizabeth I. These authorised copper tokens were square and beared the letters C.B. on one side and the city's coat of arms on the other. They are also known as Bristol Farthings. The issue of the coins did not, however, stop some rogues trying to forge them, for in March 1587 Christopher Callwey was convicted of counterfeiting the tokens and fined £5. Other swindlers were at work, for at the command of the government, the corporation bought 12,600 false tokens the following month. (John Latimer, *Annals of Bristol*, Kingsmead, 1970)

# November 18th

**1745:** Bristol Consistory Court issued an unusual faculty on this date signed by the Revd William Cary, Vicar-General of the bishopric, which granted permission for John Coopey to practice medicine in the city. The faculty was granted owing to Coopey's extensive knowledge of the subject, and as proof of Coopey's skill a tract written by him on the treatment of diabetes was referred to. It is unusual that Bristol's ecclesiastical authorities still claimed the right to issue degrees and licences of this character. A previous attempt to regulate medicine in 1670, when the Chancellor of the diocese attempted to force all surgeons to take out a licence allowing them to practice, was resisted by the corporation, who forbade compliance and the diocesan authorities backed down. Today only the Archbishop of Canterbury uses his power to award degrees. These can be awarded in the following areas: divinity, law, medicine, the arts and music. The Archbishop has had the power to award academic degrees since 1533, when the Peter's Pence Act was passed. Candidates can be awarded these honorary degrees by nomination. (John Latimer, *Annals of Bristol*, Kingsmead, 1970)

# November 19th

**1886:** William Owen, described as 'a rough looking customer', was sentenced to three months' hard labour as a rogue and a vagabond. The prisoner left the dock cursing the magistrates. (*Bristol Mercury and Daily Post*)

---

**1888:** Alexander Harris, 30, a grocer of Cotham, was convicted for selling adulterated pepper at Bristol Police Court. An inspector went into the shop and asked for a quarter pound of pepper. Analysis showed that the sample was found to contain 8 per cent sand and 10 per cent vegetable matter, which was mainly ground rice. The defendent stated that the pepper was part of the stock of the previous shop owner, and that it was his wife, and not he, who had supplied the inspector. Harris was fined 10 shillings plus costs. (*Bristol Mercury and Daily Post*)

---

**1985:** The problem with what to do with Bristol's rubbish led to a refuse transfer station being opened at Westerleigh Sidings, located to the north of the city, to take refuge away by train. The scheme ran until 2001, when the last train departed from the transfer terminal on March 30th that year. (Colin G. Maggs, *Branch Lines of Gloucestershire*, Alan Sutton, 1991 / www.bristol-rail.co.uk)

# November 20th

**1997:** The statue of Rajah Rammohun Roy was unveiled on College Green by Dr L.M. Singir, the High Commissioner for India, in the presence of the Lord Mayor of Bristol, Jack Fisk, marking the occasion of the Golden Jubilee of India's independence. Rammohun was born on May 12th 1772 in Radhengar, located in the Burdan District of Bengal. Rammohun seems to have made his fortune dealing in East India Company stock and as an interpreter. His work with the East India Company made him familiar with Western values. From 1815 Rammohun lived in Calcutta, where he published widely on political and religious subjects. On religious matters he believed that all religions are true as they teach that God created the universe, but false as religions add unnecessary and contradictory beliefs. He was one of India's leading thinkers and became known to British readers through his publications in missionary journals. Rammohun also established some of India's first newspapers, in 1822. In 1830, he travelled to England as ambassador of the Mughal emperor, Akbar II. The last three weeks of his life were spent in Bristol amongst Unitarian friends. He died on September 27th 1883, suffering from fever and inflammation of the brain. He is interred in Arnos Vale Cemetery. (*Oxford Dictionary of National Biography*, OUP / *Author's field notes*)

# November 21st

**1888:** A fatal explosion took place in the Bathurst Basin in Bristol Harbour when a Jersey ketch, *The United*, which was carrying 300 barrels of highly volatile naphtha, was ignited. Since the vessel was due to set sail within a matter of hours, the captain and crew were all on board and consequently died. A policeman was watching her within 2 yards of the quay when 'the whole cargo exploded just as the officer had been speaking to the captain and three men on the deck. The policeman was felled by a huge piece of timber from the vessel's side, and when he got up he saw the whole vessel in one mass of flames. The deck was gone and the flames were leaping to a height of 60ft.' The force of the explosion caused all the windows, over 1,000 panes of glass, of the nearby General Hospital to be smashed, and led to the closure of four wards. Through the efforts of the fire brigade, policemen and dockyard workers, the adjoining buildings were saved, including a linseed and cotton oil store, which contained many tons of oil. Nothing could extinguish the flames and the fire eventually simply burnt itself out. (*The Times*)

# November 22nd

**1859:** Clifton was well known for the problem of insufficient space in its parish churches. Joseph Leech, writing in 1843, states that the main parish church 'the rich and the non-resident occupy the reserved seats, and those few that are still normally free are filled by servants' of their masters.' Leech goes on to say, 'The rich must worship it is true, as well as the poor, and agreeable spectacle as it is to see the poor attend in truth and sincerity, the rich joining in the services of the church in humbleness and reverence are still more gratifying sight; but the poor ought not to be kept out of their own parish church – from the pews by the rich, and from the free seats by their powdered footmen.' By 1858 the incumbent of Clifton urged his parishioners of Christ Church to add isles to increase capacity. The parishioners, however, preferred to add the tower and the spire according to the original design by Charles Dyer. This was completed on this date in 1859. A workman celebrating the completion of the tower stood on his head on the capstone, a height of 212ft (64.6m). (John Latimer, *Annals of Bristol*, Kingsmead, 1970 / *The Bristol Times* / Nikolaus Pevsner, *The Buildings of England: North Somerset and Bristol*, Penguin, 1958)

# November 23rd

1880: The execution of William Joseph Distin, who was executed for the murder of a widow named Daniels with whom he cohabited, took place within the precincts of Bristol Gaol. The execution was grimly recounted in contemporary newspapers. Distin had a history of offences from drunkenness to violent assault. Prior to his execution, penitence gripped the prisoner and he slept little during the days before his execution and had lost his appetite. When he was led out to die he had to be supported by the warders and was scarcely able to stand without assistance. His last words before he was hanged were 'Lord have mercy on me!' The Lord's Prayer was read aloud by the prison chaplain as the prisoner disappeared into the well below the scaffold. The first execution at the jail was that of John Horwood in 1821, who was hanged for the murder of Eliza Balsum, a girl with whom he had become infatuated. His body was taken to the Bristol Royal Infirmary to allow surgeon Richard Smith to carry out a dissection before one of his classes. In a gruesome twist, Smith had Horwood's skin preserved, tanned and used to cover a book containing an account of Horwood's trial and execution. The book is currently held in the city's Record Office. (*The Star* / BBC News website)

# November 24th

**1940:** German bombing raids on the city started. They continued until May 15th 1944, and were known as the Bristol Blitz. Air-raid warnings sounded at 6.21 p.m., when sixty enemy planes descended on the city. The raid destroyed 10,000 homes and several prominent landmarks, including St Nicholas' Church, Dr White's Almshouses in Temple Street, Princes Theatre and the Freemasons' Hall. Joan Westcott recalls that she, her mother and grandmother were waiting for a bus back home to Kingswood when the air was filled with the sound of low-flying aircraft. 'The noise increased and at the same time a brilliant light dropped from the sky and landed about three feet away from us. Being a shy seven-year-old I whispered, "Oh! Look Mum a fairy!" My mother gasped, "No! It's a flare!" as she pushed us back to the wall of the building. We stood transfixed as other flares dropped near us; people were running, like ants, in all directions and as the noise of the aircraft increased three sailors ran up to us, picked me up and told my mother and gran to follow them.' They sheltered in an unfinished air-raid shelter. The raid continued until 12.08 a.m., when the all clear was sounded. (*Western Daily Press* / Reece Winstone, *Bristol in the 1940s*, 1961)

# November 25th

Today marks the feast of St Catherine, whose cult was particularly celebrated during the Middle Ages. St Catherine was venerated as a fourth-century martyr, who was devoted to learning. When the wheel on which she was to be broken, the Catherine Wheel, fell in pieces, she was subsequently beheaded. In the parishes surrounding St Thomas in Bedminster, a custom known as 'going-a-Kattering' was for a long time observed by spinsters and female wool spinners on St Catherine's Day. Here the women would insist on their 'right' to kiss any eligible young man in sight. (F.C. Jones, *The Glory that was Bristol*, St Stephen's Bristol Press, 1946)

———— • ◆ • ————

**1753:** George Whitfield, one of the founders of Methodism, opened a chapel in Bristol for accommodation of his followers. Like the chapel Whitfield founded in London, it was known as the Tabernacle. Whitfield recorded that the chapel was 'large, but not large enough; would the place contain them, I believe near as many would attend as in London.' When communion was celebrated at the Tabernacle, as much as two gallons of wine were needed. Seating in the galleries was separated, with a section for men and another for women. (John Latimer, *Annals of Bristol*, Kingsmead, 1970)

# November 26th

**2003:** The last flight of Concorde took place – it was a special flight from Heathrow to Filton. Thousands lined the streets surrounding Filton Airfield and around Clifton Suspension Bridge, where the plane was due to make a fly-over. Concorde 216, which was constructed in 1979, left Heathrow at 11.29 a.m. under the command of Captain Les Brodie with chief pilot Mike Bannister also in the cockpit. One hundred BA staff who had worked on Concorde were also on board. Before landing at Filton the plane flew overhead at 2,000ft (610m). The Duke of York welcomed the flight receiving the plane on behalf of the people of Bristol. The last commercial flight, when Concorde flew supersonic, took place on November 24th, flying from New York to Heathrow. Most of the passengers on this occasion were celebrities, including Joan Collins, who told reporters that, 'The first time I ever flew Concorde was a bit of a white knuckle ride. I am more used to it now, it's so wonderful to make the journey in three and a half hours.' Jets of red, white and blue water had been sprayed over the plane at John F. Kennedy Airport to symbolise the colours of the American, French and British flags in celebration of the last flight. (*The Times* / BBC News website)

# November 27th

**1758:** Actress Mary Darby was born in College Green. She was regarded as a beauty and received her first proposal of marriage when she was just 13 from a naval officer, who thought she was 16. She married Thomas Robinson but, after two years, they were both thrown into prison because of her husband's debts. On her release, she returned to the stage and was billed as 'Perdita' in a performance of Shakespeare's *A Winter's Tale*. This was watched by the Prince of Wales, who immediately fell in love with her. The Prince promised her £20,000 if she would become his mistress when she came of age. The King, embarrassed at the actions of his son, offered £5,000 to get the love letters between them back and soon the Prince's affections were transferred elsewhere. Mary moved to Paris to continue acting, where she met Col. Banistre Tarleton. When he got into monetary difficulties she travelled far to help him. The journey affected her health and she became paralysed. She wished to return to Hotwells to take the waters but had insufficient funds and died at Englefield in Surrey on December 26th 1800. (Marguerite Fedden, *Bristol Vignettes*, Burleigh Press, 1957)

# November 28th

**1919:** Designer Frank Barnwell of the Bristol Aeroplane Company first proposed a small single-seater aircraft for sale to private owners and especially for ex-servicemen who wanted to continue to fly cheaply after demobilisation after the war. The Bristol Babe biplane was born, which had a wingspan of only 19ft 8in (5.99m). Barnwell installed his own 45hp Viale Radial engine into the plane for the test flight. The first flight took place unexpectedly on this date in 1919 when Cyril Unwins, the Bristol Aeroplane Company's test pilot, intending only to do some preliminary taxiing, was forced to take off in order to avoid a flock of sheep on Filton Airfield. Development continued on the aircraft and an incomplete Siddeley Ounce engine was installed for the Paris Salon in December 1919 and priced with selling price of £400 ex-works. Later, the first two aircraft were fitted with a specially tuned and modified 60hp Le Rhône engine. Only three aircraft were subsequently built. The 45hp Viale engine was stored until 1959, when it was rediscovered in a garage at Alveston, Gloucestershire. The engine was restored by Bristol Siddeley Engines Ltd and presented to the Royal Aeronautical Society. In 1963 the engine was placed in the London Science Museum. (C.H. Barnes, *Bristol Aircraft Since 1910*, Putnam, 1970)

# November 29th

**1921:** The Whiteladies Picture House is opened by the Duchess of Beaufort. The first film shown was *Polyanna,* staring Mary Pickford. The building was designed by James Henry La Trobe and Thomas Henry Weston and included a tower with the cinema's name in concrete on the top. Inside, the entrance hall included columns of marble from Italy and a mosaic floor. There were a series of eight murals inside the auditorium which included depictions of the Pied Piper of Hamlin, the First Voyage of Sinbad the Sailor, Ali Baba in the Robber's Cave, the Magic Carpet, the Greeks setting out to rescue Helen from the Trojans, Alice in Wonderland and the New Marriage of Omar Khayam. When 'talkies' came to Bristol cinemas in 1929, the Whiteladies Road cinema held out, showing 'silent movies' and advertising itself as 'home of the silents'. Patrons, however, wanted to hear as well as see their films and eventually the cinema began to show 'talkies'. In 1978 the cinema was converted into a three-screen cinema. The cinema remained opened until 2002, when it closed despite protests from such prominent celebrities as Tony Robinson, Nick Park – the creator of Wallace and Gromit – and actor Paul McGann. The cinema remains closed at the time of writing. (Dave Stephenson & Jill Willmott, *Bristol Cinemas*, The History Press, 2005 / BBC News website)

# November 30th

**1852:** *The Times* reported an attack by a bear in Bristol on a man called Fitzgerald, who was employed on a timber yard, where the proprietor owned the animal. Fitzgerald had gone to feed the bear when the animal attacked him, forcing its teeth through the fleshy part of Fitzgerald's arm, severely lacerating the limb, which required treatment at Bristol Infirmary. It was not the only time a Bristolian was attacked by a wild animal from overseas. On September 14th 1831, John Johnson was employed by Mr Wombell as a watchman to a caravan of wild beasts that were being exhibited in Bristol. Johnson had become intoxicated and at 7 a.m. opened the shutters to the lion's cage to show his friends the animal. Since the lion was asleep Johnson tugged at its mane in order to wake it. The lion, however, using its paw, dragged Johnson against the iron bars and in an instant clawed at Johnson's arm, stripping away enough flesh from the arm so that the bone was exposed. Johnson only escaped when the lion had bitten off part of his arm. The rest of the limb was amputated at the Bristol Infirmary. (*The Times*)

# December 1st

**1841:** The opening of St Philip's Bridge, connecting the parishes of SS Philip and Jacob and Temple, took place. The bridge was designed in mock-Tudor style by Mr Gravatt. The opening of the bridge was accompanied by a large procession involving the contractor Mr Bromhead and his workmen, Filer's Brass Band, who played 'God Save the Queen', the Beadle of Temple Parish and the Temple Blue Coat Boys, the Corporation Beadle, the Mayor and his officers, Mr Gravatt, Mr Townsend the surveyor, clergy of the parishes and many more besides. After the official ceremony the bridge was open for use by the general public. (*Bristol Mercury*)

———— • ◆ • ————

**1883:** Bristol Rovers, who were then known as the Black Arabs, played their first match, a friendly, and would go on to play another nine further matches in their first season. The club was formed following a meeting of five young men in a restaurant in Stapleton Road. Their original name was derived from the black shirts worn by the players and a local rugby club known as the Arabs, who played on a nearby pitch at Purdown in East Bristol. After their first season the club gained the nickname of the 'Purdown Poachers'. (Bristol Rovers website)

# December 2nd

**1657:** A letter from Oliver Cromwell to Bristol Corporation warned of Royalist conspiracies in the city: 'Trustie and well beloved, we greete you well: remembering well the late expressions of love that I have had from you, I cannot omit any opportunitie to expresse my care of you. I do hear on all hands, that the Cavalier party designing to put us into blood. We are, I hope, taking the best care we can, by the blessing of God, to obviate this danger. But our intelligence on all hands being, that they have a design upon your cittie, we could not but warne you thereof, and give you authoritie, as we doe hereby, to put yourselves into the best posture you can for your own defence, raising your militia, by virtue of the commission formerly sent to you, and putting them in readinesse for the purpose aforesaid; letting you also knowe that for your better encouragement herein, you shall have a troop of horse sent you, to quarter in or neare your towne. We desire you to let us heare from time to time what occurs touching the malignant partie, and so we bid you farewell.' (John Chilcott, *Chilcott's Descriptive History of Bristol*, J. Chilcott, 1849)

# December 3rd

**1918:** The first choice for headmaster of Clifton College had been the Revd C. Evans but he had instead taken the headmastership of a Birmingham school. Fredrick Temple, headmaster at Rugby, recommended Revd John Percival for the post when Clifton College first opened on September 30th 1862. Clifton College was established at a meeting – with the Mayor presiding – in order to establish a first-class public school for the education of the sons of gentlemen. Under Percival this aim was achieved largely through his careful choice of masters. He left Clifton College in 1879 to become president of Trinity College, Oxford. His work outside the college was arguably more significant, including becoming chairman of the committee to found Sommerville Hall, Oxford, a non-denominational college for women and promoting the university adult education movement. From 1882 to 1887 he was canon of Bristol Cathedral where he resided during university vacations and he started Sunday evening services there. From May 1887 he became headmaster of Rugby School and was nominated to the bishopric of Hereford in January 1895. He retired in 1917 to Oxford and died on this date. He was buried in the crypt of the chapel of Clifton College. (John Latimer, *Annals of Bristol*, Kingsmead, 1970 / *Oxford Dictionary of National Biography*, OUP)

# December 4th

1814: The Bristol mail coach was robbed of several banknotes and bills to a considerable amount. The man arrested, James Walker, who went under the alias Sheridan, was also believed to be responsible for a considerable number of other mail coach robberies. When he was arrested previously, the prosecution withdrew proceedings on condition that Walker entered the 50th Regiment. However, Walker soon deserted and he was again at large. On the present occasion the parcel in question was discovered missing when the Bristol mail coach arrived at its destination, the Swan with Two Necks public house in London. Walker was soon suspected when a respectable linen draper in the vicinity became suspicious after Walker attempted to purchase some goods from his shop with a £10 note. The linen draper expressed some concern of its genuineness, whereupon Walker produced six others to the same value, and, when asked how he came by so many new notes, Walker replied that he had taken them in change from a £100 note after arriving from Salisbury. It was the information provided by the linen draper that led to Walker's arrest. (*The Times*)

# December 5th

**1958:** The first trunk dialled phone call took place today during a ceremony held at the Bristol Central Telephone Exchange, where the Queen made a long-distance phone call to the Lord Provost of Edinburgh, over 300 miles away. The call lasted two minutes and five seconds and cost only 10*d*. Under the old system, with an operator involved, the call would have cost 3*s* 9*d* and thus represented a significant saving. Trunk dialling allowed the caller to make long-distance calls without the aid of an operator and 18,000 subscribing Bristolians were the first to make use of the service. It was hoped that £15 million would be saved from halving the number of 50,000 operators currently employed by the General Post Office. The new system was later launched from a public call box the following year. The last manual telephone exchange in the UK, at Portree in the Isle of Skye, closed in 1976, making the British telephone system fully automatic. British Telecom took over the running of the telephone system from the Post Office in 1981. (BBC website / *Daily Telegraph*)

# December 6th

Before the Reformation a ceremony of the boy bishop would take place in many cathedrals and churches on this date, which is also the feast date of St Nicholas, the patron saint of children. If a bishop was present the Magnificat (Luke 1: 46-55) would be recited and at the point of the Magnificat which states 'he has put down the mighty from their seats and has exalted the humble and meek' the bishop would step down from his throne and a boy would take his place and be clothed with episcopal vestments with mitre and crosier. The ceremony was similar in parish churches although no bishop would be present. In places like Bristol, which did not have a cathedral until 1542, the ceremony took place at St Nicholas's Church where a boy, probably a server of the parish priest, was instituted as bishop and gave a sermon in the church before the Mayor and Common Council, after which the boy would pronounce his blessing on them. The authority of the boy bishop would last until Holy Innocents' Day on December 28th. The ceremony was abolished under Henry VIII during the Reformation in 1542. (John Latimer, *Annals of Bristol*, Kingsmead, 1970)

# December 7th

1880: A number of petty thefts were brought to the attention of the Bristol Police Court. Joseph Llewellyn was charged with stealing two sheets and table napkins to the value of 5s from the residence of Revd H.J Wiseman. He was interrupted by a domestic servant, whereupon he asked for some bread but was refused. His crime was discovered when the servant later discovered items missing from the pantry. Charles Morgan, an unemployed baker, was also charged with stealing a pair of stockings from a shop in Castle Street. His crime was witnessed by Henry Dutton, an errand boy, who followed Morgan and alerted the authorities. Dutton was awarded 2s 6d by the court for his trouble. (*Bristol Mercury and Daily Post*)

———— • ◆ • ————

2001: A sculpture of Hollywood actor Cary Grant was unveiled in the Millennium Square. The unveiling was carried out by Barbara James, Grant's widow. Cary Grant was born in the city's Horfield suburb. The statue was created by Graham Ibbeson from Barnsley, who was also responsible for a sculpture of Eric Morecambe. Bristol-based writer David Long had campaigned for the statue and raised approximately £60,000 towards it. (*The Guardian*)

# December 8th

1864: The formal opening of the Clifton Suspension Bridge took place with a procession of trades and friendly societies – over a mile in length – which marched through the city to Clifton Down, where a large crowd of spectators had gathered. The first to pass over the bridge were the resident engineer and bridge workers, followed by the Lords Lieutenant of Somerset and Bristol. A banquet held in the Victoria Rooms ended the day's proceedings. (John Latimer, *Annals of Bristol*, Kingsmead, 1970)

———— • ❖ • ————

1874: An ecclesiastical court case took place before commissioners appointed by Bishop Ellicott. The case started when Henry Jenkins, who doubted the presence of demonical spirits, sent a revised version of the Bible omitting passages he considered unsuitable for children to Revd Flavel Cook, vicar of Christ Church, who took little interest. Later, Cook preached a series of sermons against ritualism, which Jenkins objected to, and he wrote critically to the vicar and called to mind the book that he had sent. It was then that Cook looked at the volume and thought it 'a systematic and wicked mutilation of the bible' and consequently refused to let Jenkins communicate at his church. The court upheld Cook's actions owning to Jenkins' sceptical views of the devil, although the judgement was later overturned on appeal. (John Latimer, *Annals of Bristol*, Kingsmead, 1970)

# December 9th

**1824:** The unwrapping of an Egyptian mummy took place at the Bristol Institute. The unwrapping was undertaken by Dr Pritchard, surgeon Dr Grapper and Richard Smith, the curator, and witnessed by an invited audience. The audience was limited to the institution's shareholders, honorary fellows and associates, and friends of Mr Ganard, the donor of the mummy. Despite these restrictions, several people were able to gather for the event. The mummy had been taken from a catacomb in Thebais. The coffin was full of hieroglyphs and when opened 'there arose a particular but not unpleasant odour'. The body was wrapped in many layers of cloth with the innermost layers described as being soaked in naptha and asphaltum, with a layer of natron in order to preserve the body. When the body was revealed it was thought to be a young female. Richard Smith then pointed out the difference between the bodies preserved by antiseptics, and those converted in our cemeteries, by moisture, into the substance called adipocere. To demonstrate this point Smith showed the audience the heart of Sheriff Yeamans, who was executed in Wine Street by Cromwell's officer, Colonel Fiennes, on May 30th 1643, as 'being quite perfect, after having lost the vital spark 171 years!' (*The Times*)

# December 10th

**1933:** Every year since 1901 the Nobel Prize has been awarded on the anniversary of the death of Alfred Nobel, whose will allowed for the provision of the award, and in 1933 Paul Adrien Maurice Dirac shared the Nobel Prize for physics. Dirac was born in August 8th 1902 in Bristol and attended the Merchant Venturers School before studying electrical engineering at Bristol University. He gained his BSc in 1921 and spent a further two years at the university studying mathematics. Next Dirac studied at St John's College, Cambridge, where he gained his PhD in 1926. In 1927 he became a Fellow of St John's and in 1932 he was made Laucasian Professor of Mathematics. His work focused on the mathematical and theoretical aspects of quantum mechanics. Dirac's most significant contribution to physics was his study of wave mechanics and applying this knowledge to link the mathematically distinct theories of relativity and quantum theory. Together with Erwin Schrodinger he was awarded the Nobel Prize for physics 'for the discovery of new productive forms of atomic theory' in 1933. He was elected Fellow of the Royal Society in 1930. Throughout his career Dirac travelled extensively, studying at various universities throughout the world. He died on October 20th 1984. (Nobel Prize Awards website)

# December 11th

**1844:** Although Isambard Kingdom Brunel's ship the SS *Great Britain* was ready to steam away down the Avon to the open sea at the beginning of the year, the trip could not be made as the necessary Act of Parliament required to widen the Cumberland Lock had not been passed. It was not until December 1844 that the Great Western Steam Ship Company removed masonry in the Cumberland Basin locks and a footbridge across the lock, allowing access for the *Great Britain*. A high tide was also necessary to carry the ship high in the lock and the first attempt to pass the ship through the lock was made on this date. The east wind meant that the tide was much lower than expected and when she was three-quarters of the way in, the ship scraped the side of the lock. She was pulled back out of the lock and frantic work on widening the lock was made to ensure that the *Great Britain* made it out on the last spring tide of the season. Fortunately the alterations worked, for the following day the SS *Great Britain* was finally towed downriver towards the Bristol Channel. (Adrian Vaughn, *Isambard Kingdom Brunel*, John Murray, 1991)

# December 12th

**1705:** Sir William Lewis made a representation to the council, complaining 'that the great noise made by trucks in this city by means of the iron materials on about them is a great annoyance to the inhabitants of the city thereof.' The meeting resolved that no carts of this type should be permitted and the only iron materials allowed would be the banding of iron around the wheels. A fine of 3s 4d would be levied for perpetrators of this new offence. Despite Sir William's attempts, great difficulty was had in enforcing the new bylaw, which was frequently broken. (John Latimer, *Annals of Bristol*, Kingsmead, 1970)

**1815:** 'Mr Stokes, a pedestrian at Bristol, has just accomplished an undertaking of walking 1000 miles in twenty successive days. He has done this with the greatest apparent ease. It would seem from this and with other specimens, that the man is hardly aware of his full capabilities. We are almost disposed to believe that as the human being surpasses all other animals in intelligence so he would be found their superior (if proper experiments were made) in every possible combination or application of strength, active and passive.' (*The Times*)

# December 13th

**1860:** A daring robbery took place at the Broadmead premises of Mr James Jacobs, pawnbroker, silversmith and jeweller. An estimated £800 worth of jewellery was taken. The rear of the property was protected by a 12ft-high wall, which was covered in glass. Amazingly no glass was broken to indicate where the thieves may have clambered over. The locks on Jacob's property 'were hardly of so secure a character as to have been desirable', which would have allowed the thieves to enter without a great deal of violence. It is possible that the maid may have forgotten to bolt the outer door. A lock was taken off a door communicating with the shop parlour and from here a window pane was removed from another door which led to the shop in order to gain access. A quantity of jewellery was taken but, amazingly, the robbers missed some valuable pledges which were left. Jacobs, a light sleeper, did not hear anything nor did the policeman on the beat see anything unusual. John and Mary Ann Lucas were the only people arrested for the robbery, but, although the police seized some housebreaking equipment, theirs did not match the marks left at the Broadmead robbery and they were discharged. (*Bristol Mercury and Daily Post*)

# December 14th

**1868:** Emma Saunders appeared at the Council House charged with stealing more than £5 from Walter Graver. Graver was on his way to the north of the country to a take up a position but was currently staying at The Patriot on Temple Street. Here he had consumed several pints of beer when a young man introduced himself and Graver agreed to go with the young man, who promised to introduce him to his sister, who 'would take good care of him'. Emma Saunders took him to a house on Church Street and plied Graver with more beer. A while later Graver was lying in the street, being woken by a police constable. It was then that he discovered that all of his money was gone. Graver could remember nothing of what happened to him prior to being found by the policeman. The magistrates were less than impressed with Graver and told him that he had paid the price for drunkenness. Emma Saunders was discharged with a caution. (Nicola Sly, *A Grim Almanac of Bristol*, The History Press, 2011)

# December 15th

**1798:** *Felix Farley's Journal* of this date contained an article on the lack of entertainment in Bristol, stating that 'the deficiency of public amusements in the populous and opulent city is not only a constant source of complaint to persons visiting it, but also the subject of frequent regret to the greater number of the respectable inhabitants.' This was not the only complaint about Bristol on this matter; a letter in *Monthly Magazine* stated that 'Perhaps there is no place in England where public and social amusements are so little attended as to here.' The writer went on to say how Bristolians were ridiculed by others for their apparent lack of taste. (John Latimer, *Annals of Bristol*, Kingsmead, 1970)

———— ◆ ————

**1925:** Flight-Lieutenant D.C. Anderson, who was flying over Bristol, had a lucky escape when his plane crash-landed onto the roof of a garage. Hanging nose down, the plane burst into flames and set the garage alight. Anderson, however, managed to unstrap himself from the plane and escaped, suffering a 'badly scorched face' and severe burns to his knee and heel. Witnesses stated that the plane hit the ground first before being bounced up and onto the roof. Four motorcars that were inside the garage were destroyed. (*The Times*)

# December 16th

**1912:** The Bristol Hippodrome opens. The theatre was designed by Frank Matcham and possessed several interesting features, including a water tank whose 100,000-gallon capacity could be filled in one minute. A single lever also raised a glass screen to protect the orchestra from the resulting spray. A variety of circus, stage and aquatic acts could thus be performed. The water tank does not survive today. The theatre also has a domed roof, which can be opened to reveal the sky and keep the theatre cool. It is a unique feature of any theatre in the UK. The rear portion of the theatre was gutted in a fire on February 18th 1947. Through the efforts of the fire brigade the fire was halted at the orchestra pit with limited damage to the auditorium. The cause was thought to be a discarded match. On December 24th 1947 the theatre was re-opened to a performance of *Cinderella*. Unfortunately the curtain failed to open during the second act and Ted Ray, who was playing Buttons, found himself ad-libbing for almost half an hour whilst members of the theatre and even members of the audience battled to get the curtains open. (Bristol Hippodrome website / www.arthurlloyd.co.uk – a music hall and theatre history website)

# December 17th

**1851:** *The Times* reported a severe gas explosion which took place in the city at around 11.30 a.m.: 'The inhabitants of Temple Street ... were much alarmed by a loud explosion, which sounded like the report of a canon. The shop windows of Mr William Hitchman, grocer, were blown into the street, as well as some of the windows of Mr King, boot and shoemaker, two doors above. In addition to these, two premises the adjoining houses were much shaken. Such was the force of the explosion that the whole of the flooring in the parlour was torn up in and the door forcibly rent form its heavy iron hinges. The house was so much shaken that Mr Hitchman was afraid it would have fallen in on him. A portion of the chimneypiece was knocked off and projected nearly through the ceiling. The windows and a great deal of the flooring of Mr King's house were also blown up.' The cause of the explosion was a leaking gas pipe in Water Lane, where the gas had penetrated into the drain running under the premises, 'and mingling with the foul air of the drain, formed an explosive mixture.' (*The Times*)

# December 18th

**1851:** An inquest took place on this date into a fatal accident at the Lower Soundwell Colliery, where a boiler exploded, killing Thomas Walker. The explosion blew up the engine house and scattered bricks and tiles in every direction, injuring another man also in the engine house. The cause of the explosion was excessive pressure in the boiler. At the inquest it was found that the boiler had no steam gauge with which to measure the pressure. Although the safety valve had been examined about an hour before the incident, the opinion was expressed that if another safety valve had been fitted then the accident need never have happened. The coroner expressed his regret that the colliery did not employ engineers as the men employed to work on the engine were ignorant as to its workings. The jury took time to reach their decision but at length a verdict of accidental death was recorded. It was also reported that the case had excited a great deal of interest in the neighbourhood and it was suggested that the only remedy for mining accidents was the appointment of a government inspector to visit the district's collieries and enforce colliery owners to carry out preventative safety measures. (*The Times / Bristol Mercury*)

# December 19th

**1800:** A lady simply known as Louisa or 'the lady of the haystack' died at Guy's Hospital in London. The origins of this story go back to 1776, when a young, beautiful girl with graceful manners called upon a house in Flax Bourton, a village just south of Bristol. Afterwards she wandered the fields and took shelter underneath a haystack. Village women saw to it that she was fed but Louisa refused the shelter of a house. Later she was removed to St Peter's Hospital in Bristol, but on her release she returned to the shelter of the haystack. She was befriended by the writer and philanthropist Hannah More, who, in 1781, ensured she was safely removed to a private asylum in Hanham. Eventually her condition deteriorated and she was moved to Guy's Hospital. Louisa never spoke of her origins, giving rise to much contemporary speculation. G.H. Glasse, writing in 1801, sought to identify her as a daughter of Emperor Francis I of Austria, who was abandoned when the emperor died. However, it is unlikely that the mystery of her origins will be solved. (John Latimer, *Annals of Bristol*, Kingsmead, 1970 / George S. Master, *The History of Flax Bourton*, Nailsea & District Local History Society, 2009 / G.H. Glasse, *The Affecting History of Louisa*, A. Neil, 1804)

# December 20th

**1629:** 'At night died Captain John Dowghtie, an alderman of Bristoll, and was solemnly buried according to his desert on the 5th of January. In respect that at his death he was the eldest captain of our trained bands, and was the first president of the military yard and a good benefactor thereunto, he was not only honoured by the captains, assistants and company of the same, but also by all the trained soldiers of our city, in warlike manner. Among whom the corporals of his own band (expressing their loves bountifully) at their own charges bestowed 74 chambers and one piece of brass ordnance, which were discharged upon the castle walls in good order, as the army marched before the corpse, coming from his house at Read Crosse along the Weare; from thence he was carried to Alsaincts Church, where after sermon at his interring all our musketeers gave him 3 volleys of shot, which were presently seconded by 6 pieces of great ordnance in the Marsh which were heard far off as strangers affirmed.' (William Adams, *Adams's Chronicle of Bristol*, J.W. Arrowsmith, 1910)

# December 21st

**1720:** Scorpio Africanus, a pageboy to Charles William, Earl of Suffolk, died. At this time Bristol was heavily involved in the slave trade, where ships would sail from ports such as Bristol to West Africa carrying manufactured goods in exchange for slaves who would then be shipped to the Carribean Islands, where they would work on plantations of sugar, cotton and tobacco. These goods would then be shipped back to Britain. Scorpio Africanus was an exception to this in that he ended up as a pageboy in a stately home rather than a plantation. At the time it was fashionable to have such boys as curiosities and to give them Roman-sounding names. The inscription on his gravestone, located in Henbury churchyard, shows clearly contemporary attitudes: 'Here Lieth the Body of SCORPIO AFRICANUS Negro Servant to ye Right Honerable Charles William Earl of Suffolk and Brandon Who died ye 21 December 1720, Aged 18 Years. I who was born a PAGAN and a SLAVE Now sweetly sleep a Christian in my grave, What tho' my hue was dark my grace to me my Lord on Earth has given To recommend me to my Lord in heaven, Whose glorious second coming here I wait With Saints and Angels to Celebrate.' (*Author's field notes*)

# December 22nd

**1847:** During the course of 1847 three new churches were built to accommodate the expanding population. The churches were all by Bristol architect S.B. Gabriel and the first was consecrated on this date in 1847. St Mark's, Lower Easton was consecrated on May 18th 1848 and St Jude's, Poyntz Pool was opened in June 1849. The three buildings cost £2,500 each. St Simon's is now home to the Greek Othodox Church of St Peter and St Paul. Its spire, originally 121ft tall, has been truncated, as the orthodox community were unable to secure funds for its repair. Inside, a number of the Anglo-Catholic fittings survive, augmented by icons and rich fittings. St Mark's Church was originally designed by Charles Dyer, who died before the building was completed, and so Gabriel supervised the work until completion. The church is designed in a neo-Norman style, which was popular between the mid-1840s and the mid-1850s. The final service of Holy Communion was held on May 18th 1984 and the building has now been converted into supported housing. St Jude's was also converted into housing in 2004/5. (John Latimer, *Annals of Bristol*, Kingsmead, 1970 / Nikolaus Pevsner, *The Buildings of England: North Somerset and Bristol*, Penguin, 1958 / www.churchcrawler. pwp.blueyonder.co.uk/pmdraper10/bristol1.htm – a website dedicated to Bristol's churches)

# December 23rd

**1904:** At 9.55 p.m., the 3.45 p.m. train from Crewe to Bristol ran into the 11 a.m. goods train from Pontypool Road at Stapleton Road. The goods train had just begun to move forward when it was struck by the passenger train. The collision caused the goods train, consisting of locomotive, tender, thirty-nine wagons and brake van to become detached and the part of the train moved off with the driver unaware of the accident. Six wagons remained at the scene of the accident; one truck, the seventh from the tail end of the train, rolled forward and came to a halt at the Stapleton Road signal box. The separation of the train was caused by the couplings become detached from the force of the impact rather than the couplings becoming broken. Fortunately the driver of the passenger train was slowing down owing to signals ahead being at red and no one was seriously injured or killed. Many of the passengers were able to transfer to another train whilst others were able to walk the short distance back to Stapleton Road station. The cause of the accident was put down to an error by the signalman allowing two trains on the same stretch of track. (*Accident Returns* published by the Board of Trade)

# December 24th

**1843:** Joseph Leech gives this account of attending St Thomas' Church: 'Like Christmastide today it was not the '"frosty and kindly" of other days – for no one seemed cold, and all most unnaturally temperate.' Yet there the holly berries 'were peeping out in little clusters from amongst very green and hardy leaves.' Coming inside the church, Leech is shown to a 'commodious' pew. From here he describes the church interior. The classical architecture of the church contained square box pews arranged so 'that people have a sociable and most neighbourly way of looking in one another's faces,' nevertheless, it 'imparts a certain appearance of irregularity to the whole.' Leech described the congregation as being 'ranked under the class called comfortable.' His view of the chancel was restricted by the pulpit, reading desk, a row of red curtains, and 'a lofty churchwardens' pew'. The two churchwardens, perhaps stereotypically, were described as 'grave-looking' and 'who seemed all as demure as if the parish were in debt'. The sermon was based on the book of Revelation and Leech admitted that he felt nervous at this point 'lest the preacher should get into any kind of those extraordinary speculations which sometimes result in any rash attempt to unravel the figures and terms of that mysterious book.' (*Bristol Times*)

# December 25th

**1654:** During the Protectorate, Oliver Cromwell decreed that Christmas Day should be a day of national fasting rather than a day of celebration. However, the ordinance met with stout resistance from some quarters. A riot in Bristol broke out on December 18th 1654 after some city apprentices took offence at Quakers and tried to force them to shut their places of business. The following day magistrates of the city, after being defied by a mob, gathered around the Tolzey and issued a proclamation commanding that all persons refrain from civil disorder. Despite this the disturbances continued on subsequent days involving around 1,500 people with cries for the exiled king, Charles Stewart. On Christmas Day another proclamation was issued in the name of the Protector, requiring that all apprentices return to their occupations and that the shops should remain open upon this day. This had an adverse reaction with rioting by the apprentices, which was openly encouraged by their employers. The citizens were said to have been in 'much affrightment' as troops were brought in to supplement the authority's efforts and the disturbances at length abated. (John Latimer, *Annals of Bristol*, Kingsmead, 1970)

# December 26th

**1822:** Bristol historian John Latimer records that on Boxing Day a fair was held outside the gate and was known as the Horn Fair. 'It took its name from a grotesque looking gingerbread cake known as "the horn", which was made to represent a man's head and shoulders, with two trumpets branching out from his back; they varied in size from a few inches to a yard long ... The fair was held in Wade Street. Stalls were pitched on the sides of the road ... gilt horns were everywhere by hundreds. It was a wild, noisy affair, notable for petty gambling ... From morning till night groups of pleasure seekers wandered up and down amongst the stalls, staking their pence until their pockets were emptied.' (John Latimer, *Annals of Bristol*, Kingsmead, 1970)

———— • ◆ • ————

**1869:** A stampede occurred at the New Theatre, Park Row, as the doors were opened to admit people to the Christmas pantomime. Fourteen people died in the incident. Those already inside the theatre were oblivious to the carnage going on outside and it was decided to let the performance continue lest further panic be induced inside the theatre. (John Latimer, *Annals of Bristol*, Kingsmead, 1970)

# December 27th

**1814:** Joanna Southcott was born in Devon on April 25th 1750, the daughter of a tenant farmer. As a child she developed a habit of interpreting everyday life though the perspective of biblical scripture. In 1792 she experienced visions and a voice in her head predicting the future. Her fame grew locally in Devon after she correctly predicted the death of the Bishop of Exeter in December 1796, and the crop failures of 1799 and 1800. In 1801 she used her life savings to print 1,000 copies of a book entitled *The Strange Effects of Faith*. This raised her profile nationally and in Bristol her writings were advertised from 1805. At this time her followers in Bristol rented a room in Colston's House where the Revd Samuel Eyre read and explained her prophesies. Bristol was also where she retired to after much ridicule in newspapers. In 1814 she claimed that she was about to give birth to Shiloh, interpreted by some to be the divine incarnation predicted in Genesis. She died on December 27th 1814 and a subsequent autopsy showed that she was not pregnant, which shook the faith of her admirers in Bristol. The furniture of the Colston House room in Bristol was seized for rent and sold in the street. (John Latimer, *Annals of Bristol*, Kingsmead, 1970 / *Oxford Dictionary of National Biography*, OUP)

# December 28th

**1807:** Paul Falconer Poole, artist, was born at 43 College Street. Poole received little education and was largely self-taught. In November 1829 he moved to London and exhibited at the Royal Academy. He was soon giving guitar lessons to landscape artist Francis Danby's wife. Hannah Danby left London for Paris the following year in order to escape his creditors and Poole went to North Wales almost certainly with Hannah. By August 1831 the two of them visited Bristol seeing almost no one. At this time Poole concentrated on producing routine pieces typically of smiling country girls and their childen posed against rocky streams and is the work for which he is best known. These pictures were to be found salesrooms but were rarely exhibited. In 1837 he once again exhibited at the Royal Academy and continued to do so annually until his death, by which time he was once again living in London. Following the death of Francis Danby he married Hannah in 1861. He died at his home on September 22nd 1879. (*Oxford Dictionary of National Biography*, OUP)

———— • ————

**1946:** Bristol City lost 9–0 in a Division Three (South) game against Aldershot played at Bristol City's home ground at Ashton Gate. It is their worst loss in a league match. (Bristol City website)

# December 29th

**1853:** John Green had been working at Soundwell Colliery at a shaft, which took up water from the mine, when the rope carrying a bucket broke. The bucket fell 200 fathoms, hitting Green, who had been working below. Joseph Wiltshire, Banksman at the colliery and the man who had made the spliced rope, was of the opinion that the rope was securely made. The government inspector Mr H. Mackworth has serious concerns over the mine. Mackworth had visited the pit several times before the accident, making several recommendations regarding the security of the ropes in the lower pits. He also tested the rope that had broken in the accident but found that it was of average strength and that the condition of the rope was near to the proper standard. However, a hinge or splice had been inserted into a part of the rope that appeared decayed, which indicated the unsoundness of the rope, and the rope was over three years old, when it should have been replaced. The hinge that was put on the rope was unusually short and the rope severed where the hinge caught on part of the shaft. For failing to ensure the adequate condition of the rope, Mackworth blamed the proprietors for the accident. The jury's verdict was 'accidental death'. (*The Times*)

# December 30th

**1846:** *The Lancet* of January 16th 1847 printed a letter from the senior surgeon at Bristol General Hospital, Dr James Goodall Lansdown, who had carried out an operation on this date on a young man to amputate his left leg above the knee. It was the first operation in Bristol to use a general anaesthetic, which had only been demonstrated in London a few weeks previously. *The Times* describes the way in which the anaesthetic, ether, was used at the operation. A bladder was filled with an ounce of ether and once the ether vaporised it was administered with an ivory mouthpiece attached to the bladder and 'as soon as the patient is ready for the operation, close his nostrils, introduce the mouthpiece and close the lips around it with the fingers. He must now breathe into and out of the bladder, and in about one or two minutes, the muscles of his lips will begin to lose their hold. This is the moment the first cut is to be made. In two or three minutes, the effect will begin to disappear; the mouthpiece should again be introduced, and this repeated as often as required.' (www.johnpowell.net/weller.htm – a copy of an article that first appeared in *The History of Anaesthesia Proceedings; 1999*)

# December 31st

**1839:** Richard Vines, along with four others, was convicted to hang for his role in the Bristol Riots, which resulted from the rejection of the Parliamentary Reform Bill by the House of Lords in October 1831. The day before the execution, Vines was reprieved owing to his insanity and allegations that one of the witnesses, used to convict Vines, was guilty of perjury. Instead Richard Vines was sentenced to transportation for life to Australia. He was taken on board the *Justitia* hulk on March 8th 1832, where his behaviour was regarded as 'orderly'. On April 4th, along with 199 other prisoners, he sailed in the *England*, arriving in Hobart Town on July 18th. There, Vines went to work for a Dr B. Wilson, staying there for four years before absconding. His time with Dr Wilson was not without incident as Vines committed several punishable offences, with spells in a chain gang, imprisonment and flogging. He was caught and further attempts to escape his captivity resulted in two years imprisonment with hard labour and a flogging of '75 stripes'. On October 20th 1839, Vines began a twelve-month spell on the Hobart Town Surveyor's Gang but died on this date before completion of his sentence. (Geoffrey Amey, *City Under Fire: The Bristol Riots and their Aftermath*, Lutterworth Press, 1979)